Three Knots
to Nowhere

Three Knots to Nowhere

A Cold War Submariner on the Undersea Frontline

TED E. DUBAY

McFarland & Company, Inc., Publishers
Jefferson, North Carolina

LIBRARY OF CONGRESS CATALOGUING-IN-PUBLICATION DATA

Dubay, Ted E.
   Three knots to nowhere : a Cold War submariner on the
undersea frontline / Ted E. Dubay.
     p.   cm.
   Includes bibliographical references and index.

   ISBN 978-0-7864-7874-3 (softcover : acid free paper) ∞

   ISBN 978-0-4766-1404-5 (ebook)

   1. Dubay, Ted E. 2. Submariners—United States—
Biography. 3. United States. Navy—Submarine forces—
Biography. 4. Henry Clay (Submarine) 5. Nuclear
submarines—United States—History—20th century. 6. Naval
reconnaissance—History—20th century. 7. United States—
History, Naval—20th century. 8. Pacific Area—History,
Naval—20th century. 9. Cold War—Biography. I. Title.
   V63.D83A3 2014
   359.0092—dc23
   [B]   2014002545

BRITISH LIBRARY CATALOGUING DATA ARE AVAILABLE

On the cover: SSBN Deterrent Patrol insignia (United States Navy)

Manufactured in the United States of America

McFarland & Company, Inc., Publishers
  Box 611, Jefferson, North Carolina 28640
   www.mcfarlandpub.com

Table of Contents

Acknowledgments

My appreciation goes to all of my past shipmates. I extend extra thanks to those who maintained a relationship after my discharge from the United States Navy. You are a special breed of people. I could not have written this book without any of you. Special gratitude is in order to the individuals who allowed the use of their names, nicknames, and images, and who provided photographs. Your support added a personal element to this work.

I used every means at my disposal to contact Robert Montross, Tommy Lee Connell, Charlie Vannoy, Robert Frechette, and Stan Wryn. Regretably, my efforts were fruitless.

I also employed pseudonyms, if the situation could be considered embarrasing.

Above all, several exceptional individuals, Ludima Gus Burton, Leona Dubay Lane, Maria Maryeski, and Dr. Edward Monroe Jones, gave their time, support, and technical expertise.

I would be remiss without out acknowledging my father, Frank Dubay, Sr. He was a remarkable man. Dad was my hero in every sense of the word. If I become half the man he was, I can hold my head high. His younger brother Harry Dubay inspired me to join the submarine service. These two men were the perfect examples of the Greatest Generation. My only regret is they passed on to a better place before my completing this book.

A final thank you goes to my mom, Mrs. Leona Gus Dubay. Her support and love were always unwavering. She always makes me feel special.

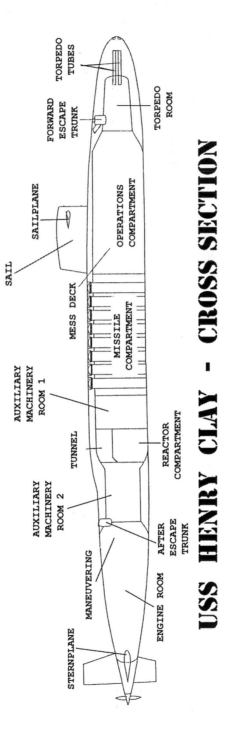

USS HENRY CLAY - CROSS SECTION

TORPEDO TUBES

FORWARD ESCAPE TRUNK

TORPEDO ROOM

SAIL

SAILPLANE

MESS DECK

OPERATIONS COMPARTMENT

MISSILE COMPARTMENT

AUXILIARY MACHINERY ROOM 1

TUNNEL

REACTOR COMPARTMENT

AUXILIARY MACHINERY ROOM 2

AFTER ESCAPE TRUNK

MANEUVERING

STERNPLANE

ENGINE ROOM

Preface

Several years ago, my granddaughter Annie Thompson and I took a trip to the United States Submarine Museum in Groton, Connecticut.

Our outing was merely an adventure for Annie. For me, I hoped it would revive long-buried memories of my Cold War submarine experiences.

While driving, I silently tried to recall facets of that portion of my life. My reward was faint recollections that floated in my mind like the fog swirling around the car. The memories were teasingly present, yet elusive.

When we arrived at the museum, the sight of a fleet ballistic missile submarine's missile hatch further tickled long-buried recollections.

I led Annie to a window on the museum's second level. We looked out. An eerie scene greeted us. The fog had intensified and we could barely see the faint profile of the USS *Nautilus*, the museum's star attraction. Just as the haze was enshrouding the submarine, a similar effect shielded memories of my naval service.

We exited the building and walked down a pier towards the *Nautilus*. The submarine gradually emerged from its foggy shroud. I took it as a good omen. If all went well, the Cold War experiences cloaked in my mind would likewise materialize.

Annie and I entered the submarine via a stairway at its front end. The modified opening replaced the original watertight hatch and vertical ladder. Other than changes to the entrance, items removed for security purposes, and protective Plexiglas over some of the equipment, everything was the same as when the *Nautilus* was on active duty.

The crowded Torpedo Room, narrow passageways, cramped bunks, and nearly everything painted Navy gray, caused more and more memories of my submarine service to flash and fade.

While leaving the *Nautilus*, I noticed the sailor assisting with the tours was wearing a ship's patch for the Fleet Ballistic Missile submarine USS *Henry Clay*, SSBN 625.

I said, "Hey, buddy. I was on the *Clay*. Where is she now?"

Looking at me as if I had three heads, he stated, "Holy Loch, Scotland. Just like always."

"When I was on the *Clay*, her homeport was Pearl Harbor and she operated out of Guam."

Taken aback, he blurted, "Wow. That was a *long* time ago!"

He was correct. I served in the United States Navy from July 1966 through August 1972. The last four years were on the USS *Henry Clay*.

Although Annie enjoyed the tour, it had a different effect on me. I began circling back to a self-defining portion of my life.

After returning home, I rummaged through the attic and found a dusty box filled with a plethora of materials related to my time in the Navy. Buried in the back of a closet were several photo albums from the same era.

Fueled by the material, a sporadic hodgepodge of memories emerged from the recesses of my mind: diving to test depth, transit through the Panama Canal, jam dive, Hawaii, Guam, rigged for ultra-quiet, hiding from Russian submarines, Ah-oooo-gah! Ah-oooo-gah! Dive! Dive!

As the evening passed, the crack in the dam holding back memories of my naval service continued to open. More and more recollections flowed through. At long last, my odyssey from shy adolescent to confident submariner, what it was like serving in the submarine service during the height of the Cold War, and how I coped with the experience slowly emerged.

I could finally look back. The circle was complete.

Then I had a troubling thought.

My submarine service memories were lost for a long time. The holes submarines valiantly punched through the oceans during the Cold War no longer exist. Would my reclaimed memories suffer a similar fate by ebbing away like fading echoes, never to return?

I began reading every submarine-related book I could find. They disappointed me. None captured the true submarine experience.

I also joined the United States Submarine Veterans Incorporated. The organization gave me the opportunity to tour present-day submarines and get a feel for crew culture. I found that the present-day submarine service was a different life from the one I experienced. It is a softer, kinder culture. There are other changes. Somewhere along the line, the Navy replaced the traditional ah-oooo-gah diving alarm with a siren. Computers replaced mechanical controls. Instead of a helmsman and planesman using their experience and senses fighting the elements to maintain depth control, sailors perform the same task with touch-screens and computers.

I was inspired to write this book, because of the evolution of the submarine service and the inadequate written documentation of Cold War–era submarine duty. Not only would it help other ex-submariners reconnect with their past, it would entertain and educate laypersons about the secret life of submarines.

My recollections, photographs, and box of artifacts were a good starting point. If the book was going to portray the full breadth of the experience, I needed more.

I began searching for past shipmates. The arduous process was worth it. I found all of my closest buddies. We now gather at reunions and share past joys, sorrows, good times, and hardships. It is as if we never parted. Serving together, isolated from the world for months at a time, created a bond that can never be broken. These wonderful individuals also provided valuable material that added to the quality of this book.

Like Richard Dana's *Two Years Before the Mast*, the work portrays the experience from an ordinary sailor's perspective. His tale takes place on a sail-driven merchant vessel. This account occurs aboard a submerged nuclear-powered warship and focuses on its extraordinary enlisted men— the backbone of a submarine crew. It is an autobiographical portrait and all events are true, to the best of my knowledge and belief. In order to paint the proper picture, it was necessary to include unclassified technical information. A tour through the *Henry Clay* describes the actual layout of the submarine. There is one deviation from an accurate portrayal of life on a submarine. I left out the salty language submarine sailors take great pride in using.

Introduction

After volunteering for submarine duty, I quickly discovered the obvious: the men of the United States Submarine Service are the cream of the crop. Less than one percent of the United States Navy serves in the submarine service. Having men such as these consider me a fellow submariner is an honor.

There is a reason the crew of a submarine is all volunteers: a submerged sub is one mistake or equipment malfunction away from never returning to the surface. The fates of the USS *Thresher* and the USS *Scorpion* are stark reminders of that fact.

In addition to living with danger, submarine sailors endure seclusion, cramped quarters, and no sunlight or fresh air for months. Only extraordinary men can survive and thrive under these conditions.

Dr. Joyce Brothers, in part, provided this assessment of submariners:

Togetherness is an overworked term, but in no other branch of our military service is it given such full meaning as in the "silent service."

In an undersea craft, each man is totally dependent upon the skill of every other man in the crew, not only for top performance, but for actual survival.

Are the men in the submarine service braver than those in other pursuits where the possibility of a sudden tragedy is constant? The glib answer would be to say they are. It is more accurate, from a psychological point of view, to say they are not necessarily braver, but that they are men who have a little more insight into themselves and their capabilities.

They know themselves a little better than the next man. This has to be so with men who have a healthy reason to volunteer for a risk. They are generally a cut healthier emotionally than others of a similar age and background because of their willingness to push themselves a little bit further and not settle for an easier kind of existence.

We all have tremendous capabilities but are rarely straining at the upper level of what we can do; these men are[1] [see end of Introduction].

My experience with the USS *Henry Clay*'s sailors matched Dr. Brothers's assessment. I trusted them and they never failed to perform as professionals.

The *Clay* also earned my respect.

I found out about the demise of the USS *Henry Clay* from a one-line sentence buried in a Web site on the Internet. Rumors that her end was near or had already occurred were circulating for some time. Previous attempts to discover the facts were fruitless. A tight-lipped society protected her and those not in the proper circle were not privy to relevant information. When I learned the details, it was comforting to know she succumbed peacefully to old age.

She and I were close, very close. We parted amicably with neither harboring hard feelings.

Given a man's name at birth, she wore it proudly and no one questioned her femininity. I remember her as vibrant, alive, and full of activity. Few would call her beautiful but she was graceful and noble in her own way.

The *Henry Clay*'s ability to dispense unimaginable fury made her one of the major players in keeping the peace during the Free World's Cold War with the Soviet Union. This lady and her crew were the quintessential example of speaking softly but carrying a big stick.

Former United States Secretary of State, General Colin Powell, Ret., summed up the importance of the FBM fleet with this tribute:

> No one has done more to prevent conflict—no one has made a greater sacrifice for the cause for peace—than you, America's proud missile submarine family. You stand tall among our heroes of the Cold War.
>
> America's leaders place special trust and confidence in the members of their submarine force. You go to sea entrusted with weapons of incredible destructive power. You go to sea propelled by power plants of unbelievable sophistication. You go to sea armed for Armageddon, while charged with the solemn responsibility of preventing it. No other members of America's Armed Forces have been given so great a burden of responsibility as the sailors of the Ballistic Missile Submarine Force. No other members of America's Armed Forces have so earned America's trust.
>
> Our SSBN patrols continued as the Cold War continued. The Berlin Crisis came and went. The Cuban Crisis came and went. The Vietnam War came and went. Through it all, the sailors of the Submarine Force continued to guide their craft far beneath the surface of the ocean, deterring a Third War that so often looked like it was threatening to break out and destroy us all.
>
> You did your job well. The terrible War we feared never came.[2]

Commissioned on February 20, 1964, the *Henry Clay* had an active career that lasted 26 years. Her decommissioning occurred on November

5, 1990. She entered the Nuclear Powered Ship and Submarine Recycling program, and her scrapping was complete on September 30, 1997. It was an ignoble end to a grand lady's existence.

Now she is resting peacefully in the afterlife. Not enough mourn her passing and, unfortunately, many actually rejoice in her departure into oblivion. How sad. Those who are pleased do not understand her true virtues.

My time in the Navy, especially while assigned to the *Clay*, was a unique experience. I have no regrets. If given a chance to go back in time and do it again, I would.

One of the last remnants of the USS *Henry Clay*. The author holding a piece of her hull. From the archives of Ted E. Dubay (September 2012).

Notes

1. Dr. Joyce Brothers, "Why They Behave That Way—Risk Is an Inspiration in Submarine Service," *Milwaukee Journal*, April 20, 1963, 1.

2. Colin L. Powell, "Remarks by General Colin L. Powell, Chairman of the Joint Chiefs of Staff, at the Ceremony for the 3000th SSBN Patrol," *The Submarine Review*, July 1992, 5–8.

Chapter 1

Battle Stations

Suddenly the submerged submarine's speakers shrieked. Immediately following was a terse announcement: "Man Battle Station Missile. Set condition 1SQ. Spin up all missiles."

It was midsummer 1971 and three days past Hump Day, the scheduled halfway point of one of my Cold War Fleet Ballistic Missile submarine patrols.

The USS *Henry Clay*, SSBN 625, was patrolling the Cold War's front line beneath the western Pacific. As she maintained a stealthy three-knot pace, her motion through the sea was imperceptible.

Prior to the announcement, tranquility prevailed—humming electronics, droning pumps and electric motors, whooshing ventilation systems, and whining turbines. I, along with one-third of the crew, was sleeping. Another third were performing assigned maintenance, working on qualifications, or finding ways to combat boredom. The remaining men were on watch, diligently operating and monitoring the complex systems needed to keep the FBM functioning.

Awakened by the announcements, I heard the click-click-click of my rack's privacy curtain sliding open as the submarine's bow tilted up during its ascent to launch depth.

I, a twenty-two-year-old nuclear-trained electrician, shook the cobwebs from my head. It only took a moment to realize I was aboard the most powerful weapon on Earth. Protection of the United States of America and the responsibility of safely operating a nuclear powered submarine were in direct contrast with my idyllic youth in rural Hickory Township, Pennsylvania. Back then, I did not have a care in the world. The simple life reflected my behavior. I was shy, naive, and a mediocre student. Joining the Navy transformed me. Admiral Hyman Rickover's highly intensive nuclear propulsion program and qualifying in submarines turned me into an outgoing, confident, and highly respected knowledgeable submariner.

My mind focused on the present. I dove out of my rack, joining the crew's scripted pandemonium. It was a struggle to maintain my balance on the sharply angled deck. Second Class Machinist's Mate Bob "Red" Southerland and I battled for the same portion of the narrow passageway.

Southerland was slim, smooth-talking, red-haired, fair-skinned, and from Alabama. In the glow of the dimmed compartment lighting, I could see he was sporting sleep-rumpled hair and a day's growth of stubble. His six-foot-three-inch frame was a distinct disadvantage for maneuvering in a confined space. After bumping his head on a light in the overhead, he muttered a few choice expletives and moved. I, at 5'6", occupied the vacated space.

Southerland and I met late fall 1967 while students of U.S. Naval Nuclear Power School, Bainbridge, Maryland. He was a typical selectee: highly intelligent, looking for his life's direction, and not afraid of a challenge. We were both single and lived on the base. Pickup basketball was our common thread. Even though we went to the same nuclear power school prototype, the long hours and rotating shift schedule prevented our socializing. While we were attending submarine school, New London/Groton, Connecticut, basketball brought us back together. When we were assigned to the same crew of the USS *Henry Clay*, our camaraderie grew into something special and we became lifelong friends. As individuals, we were professionally and socially Yin/Yang. This worked well for us. He was a machinist's mate, making him an expert in mechanical systems. I was an electrician and had expertise in a different technology. Southerland had a partying nature. My subdued demeanor created a good balance.

The battle station announcement made adrenaline rush through me. After grabbing lint-free coveralls, I quickly threw them over tee shirt and skivvies. Slipping on shoes, *sans* socks to save time, I ran to my battle station. Hot on my heels was Southerland.

As the FBM rose to launch depth, I was running aft and downhill through the middle level operations compartment. I encountered Auxillaryman Tommy Lee Connell, who was rushing forward. Even though both of us were thin, we had to squeeze past each other in the narrow passageway.

I reached the hatch between the operations and missile compartments. Grasping the bar over the opening, I swung my body feet-first through the hole, much like a trapeze artist. I landed on my feet, and continued at a rapid pace down the submarine's port walkway. Southerland followed suit. At the aft end of the middle level missile compartment, I bounded up the stairs and ran through upper level machinery 1. The short distance through the reactor compartment tunnel only took a few seconds.

At the hatch between the tunnel and machinery 2 upper level, I met one of the forward non-quals. He was in the engineering spaces working on his submarine qualifications. Because of the hatch's small size, only one person can pass through. The man was a higher military rank, but deferred to me because I was qualified in submarines, a procedure that adhered to submarine protocol.

Within a minute of awakening, I was in maneuvering, the control room for the reactor and engineering equipment. My clothes were damp with sweat. It was a combination of exertion and the engine room's extreme heat and humidity.

I relieved Second Class Interior Communications Technician Charlie Schweikert. He was manning the Steam Plant Control Panel (SPCP) as the throttleman. Although Schweikert grew up mainly in the South, he did not associate with any particular part of the United States. His father was in the Air Force and continually moved the family around the country. Schweikert had blond hair and a wiry five-foot-seven-inch frame, and was as good-natured as anybody I have known. He had a passion for periscope liberty and partook in the activity whenever possible. His craving was so strong, he sometimes had the messenger of the watch wake him just for the possibility of seeing beyond the submarine's confines. Schweikert's most enduring traits were an excellent dry wit and a great sense of humor. In this instance, due to the gravity of Battle Station Missile, he was all business. After he gave me a rundown of the watch station's status, I controlled the speed of the submarine, as directed by an officer located in the boat's control room.

Schweikert hustled to his own battle station.

Southerland relieved Bill "Willy Tat" Souder as the upper level engine room (ULER) watch. Souder, a short man with a buzz haircut, hated the nickname, but endured it without complaint. As with Southerland, we became acquainted at Bainbridge. Souder was a pleasant and fun companion.

Also in maneuvering was Electrician's Mate First Class Rich Lewis. He manned the electric plant control panel (EPCP). A native of Buffalo,

New York, Lewis was 5'10" and a paunchy 250 pounds. His nickname was "Hogbody." Unlike Souder, Lewis embraced the moniker. Beneath the plump exterior and round face, he was a mass of muscle. There was not an ounce of fat on his legs. Adonis would have been proud of them. Physique-wise, Lewis and I were opposites. I was 140 pounds; in other words, a runt. My pre–Navy athletic experience consisted of being the manager of my high school football and basketball teams. I also participated in intramural track and briefly held Hickory High School's high-jump record. Lewis was an excellent athlete. He was a nose tackle and middle linebacker when attending Baldwin-Wallace College. Lewis was a top-notch electrical operator and had a subtle sense of humor. I spent many nice times socializing with him, his wife and young son.

The submarine was hovering at launch depth and poised to fire her lethal projectiles. All hands were ready to carry out their particular duty. The outward appearance of Lewis and Southerland was amazingly calm, a true testament to their professionalism and training. Like me, were they successfully suppressing feelings of anxiety?

Was this just a drill? We did not know. Sometimes the announcement to man battle stations included the phrase "for WSRT" (Weapons Systems Readiness Test). In those cases, we knew it was not a prelude to war. This time the statement was not included. Because we set Condition 1SQ (the *Clay*'s highest level of preparedness and having the missiles ready for launch), I could not discount the possibility that a nuclear confrontation was about to begin. The prospect weighed heavily on my mind.

Passing minutes seemed like hours as I waited in limbo. My worst fear was having the deck drop out from under me as the *Clay* dispatched her deadly missiles. I hoped and prayed battle stations would end with our merchants of destruction still nestled in their tubes.

As the minutes crept along, I could not help thinking about why the crew of the USS *Henry Clay* was in this unenviable situation. I normally suppressed the thought, but Battle Station Missile brought it into the forefront.

Chapter 2

Troubled Times

It was the height of the Cold War. Tensions rose and ebbed with unpredictable frequency.

The United States deterred an all-out war by employing a nuclear triad of counterstrike capabilities.

One component was the Air Force Strategic Air Command's (SAC) stable of bombers. Some were always in the air. Others relied on their ability to scramble and strike the perpetrator of an attack.

The second was nuclear-tipped intercontinental ballistic missiles (ICBMs) hidden throughout the United States in underground silos.

The most important arm of the triad was the existence of 41 American Fleet Ballistic Missile (FBM) submarines, dubbed Forty-one for Freedom. The USS *Henry Clay* was the 22nd FBM built.

The *Clay* carried sixteen nuclear-tipped intercontinental ballistic missiles. These birds of death had a range of over 2000 miles. Each Fleet Ballistic Missile submarine contained more firepower than all the bombs dropped during World War II. That made the *Henry Clay* the most power-ful weapon on Earth. If we had ever been required to launch our nuclear-tipped projectiles, it would have been Armageddon.

Stealth was an FBM's secret to success. A war patrol consisted of cruising submerged at a virtually silent speed of three knots, for at least two months. FBMs did not go anywhere in particular. After randomly roaming the ocean, at the end of a patrol the USS *Henry Clay* returned to her starting point, Apra Harbor, Guam, essentially having gone nowhere.

The Soviets employed every means possible to find America's FBMs. They had aircraft, surface ships, and submarines continually searching the seas. Their huge fleet of nuclear and conventional hunter-killer sub-marines was my biggest fear. These stealthy compatriots snuck through the seas and hid in underwater sea-lane choke points trying to detect FBMs. If lucky enough to find us, they would try their best to follow. A Soviet attack boat having the *Clay* in its crosshairs would be a no-win situation for us if hostilities broke out. Our 20-knot-plus top speed was no match for a greater than 40-knot torpedo.

The loss of one FBM would not compromise this portion of the triad. Two-thirds of the forty-one were always hiding on station, ready to launch a massive counterstrike.

The United States Navy achieved this remarkable record by staffing every FBM with two complete crews, the Blue and Gold. I was on the *Clay*'s Gold Crew.

Each crew rotated on a three-month cycle. When the Gold was on patrol, the Blue underwent refresher training. After the *Clay* returned to port and we conducted a three-day turnover, the Blue Crew relieved us. Then the Gold Crew flew back to Hawaii for 30 days of rest and relaxation (R & R). While the Gold Crew enjoyed their hard-earned rest, the Blue Crew spent the same period performing a refit of the *Clay*. This consisted of making repairs and checks, thus ensuring the submarine could endure the rigors of patrol. Restocking the submarine with a 90-day supply of stores also occurred during refit. When the Blue Crew left on patrol, the Gold Crew commenced refresher training. The cycle repeated itself over and over. This pattern allowed the *Clay* to be on station eight out of every twelve months.

It was a thankless job, but the *Clay*'s war patrols were indispensible in maintaining world peace.

The sound of Lewis recording his hourly readings brought me back to the current condition. This meant that the *Clay* had been at battle stations for almost an hour, with no end in sight.

I silently manned the throttleman position. In addition to vigilantly monitoring the steam plant control panel instruments, with senses like hair triggers I tried to pick up the slightest clue of the situation. It was impossible. The *Clay*'s hovering system was working flawlessly to keep the FBM at launch depth. The submarine was so motionless, we might as well be home in our living rooms. All other elements of the *Clay*'s operation were equally mute.

Lewis broke the tension when he said, "Boy. I'm glad we just push this thing around."

I responded, "I'd be happier if the pushin' we're doing is for making going home turns."

Lewis added, "Look at it this way. Maybe we're in the process of earning another Unit Commendation award. They never told us exactly why we merited the last one. We might be doing it again. This must be one of the reasons submarine duty is called the silent service."

The limited dialogue was enough to ease my tension. Not long afterwards, I rejoiced when hearing the message to secure from battle stations.

Schweikert soon appeared and relieved me as throttleman.

As I was leaving maneuvering, he said with a sly grin, "Looks like we stared down the Russians and *they* blinked. Again."

I headed forward retracing my previous path, engine room, upper level machinery 2, tunnel, and upper level machinery 1, at a leisurely pace. I sped up when passing through the missile compartment. Mixed feelings swept through me. It was frightening knowing the awesome destructive power the *Clay* was capable of delivering, although that was probably why our missiles were still nestled in their tubes.

I slowed down after entering the middle level operations compartment. My track took me past the mess deck and CPO quarters, then down the stairs into crew's berthing. When I arrived at my rack, I surveyed the surroundings. Berthing's lights were off, as they were when the alarm sounded more than an hour ago. Many men were already lying down with their curtains closed.

Across the passageway, I heard Southerland snoring. His height made him a couple of inches too long for the rack and his feet protruded into the passageway.

I resisted the temptation of tickling his foot. Sleep was a sacred item on a submarine. It was bad enough that Battle Station Missile disturbed our rest.

I took great pride in my ability to arise out of a dead sleep and quickly transition to fully alert, ready to carry out complex and critical actions in a matter of minutes. Then I could go from the pinnacle of vigilance to fast asleep in an equal amount of time. It was a difficult task, but the defense of America was at stake.

The stress of battle stations had a profound effect upon me. It made me reflect about how I ended up in such a bizarre, yet rewarding situation.

Chapter 3

Odyssey

I grew up in Hickory Township, a small rural Appalachian community in western Pennsylvania.

Although steel mills in nearby towns fueled the local economy, the area was in chaos. Sporadic family-straining strikes and downsizing work forces ran rampant. The American steel industry was deteriorating.

Given these circumstances, one thing was a certainty. I was determined not to spend my life as an uneducated worker in a dangerous, dirty mill with an unstable future.

Even though I took college preparatory courses, formal education beyond high school was not an option. In addition to the huge financial burden, an English teacher convinced me that I had no chance of handling college courses. In retaliation, I investigated each military service to determine which would provide the best educational opportunity. This approach had the added benefit of being at the government's expense.

After much deliberation on my part, Admiral Hyman Rickover's extremely intensive and secret Naval Nuclear Propulsion Program became my ticket out of that depressed region. The Navy recruiter reinforced the selection by claiming that my scores during the initial screening were very good and I had great intellectual potential. Recruiters across the country fed the same line to thousands of others. We ate it up and felt like geniuses.

The decision gave me four options.

There was the possibility of making the military my career.

Depending on the results of placement and aptitude screening, the Navy would train me as an interior communications technician (IC), machinist's mate (MM), electrician's mate (EM), or electronics technician (ET). All offered potential careers after the Navy.

Third, the twelve months of nuclear training was the equivalent of two years of college. Many considered it the most difficult academic curriculum available. Nuclear Power School could provide the foundation for a career in the civilian nuclear electrical generation industry.

If none of these worked out, I could go to college on the GI Bill.

Joining the Navy had another benefit. I evaded serving in Vietnam.

In addition to academic requirements, the Navy imposed a six-year minimum enlistment obligation for nuclear power program eligibility. Being only seventeen, I was a "kiddy-cruiser." This meant my base obligation was three years of service. I had to commit to an extra three years to receive the additional education.

I entered the United States Navy in July 1966, a month after graduating from Hickory High School as a naive seventeen-year-old country boy with no marketable skills. A bus transported me to the Great Lakes Naval Training Center, North Chicago, Illinois. Upon the recruits' arrival at boot camp, the Navy subjected us to more testing. For me, the two most important exams were a general knowledge (GCT) and a mathematical test (ARI). I needed a combined score of greater than 120 to ensure my qualification for the Navy nuclear program. Knowing that 115 was the minimum combined score to become an officer added to my stress. To my relief, I easily scored well above the required value.

Typical of the other service boot camps, it taught basic military protocol. Every so often, boot camp subjected us to seemingly absurd situations. These instilled self-control, and weeded out those unable to cope.

Two incidents stood out.

The first was during one of our daily 0600 inspections. Somehow, I got dirt on my left thumb and forefinger. On the way to inspection, those digits brushed against my otherwise immaculate white uniform, smudging it in two places. The pose we assumed for inspection compounded the problem. With fingers pointing up, the thumb of the left hand hooked into the collar of my undershirt, exposed the garment's inner edge. When the inspector stood in front of me, I expected him to slap my hand, signifying I passed inspection. Instead, he pointed out the dirty spots on my uniform.

Then he grabbed my undershirt, pulled it up to my eyes, and screamed, "What the hell is this?"

Seeing the brown smudge and knowing I failed inspection, I felt my heart sink into the pit of my stomach.

The inspector ordered, "Stand over there with the rest of the scrounges."

An aide marched our ragtag group to the brig and showed us the imprisoned sailors shuffling around in their shackles. Then he told us we would join them if we failed to square ourselves away. I passed the remaining inspections and never experienced the true consequences of being a habitual scrounge.

The second situation actually made me fear for my safety. It happened during Service Week. During the five-day period, I helped staff boot camp's fire training school. Most of the time, my duties consisted of cleaning the school's facilities.

One task was not mundane.

The recruits learning firefighting skills got sweaty and dirty while combating fires. As trainees washed for lunch, my job was ensuring they did not use more than one paper towel. Not knowing this limitation beforehand, many removed shirts and scrubbed everything above their waists. Dripping wet, they stepped over to the dispenser.

Despite being 5'6" and 115 pounds, I told them, "You're only allowed one paper towel."

Hiding my shaking knees as many men hurled glares, curses, and threats of bodily harm, I repeated the statement again and again. To their credit, I escaped unscathed and no one ever used more than one.

In September of 1966, I reported to electrician's mate "A" school, administered at the Great Lakes Naval Training Center. It trained me to be a repair electrician.

Towards the end of the training, we received orders to our next duty stations. For me it would be an interim stop to gain fleet experience prior to attending Nuclear Power School. My orders had me reporting to the submarine tender, USS *Fulton*, AS-11, New London, Connecticut. She was the oldest submarine support ship in the fleet.

Several days later, the nuclear liaison officer summoned me to his office. The man informed me that he had sent a letter to Washington dropping me from the nuclear program and canceling my three-year enlistment extension. When asked why, he told me I could not pass electrician's school, even if I got 100 percent on every remaining test. This did not make any sense because I had never scored lower than 80 percent. He said I was wrong and that my average was 54 percent. After researching the issue, we discovered a transposition error. I was carrying a passing grade.

He then said, "I've already sent off the letter. You can get back in the nuclear program, but you have to do it now."

I told him I was not going to make a decision right then and there, but would return in the afternoon. After much deliberation, I decided that fate was telling me something. Spending three years on a ship that hardly roamed from her home port of New London was an excellent duty station. This outweighed having one of my potential career options eliminated.

I returned as promised and informed the nuclear liaison officer of my decision.

He strongly reiterated his previous statement, "If you don't get back in the nuclear program now, you can't ever get back in."

At this point, he was ticking me off. I told him that my decision stood and went back to class.

On February 10, 1967, I graduated from electrician's mate "A" school and earned the designation electrician's mate fireman apprentice (EMFA).

I reported to the *Fulton* on a cold, blustery Saturday in February 1967. After disembarking from the train, bundled in my peacoat, I walked up to one of the taxicabs parked outside Union Station in New London, Connecticut.

The cabbie asked, "Where can I take you, buddy?"

"The USS *Fulton.*"

"The *Fulton*? The *Fulton*'s in Puerto Rico!"

My legs went weak with anguish. It was just before noon and my orders required me to report by 1600 hours (4:00 p.m.). I was worried that I'd be absent without leave (AWOL). The driver realized my predicament and offered to take me to the submarine base or electric boat, both in Groton. Not panicking, I decided to follow my orders as closely as possible, which stated "USS *Fulton*, State Pier, New London." I told the cabbie to take me to State Pier.

It turned out to be a good decision. The *Fulton* left a skeleton force, called the Yellow Crew. They supported the boats in Submarine Squadron Ten. The squadron was expecting me, much to my relief.

The Yellow Crew's quarters were noninsulated and drafty Quonset huts, with double deck bunk beds. Since it was late winter, the hut's heaters barely kept the indoor temperature tolerable. I chose a top rack, because heat rises. The provided sheet and Navy wool blanket were so inadequate I slept in my clothes, plus a wool sweater. One morning, we woke up to a snowdrift halfway down the hut. Someone had not shut the back door properly.

One cold gray New England morning, I was with several Yellow Crew sailors tasked with mooring the USS *Nautilus*. She was in the prime of her active duty and setting numerous records. We huddled on the dock waiting for the submarine to come into view. Dressed in bell-bottomed dungarees, work jackets, and black woolen watch caps, we stomped feet and flapped arms attempting to keep warm. Our breath formed clouds of condensation with every exhalation.

The elements were quickly forgotten when the *Nautilus* came into view. The sleek submarine was smoothly slicing through the murky water of the Thames River. Ice from wind-whipped spray almost completely covered her conning tower and those stationed in it. Just as when they were under the icecap on a recent trip to the North Pole, the sailors appeared oblivious to the frosty coating.

I stared silently in awe of these brazen but stoic men. They were submariners, members of an elite force.

About a month later, the *Fulton* returned to New London. I and the other members of the Yellow Crew moved onboard.

Within a few days, the *Fulton*'s administration summoned me to the ship's office for a review of my service record.

During the meeting, the personnelman remarked about a three-year enlistment extension.

I shook my head to the negative and related the discussion I had had with the nuclear liaison at electrician's mate school.

Holding up the documents and pointing, he said, "I'm no lawyer, but see this passage? It says: binding upon successful completion of electrician school."

The man flipped to another page and said, "The grade on this form indicates you passed with flying colors."

He sent me to the ship's legal officer, who confirmed the conclusion. After they corrected my score, he explained, the extension was valid. I showed the lawyer another statement in the contract that appeared to stipulate that the Navy had to send me to Nuclear Power School.

He responded, "Yep, you're correct."

Confused, I related what the nuclear liaison officer had told me: "If you don't get back in the program now, you can't ever get back in."

He said, "I don't know anything about that, but it's easy to get back in the program. You meet all the qualifications. Just submit a chit. Here, take a couple, in case you make a mistake."

Not long afterwards, I received orders to the fall session of Nuclear Power School. My trust in the Navy's integrity dropped several notches.

USS *Fulton*, AS 11, State pier, New London, Connecticut. Also pictured are the USS *Triton* SSN 586 (outboard) and USS *Nautilus* SSN 571. From the archives of Ted E. Dubay (August 1967).

I spent the first part of my time on the *Fulton* in the deck division. My duties included cleaning, painting, and handling lines as submarines arrived and departed.

One hot muggy June day, I, still an electrician's mate fireman apprentice (EMFA), and several other young inexperienced sailors were waiting on State Pier for the arrival of the USS *Nautilus*. Second Class Boatswain's Mate Vargas, a tall muscular man, was in charge of our small contingent. We were clad in sweat-soaked dungarees and Dixie cup white hats.

Before long, the *Nautilus* came into view. Similar to the last time I helped moor her, she did not have a tug to assist in the docking process.

Curiosity overcame me and I asked why there wasn't a tug, like when the other submarines came in.

Vargas explained that she had twin screws. The others only had one. That made them less maneuverable.

Suddenly a strong gust of wind from up-river almost blew my white hat off.

I heard Vargas comment about the waves hitting her bow. The wind and outgoing tide were magnifying the river's natural current. The *Nautilus*'s OOD had his hands full.

Even though I was inexperienced, I could tell the submarine was struggling to reach the pier. The water at the boat's stern was frothing as her screws frantically beat the water. Instead of moving closer to the pier, she was farther out and losing ground.

Vargas quickly coupled two heaving lines back-to-back with a half hitch. Then he let the spiraled double-length of line hang from his left arm as his right whirled the lead-ball monkey's fist in an accelerating circular motion. Like a bola, the weighted end of the clothesline-diameter cotton line pulled the loops out of his hand as it payed out over the water. The astonishing heave easily reached the *Nautilus*. Within moments, there was a two-inch nylon line connecting the *Nautilus* and the pier. It wasn't enough and the taut line began to stretch.

Suddenly Vargas yelled, "Hit the deck!"

Instantly, all of us flattened ourselves to the wooden-planked pier.

A second later, the nylon line broke. It sounded like a gunshot. The white line whipped over our prone bodies. In the blink of an eye, it sliced a huge gash in the dock's metal warehouse. A shiver shot through my spine like an electric pulse. Had I been standing, it would have cut me in half. I silently gave thanks to my Maker for a narrow escape.

A tug finally came to the rescue and the *Nautilus* easily docked.

Mess cooking in the chief petty officer quarters was my final assignment on the *Fulton*. Being a mess cook is one of the early initiation rites that just about every sailor of my day endured. It consisted of working 16-hour days serving food, cleaning the eating area and galley, and washing all the paraphernalia associated with meals.

The same duty in the chief quarters galley was not as demanding. We had shorter hours, more responsibility, and the chiefs paid us a stipend.

While I was mess cooking, the *Fulton* provided my first time at sea. She went out for a six-day exercise. The weather during the cruise was beautiful. The Atlantic Ocean was sparkling clear and calm, even though we had transited several hundred miles south of Long Island. Most evenings, a few of us gathered on the main deck and watched the bow slice through the water. On several occasions, we saw flying fish. One day a dolphin—not a porpoise, but the fish of the same name—kept pace with the ship. At night, the sea shimmered with an eerie iridescence.

One day, another sailor and I were leaning on the port side rail looking out over the ocean.

All of a sudden, he pointed and excitedly said, "Hey, Ted. What's that over there?"

I strained my eyes, trying to determine the source of the water's disturbance.

My jaw dropped when I realized it was a torpedo and headed straight towards the *Fulton*. We were overwhelmed with shock.

A knot formed in the pit of my stomach. Had the Cold War with the Soviet Union turned into a shooting war? It was August of 1967 and tensions between both sides were high. Had the animosity finally reached a breaking point? Was a Russian submarine attacking us? Was the much-feared World War III commencing?

I watched in horror as the torpedo came closer and closer.

Alarms sang out, ordering us to battle stations. The ship heeled over as the men on the bridge tried to turn the ship out of the torpedo's path. It was too late. The torpedo was headed slightly aft of where I was standing.

Cringing and staring in disbelief, I braced myself for the explosion.

Much to my surprise and relief, it mercifully passed under the *Fulton*, without detonating.

Unbeknownst to most of the crew, we were conducting exercises with one of own submarines. It surfaced not far away. Figures emerged in the bridge of its conning tower. I saw the men waving, laughing at us, and basking in the glory of their successful attack. As much as they enjoyed themselves at our expense, the razzing was a welcome substitute for the alternative.

The next day someone spotted an object floating in the ocean. Crewmen lowered a sixteen-foot longboat into the water. It carried several of our boatswain's mates. With much bravado, one of them sat amidships armed with a carbine. As the small craft headed towards the object, the *Fulton* followed. When the ship closed in, I could tell that it was a container from a cargo ship. There were three dark shadows circling it.

Sharks.

They were huge. Each shark was longer than the boat manned by the *Fulton*'s sailors.

Our people quickly high-tailed it back to the ship. When the boat-swains clamored back aboard the *Fulton*, everyone could tell the experi-ence had shaken them to the core. Replacing their previous boldness were ashen complexions, animated gestures, and spirited comments. I over-heard the armed sailor muttering that he should have had a real gun instead of a peashooter.

What happened to the container was a mystery. Scuttlebutt circu-lated that it was a navigational hazard and used as target practice by a destroyer.

That evening, several buddies and I gathered in the crew's lounge. Our shoot-the-shit evolved into a discussion about the contents of the container. Each had an opinion of what had attracted the sharks. We agreed that the sharks' senses had detected something they considered edible. The most disturbing theory was a botched attempt to smuggle ille-gal aliens into the United States. I will never know the truth, but cannot dismiss that disconcerting possibility.

A little over a month later, I walked down the USS *Fulton*'s brow for the last time.

My first year in the Navy was fraught with challenges. Each made me maturate in different ways. Some were enjoyable. Others, such as a snapped mooring line almost ending my life and seeing a torpedo headed towards the *Fulton*, made me grateful to be alive.

I was embarking on another leg of my military journey. What did the future hold? Not knowing made me excited, yet nervous.

Chapter 4

Admiral Rickover's
Nuclear Power School

I reported to Basic Nuclear Power School, Bainbridge, Maryland, in the fall of 1967. It was the first phase of Rickover's Nuclear Power Program. Those reporting with me were designated class 67–4. That meant we were the fourth and last Nuclear Power School class convening in 1967. Attendees and graduates of the program earned the nickname "nuc," pronounced nuke. An unofficial nickname for the school was Nukie-Pu-U.

Battery upon battery of tests measured our aptitude. They served two purposes: eliminating those who had a low probability of completing the demanding program, and splitting the remainder into eight sections, or levels. Although all those making it through the final screening met the threshold requirements, those in section eight were the elite and delved a little more deeply into the subjects. Conversely, those in section one were on the other end of the spectrum. Regardless of the group, we all conformed to the same curriculum.

Some classes were purely preparatory, such as a several-week course on becoming proficient in the use of the slide rule. This instrument was the calculator of its time. It looks like a complex foot-long ruler, inscribed on both sides with numerous scales. A slide rule has three parallel sections. Making a calculation consisted of moving the middle section so the appropriate number aligned with a value on the desired scale of one of the stationary outer sections. There was also a clear sliding window with a single thin line perpendicular to the length of the slide rule. It aided in aligning numbers from one scale to another.

Another class was a six-week mathematics course that started with basic algebra and ended with calculus. This was a particular challenge for individuals like me. I had never studied anything more complex than trigonometry. In spite of such a handicap, I only got two questions wrong the entire course. One incorrect answer was a simple transcription error. I performed the calculations in my head instead of systematically on paper. Those classes and making that type of error taught me how to study and methodically work through problems.

The courses included classical physics, thermodynamics, reactor chemistry, metallurgy, radiation protection, nuclear physics, and reactor core design.

This portion proved to be as challenging as promised. There were

The author at the entrance to Nuclear Power School, Naval Training Center, Bainbridge, Maryland. From the archives of Ted E. Dubay (spring 1968).

eight hours of class every day. Two to four hours of daily self-study followed the instruction. Study hours were also in the classroom, because the material presented to the students was classified military information and could not leave the building.

In the final segment, officials segregated the trainees by job classification: mechanic, electrician, and electronics technician. During these, we received specific training in reactor and system operation geared toward our specialty.

Many could not sustain the frenetic pace. One of my classmates succumbed to the stress and committed suicide. Others failed out in all phases of the school. Nuclear Power School used the 4.0 scale. Any score less than 2.5 was a failure. A ditty circulated through the student population with regard to grades: 2.5 and survive, 2.8 and skate.

There were few breaks. I was determined to pass. Passing would keep all of my original four options open. I spent most evenings preparing for the next day's classes.

To maintain my sanity, I would occasionally steal away and play basketball. In one pickup game, I teamed with a tall red-haired player. I was a good outside shooter and he was excellent under the basket. In addition to our complementary playing styles, we had great chemistry. It was the beginning of my friendship with Southerland. We tried to team up whenever possible.

Sometimes, weekend evenings found Southerland, Souder and me at Fiddler's Green, the base enlisted men's club. Beside the inexpensive 3.2 beer and a drinking age of 18, it had another attraction. Wave boot camp resided at Bainbridge and the female recruits got liberty.

I had another outlet to ease the stress of Nuclear Power School. My older brother Frank attended college in Philadelphia. It was a two-hour bus ride from Bainbridge. Visiting my brother allowed a complete escape from military associations. We played sports during the day and attended school-organized activities such as dances in the evening. On the few occasions I could make an escape, I'd leave base Friday and return Sunday afternoon so I could spend the evening preparing for Monday classes.

Nuclear Power School was in an otherwise abandoned part of the base, far from any of the other active factions. Due to the intensity of the lessons, school officials relaxed many normal military requirements and we enjoyed privileges the others on the base did not have. Because of our elite training, we displayed an unwarranted aloofness. These factors created animosity between the nucs and the other sailors at Bainbridge.

After lunch one day, a large contingent of nucs was waiting for the bus to take us back to school. Several groups of radioman trainees marched by.

Somebody in our group mockingly sang out, "I love a parade."

In response, one of the radiomen's leaders called his class to a halt and approached us demanding, "Who said that?"

About 30 of the nucs independently responded with, "I did!"

We surrounded the little group.

The man's eyes grew wide as he recognized the error of his actions. He rapidly and meekly marched his subordinates out of our clutches.

Twenty-four weeks after the start of Nuclear Power School, an eight-hour comprehensive written exam (comp) provided the grand finale. Elimination was the fate of many who were unable to score greater than 2.5.

As a sidelight, Rickover thought the Comprehensive Exam scores for 67–4 were too low and demanded a re-grade. I believe he liked to show off how smart *his* people were. He had his standards, because no one who failed the first grading passed after the second review.

I finished the school with a 3.144 average.

I spent the last half of Nuclear Power School at the U.S. Naval Nuclear Power Training Unit (NPTU), Windsor, Connecticut. It was a prototype of a submarine nuclear power plant, associated electrical generation, and steam propulsion equipment. Sailors simply called it prototype. It was one of three similar training facilities. The Windsor site was designated S1C. The "S" stood for submarine, the "1" meant it was the first of its type, and the "C" denoted that Combustion Engineering, Incorporated, had built it. Located in Idaho was S5W, the fifth submarine Westinghouse design. Situated in Saratoga Springs, New York, D1G was the initial General Electric reactor design for destroyers.

I reported to S1C, Windsor, Connecticut, on May 6, 1968. I thought the security was tight at Basic Nuclear Power School, but it was nothing compared to prototype. It bordered on paranoia. Trainees had to live off base. When traveling to and from the site, the Navy required us to wear civilian clothes. This made it more difficult to determine how many men were in training. When onsite, trainees changed into dungaree uniforms with blue ball caps, and wore white pinned-on nametags.

From the moment we reported, the staff dispersed warnings about Russian spies. They could be anybody. We should be especially suspicious of people who seemed too friendly. One of the examples of subversive activities concerned a sailor from a Fleet Ballistic Missile submarine who sold nuclear technical manuals to the Soviets. I found out much later that he was a crewmember of the USS *Henry Clay*.

As in Bainbridge, we studied onsite, because of the classified nature of the training materials.

The first phase of prototype consisted of 10 weeks of classroom instruction on S1C's systems and components. There were eight hours of classes followed by four hours of mandatory study, five days a week.

Saturday study sessions were mandatory when a student could not maintain the proper grades. If this did not improve academic progress, school officials restricted him to the site and he had to live in Quonset huts, nicknamed the Hymie Hilton. Confining students to the site allowed maximizing study by eliminating behaviors that had a negative effect on the learning process, such as drinking and staying out late.

My determination to complete the training kept my performance at an acceptable level.

To counteract the intense instruction, I frequented a Hartford nightclub. One night, I met Kathy. We hit it off from the start. Our dates and the time we spent with her family helped ease the stress of the demanding curriculum.

On May 27, 1968, bad news circulated throughout S1C. The submarine USS *Scorpion* and her crew of 99 did not arrive in port as scheduled. Rumors of her fate quickly spread. They ranged from a Russian submarine sinking her with a torpedo to an explosion in the *Scorpion's* battery.

Many of the sailors at S1C were destined for submarine duty. We followed the sparse news reports with great interest. The official Navy position was that the submarine was "delayed." A week later the Navy upgraded *Scorpion's* status to missing. After a few more days, the Navy classified her as lost, but without stating a cause.

I understood submarine duty was dangerous. The incident really brought the danger to the forefront. Many men considered non-volunteering (commonly termed non-volling) from submarines. Only a few actually acted upon it.

In spite of the tragedy, training proceeded as scheduled. The expectation was that we remain unaffected by the knowledge of one of our submarines being lost with all hands. For me, I summoned the necessary fortitude and did not let the tragedy have a negative effect on my academic performance.

The school's staff divided those who made it through the first part of prototype into four operating crews. The trainees worked rotating shifts. The day and evening shifts were 12 hours. Night shift was 10 hours.

Prototype's second half consisted of 16 weeks re-studying systems and components, with an emphasis on in-rate areas and more in-depth instruction. Standing instructional watches and accomplishing watch standing practical factors, such as operating equipment and responding to plant casualties, were the bill of fare. Inferior academic achievement of not progressing through qualification cards fast enough carried the same penalty as the classroom portion: a reserved room in the Hymie Hilton.

During this portion of the training, my mom's parents died within weeks of each other. I was very close to them and deeply saddened. Due to the pace of the instruction and the need for nucs in the fleet, school officials would not grant permission to attend my grandparents' funerals. As with the loss of the *Scorpion*, the events were not supposed to affect my performance. In spite of the expectations, my grades suffered a severe drop-off. The school imposed two penalties. Officials withdrew the recommendation for me to advance to third-class electrician's mate. They also sentenced me to the maximum extra mandatory study hours, without having to move into the Hymie Hilton. The worst effect was not having time to spend with Kathy. We maintained our relationship over the phone for a few weeks, but it was not enough and we broke up.

My resolve to make it through Nuclear Power School carried me through this tough time. I worked hard and my grades rebounded. Before long, school administrators reduced my mandatory study time.

After completing all qualification requirements, which some did faster than others, each trainee had to pass a final comprehensive written examination. If students overcame that obstacle, a several-hour oral examination awaited them.

When trainees passed all exams, their qualification was complete and a pink nametag replaced the white one. Earning a pink tag was the source of pride. It essentially became the diploma for completing Nuclear Power School, because there was no certificate. The only ritual conducted was having your pink tag crumpled by those who had already received their own. The order of qualification was evident by the condition of the tag. The first man to qualify had a pristine tag and the last had a mutilated one. I hate to admit it, but mine was very wrinkled. I took it in stride and was proud to complete the demanding program with a final score of 3.035.

Sans a graduation ceremony, the S1C contingent of 67–4 departed prototype on November 8, 1968. A group of us destined for submarine school engaged in a discussion about our orders.

Some were confused. The orders said Submarine School, New London–Groton, Connecticut. They wanted to know why there were two towns.

Having served in the area on the USS *Fulton*, I had the answer. The submarine base and sub school are located in Groton, across the Thames River from New London.

In 1915, when the submarine base became an entity, the boats docked in Groton. Due to a lack of buildings in Groton, the administrative offices were in New London. By the time the staff moved and joined the submarines, it was too late. The mailing address in New London was too well established. It was a lot easier to add Groton than eliminate New London. Hence, Submarine School, New London-Groton, Connecticut.

Southerland shrugged, "Guess I'll see y'all and the rest of 67–4 in Groton."

Holding the submarine school orders ignited excitement and nervousness. I was about to join an elite force, but as the loss of the USS *Scorpion* drove home, submarine duty is dangerous.

Chapter 5

Submarine School— The Final Preparation

Class 67–4 arrived at submarine school in November 1968. The school convened classes every two months and we had just missed the latest class-up. The next class would begin early January 1969.

In the interim, Class 67–4 performed menial chores. The petty officers stood barrack master-at-arms watches. One day, we loaded several tons of lead ballast into the bowels of the submarine rescue vessel, USS *Skylark*. It was a somber experience. She was escorting the USS *Thresher* on the submarine's fateful last dive. I, still an electrician's mate fireman, mostly swept barrack floors and did groundskeeping tasks. Compared to the rigor of Nuclear Power School, it was like a vacation.

Southerland and I reunited on the basketball court. We ended up playing for the welding school team in the submarine base league, although neither of were training to be welders. The league's cream of the crop was the Submarine School Raiders. They won the championship. I think Southerland had enough talent to play for the Raiders, but he chose not to pursue that avenue.

I began Basic Enlisted Submarine School on January 6, 1969. The curriculum was a combination of classroom instruction and hands-on activities.

The classroom portion presented the basic operation of the systems in a 640-class Fleet Ballistic Missile submarine. Unlike Nuclear Power School, I found the tests easy and did not have to study.

The hands-on instruction consisted of submarine firefighting strategies and damage control techniques such as stopping leaks using emergency methods. I was particularly interested in learning how to stop piping leaks. Unofficial reports said the initiating event leading to the sinking of the USS *Thresher* was a leaking seawater pipe.

I did not find much value in the hands-on training of operating a mock-up of a conventionally powered World War II submarine's rudder and diving planes. In defense of the Navy, the U.S. submarine fleet still had a considerable number of conventional boats. Still, the logic baffled me. Non-nuclear-trained students spent a day at sea in a conventional submarine. School officials waived that requirement for nucs and we missed the experience.

By administrating a thorough medical exam, the school also weeded out those who could not pass the rigorous submarine duty requirements.

Everyone also underwent a pressure test equal to the depth of 100 feet. This was as much a psychological check as physical. In addition to monitoring the trainee's ability to equalize his ears, the instructor watched for signs of claustrophobia. During my test, one sailor kept saying that his ears were not equalizing. The instructor did not take the complaints of pain seriously until the trainee's eardrum burst and blood flowed out his ear. Our instructor calmly returned the chamber's pressure to normal and let the sailor out. We resumed the test and never saw the injured man again. I learned an important lesson from the experience. If stranded in a sunken submarine, it was better to bust an eardrum and escape, than die.

While at submarine school, I took the scheduled semi-annual rating exam for third-class electrician's mate. I had missed my last opportunity to advance from electrician's mate fireman, due to my temporary inferior academic performance at prototype.

Towards the end of submarine school, we took a written psychological test. It was the standard exam with provided responses that ranged from "Sounds like me" to "Does not sound like me." There were a few special questions thrown in. One, I will never forget. It asked, "How do you relate to the following?—I would launch nuclear weapons." My wishy-washy response was "Sounds somewhat like me." It must have been satisfactory, because I qualified for submarine duty.

The last day of class, the instructor stood in front of my class and read everybody's name and next duty station. To my surprise, some men received orders to surface ships. I rejoiced. My next assignment, along with Southerland and Souder, was the USS *Henry Clay* SSBN 625—a real submarine.

Class 67–4's final activity together was a party at the base enlisted men's club. Although the Connecticut drinking age was 21, one of our classmates was at the door checking IDs. Regardless of his age, any member of 67–4 got in. We had a grand and sentimental time saying our goodbyes, not knowing if we would ever see each other again. I left the function highly inebriated. Between the club and my barrack, I encountered a patch of ice. As soon as I stepped on the slick surface, I fell on my butt. Like my determination to make it through Nuclear Power School, I vowed to walk over the icy surface, not walk around or crawl off. It probably took 15 minutes, but I succeeded.

After submarine school, I used a week of leave and returned to Hickory Township to visit my family. It was nice seeing them, especially since I would not have another chance for quite a while. My older brother Frank even came home from college. My younger sister Leona was especially happy. She is 11 years younger than I am, but we have always been close. She is such a pleasant person, my family nicknamed her Sweetie. My brother Curt is two years older than my sister is and involved in the sciences. During my 1969 spring visit, he was into model rockets. Even though it was early March, mild weather prevailed. The four of us had a lot of fun launching the projectiles.

That evening it occurred to me how Curt's rockets were the exact opposite of those carried aboard the USS *Henry Clay*. His were harmless, aimless toys, and those on the *Clay* were accurate weapons of mass destruction.

The excitement of my impending entry into the world of submariners tempered the enjoyment of my family's company and the relaxing environment. After reporting to the *Henry Clay*, I would be protecting the nation aboard the most powerful weapon on Earth and be a member of the elite United States Submarine Service.

I had spent my whole life preparing for that moment. Like a college athlete drafted by a professional team, I was moving up to the big leagues. I would finally put all my training to use at the highest level.

Chapter 6

Reporting to the USS *Henry Clay*

Anxious to begin my new career, I arrived at the Charleston Naval Shipyard, Charleston, South Carolina, on March 13, 1969. I parked outside the *Henry Clay*'s administrative office. I felt like my chest would burst from the pride that welled inside. I was about to officially join the ranks of submariners on an awesome wonder.

Finding the office, I walked in, introduced myself, and presented my paperwork to the duty yeoman. A tall lanky man greeted me. His frame did not seem like it would fit into a submarine very well.

The processing went smoothly. The yeoman gave me instructions about when and where to report the next morning. He gave me a map of the base and circled the *Clay*'s barrack. As I was about to leave the ship's office, a sailor dressed in dungarees walked past the door.

The yeoman called, "Hey, wheatgerm. Come meet our newest non-qual puke."

The man entered the office and the yeoman introduced him as second-class electrician Bob Davis.

I sized up the sailor. Davis was large and muscular. I judged him as being six foot tall and 240 pounds. He moved with the power and grace of an athlete. Jet-black hair adorned his head. He had a sinister Fu Manchu moustache, but I detected a friendly twinkle in his eyes. After some small talk, I discovered he was affable and happy to have me as a shipmate. He had been on the *Henry Clay* for a year and was qualified in submarines. He was from Florida, but didn't have a Southern accent. Davis was married and had a young daughter. He was a member of the *Henry Clay*'s champion football team. Davis played middle linebacker and running back. He was a devastating blocker in addition to being fast. After leaving the *Clay*, he was a Navy handball champion.

Davis greeted me warmly. He saw the map in my hand and showed where the *Henry Clay* was in dry dock. Before hustling away, he made a comment about probably becoming my sea daddy.

Instead of going directly to the barrack, I went to find the *Clay*.

She wasn't far. I stood at the edge of the dry dock.

At first glance, her size impressed me. At 425 feet from bow to stern, she was considerably longer than a football field. The beam, her width at the broadest point, was 33 feet. That is about as wide as a standard two-lane road. These proportions, long and narrow, gave her the gift of speed, a much-needed attribute in the world of submarine warfare.

The *Clay's* top speed is classified information. While she was in service, the Navy forbids us from revealing more than the following statistics: she is faster than 20 knots, dives deeper than 400 feet, and is capable of carrying nuclear weapons.

Due to similar security concerns, the government did not allow taking photos of many areas of her interior. I have to admit the rule was not strictly enforced, and there are some closely guarded contraband pictures floating around.

Pride welled within me. The submarine was a sophisticated marvel of technology and one of the most powerful weapons in the world. Soon I would be learning all her systems and operating those within my area of expertise.

The *Clay* was black, and unlike her surface ship counterparts, did not display a name or hull number. The color helped hide the FBM from aerial surveillance. Not having any distinguishing markings was an attempt to thwart enemy efforts of identifying her, both at sea and in port.

Her rounded bow sloped up in a smooth curve. About one hundred feet from the tip of the submarine was the front of the sail, sometimes called the conning tower or fairwater. It was eighteen feet tall and extended aft for another forty feet. If viewed from above, the sail had the shape of a teardrop, with the fat end forward. It was ten feet wide at its broadest point and acted as a stabilizer. At the top and forward end of the conning tower was the bridge. When the *Clay* was on the surface, officers directed the operation of the FBM from this high point. Aft of the bridge were retractable gray and black camouflage periscopes, antennas, and the snorkel mast. Towards the front and at the bottom of the sail was a round open hatch. It permitted access into a tube, which connected the bridge and submarine.

Towards the leading edge of the conning tower and twelve feet from the deck were the sailplanes. There was one on each side of the sail and each extended out fifteen feet. They functioned much like an airplane's ailerons, by tilting up and down to help the submarine change depth.

Immediately aft of the sail was a long flat surface. It was the missile deck. Along its upper surface, I could see the outline of each launch tube's hatch and a squiggly track imbedded in the center of the deck for attaching safety lines. Towards the end of this area was an open personnel access hatch.

The missile deck ended with the turtleback, and the top of the submarine then gently angled down. I recalled hearing the term turtleback in submarine school. The name seemed strange at the time. When the turtleback was seen firsthand, the title made perfect sense.

Several feet further aft of the turtleback was another escape hatch, which was open. A trio of black 3-inch diameter electrical cables snaked from a distribution box and disappeared into the opening. The cables provided electricity to the submarine. When the cables were in service, the *Clay* did not need her onboard electrical generating equipment.

The round hull of the boat dipped and narrowed as it continued aft. At the end of this span was the rudder. To the left and right of the rudder and a few feet below were the stern planes. They were similar to the sailplanes.

The submarine's classified propeller was not in place. Even if it were, a tarp would conceal it. The specialized design of the screw was a closely guarded military secret. Taking a photograph of it would incur severe punishment.

The Walker spy ring finally compromised the propeller's design. Subsequent Russian submarines that used similar style screws earned the informal nickname of Walker-class boats.

Pride welled within me as I walked away from the marvelous wonder. In the six-man barrack room, a surprise awaited me. There was Southerland stowing his gear.

Things got even better the next day. After quarters, Davis introduced me to my Electrical Division (E-Div) peers.

As soon as I met Second-Class Electrician's Mate Rich Marchbanks, I could tell he was extremely intelligent and driven to excel. Marchbanks was a hot runner and a Super-Nuc. Always striving to finish number one in any training attended, he rarely fell short of his goal. This included Nuclear Power School. He had a mischievous sense of humor and was very personable. Marchbanks would go on to become E-Div's leading petty officer (LPO). He always treated those under him with respect and did not assign jobs unless they were necessary. He never hesitated to work alongside his subordinates, regardless how unpleasant the task. It was hard to get mad at him even when we were bone-dog-tired and grumpy. Marchbanks eventually shared a Honolulu apartment with Southerland and me.

My other E-Div peers included electricians Rich Lewis, Greg Metzgus, Charlie Ballard, Interior Communication Technicians Charlie Schweikert, and Dick Treptow.

COB Chief Cal Cochran searched me out and issued my submarine qualification card and *Henry Clay* piping tab. He had good news. The *Clay* was going to shift from the Atlantic Fleet to the Pacific and be homeported in Pearl Harbor, Hawaii, after her overhaul.

I could hardly believe my good fortune, first class shipmates, and Hawaii in my future.

After quarters, Davis offered to give me a tour of the *Clay*.

Chapter 7

Inside the *Henry Clay*

As Davis and I walked to the *Clay*, I tried to remember what they taught in submarine school. Disjointed facts swirled in my mind as I attempted to form a mental picture of her interior. FBM submarines had six compartments. Each had a plethora of equipment crammed into it. Watertight bulkheads and doors separated the compartments. The largest open area was the crew's mess, where the crew ate, watched movies, and conducted group activities. If I was standing on the deck of the upper level of any compartment, the top of my head was below the surface of the water.

Although it only took a few minutes to make the walk, by the time we arrived at the *Clay*, my mind was a jumble of facts.

At the edge of the dry dock, we encountered a thin young sailor dressed in Navy dungarees. He was sporting a third-class crow. His Dixie cup white hat sat on his head at a seasoned salty angle.

Davis introduced us. Tommy Lee Connell was an A-ganger. He was from the South and came to the *Clay* from the USS *Trout*, SS 566.

Connell shook my hand and good-naturedly drawled, "By the way, do you know that nuc is only half a word? Heh. Heh."

His remark made me wonder about submarine crew camaraderie.

Davis and I walked to an open hatch on the port side of the sail. I entered the opening. Inside was a shaft extending up to the bridge, and down into the submarine. While descending the metal ladder into the submarine, I quickly forgot Connell's words. An unidentifiable unpleasant odor invaded my nose and it wrinkled in defense.

Davis, already at the bottom of the ladder, saw my reaction, laughed, and said, "Welcome to submarines. All submarines smell this way."

He then related a story about drunken sailors trying to bring a skunk aboard their submarine. The inebriated men came staggering back to their boat. One of them had a live skunk under his arm. After they crossed the gangplank and started bringing the animal below decks, the topside watch confronted them. For every reason to discourage the act, the drunks had a retort. Finally, in exasperation, the topside watch commented on the smell. The drunk with the skunk said that it would get used to it, just as he did!

The nearby periscope stand and seats for driving the submarine meant we were in the attack center. While Davis was leading me towards the front of the boat, the disagreeable odor began fading. Were my olfactory senses adapting?

I gawked around trying to comprehend all the new exotic sights and sounds. What I saw did not match the mental image I had forged at submarine school. The inside of the submarine, in contrast to the impression of the *Clay* from the outside, was small and crowded with equipment. Southerland, at 6'3", would have a tough time not banging his head.

After traveling through a maze, we reached the watertight door leading into the torpedo room, the most forward section of the *Clay*.

While negotiating the opening, I banged my head on the upper edge of the frame. Surprisingly, Davis didn't make fun of me.

Instead, he said, "That's something else to get used to. No matter how long you've been aboard, it will happen every once in a while."

I stopped and surveyed the obstacle. The opening in the bulkhead was an oval about three and a half feet high by twenty inches wide. A two-inch thick metal lip encircled the cavity. I had hit my head on its upper edge. The hatch's lower lip was 18 inches from the deck. To pass through, a person needed to step over the lower lip and duck under the top.

Davis noticed I was not following and came back.

He instructed me to open and close it. The sooner I learned how to seal off a compartment the better. The first rule of damage control was isolating the problem. If there was an uncontrolled fire or flooding, the crew had half a chance of surviving if the casualty was contained to one compartment.

Facing aft, the hatch hinge was on the starboard side. A spring latch held it open. It swung into the torpedo room. I pulled the door towards me. The lip of the opening provided a sealing surface for the closed door. A slightly curved chrome bar with a ball-shaped knob on either end pivoted around the door's middle and was the operating mechanism. When I rotated the bar in one direction, dogs (clamps) moved to hold the door closed. When shut, it was as strong as the bulkhead. Turning the rotating handle in the opposite direction retracted the dogs. Situated just above the operating mechanism was a small glass viewing port, for observing the adjacent compartment. It did not take long to familiarize myself with the door's operation. Whenever the *Clay* was in port, the crew left the hatch open.

There were four torpedo tubes on the compartment's forward bulkhead. Several empty torpedo racks were on the port and starboard edges of the area. The compartment had one level and there was no room to spare. In addition to equipment, several bunks helped fill the space. Davis pointed out the forward escape trunk in the overhead and a torpedo loading hatch along with its support equipment nestled aft of the trunk.

He mentioned that the cooks stored cases of eggs in the torpedo room's nooks and crannies. It was one of the cooler parts of the boat and relatively close to the galley.

Reversing direction, I had to pass through the watertight door again. Remembering my last experience passing through the obstacle, I made a special effort to ensure my head did not have another painful encounter. This time my noggin escaped unscathed. Unfortunately, I was paying so much attention to the top of the hatch I ended up barking my shin on the lower lip. After flinging a few well-deserved meaningless intensifiers at the object, I concluded it was much less painful to rap my thick skull than bang my shins.

I didn't ask what kind of impression I was making. Davis was probably having doubts about my future as a submariner. To his credit, he did not show any outward signs of that opinion.

We continued down the narrow passageway of the middle level of the operations compartment. On the starboard side was the wardroom. I stopped and looked through the open door. Several plaques adorned the wall and a long table was in the middle. The chair at the forward end of the table stood out. It had arms. I deduced it was the captain's seat.

There was an opening in the forward bulkhead of the wardroom. I saw a small kitchen through the conduit. Davis said it was the officers' pantry. Stewards obtained a portion of the food prepared in the main galley, added a bit of garnish, and served the officers.

Across the passageway from the wardroom were the junior officer staterooms. Three to four men shared each one. The area had a communal toilet and shower. Stewards took care of officers' personal needs, like doing their laundry, making beds, cleaning staterooms, serving meals, and shining shoes. The *Clay* had one Filipino steward. He was a foreign national. That meant he could not go into the engineering spaces, sonar shack, radio room, or any other space with classified equipment. The restriction prevented him from qualifying in submarines.

Farther aft on the port side were the trash disposal unit (TDU), the boat's walk-in refrigerator and freezer, galley, and the area where the crew ate, called the mess deck.

On the starboard side and across from the forward entrance to the mess deck were the chief's quarters. Sailors affectionately called it the goat locker. Just aft of the chief's quarters was a blank wall with a closed door. Davis opened the door, revealing the submarine's main ventilation room. Filling the space were fans and duct work. Seeing the room's crowded condition, I asked if the fans were reliable.

He chuckled while giving me a sly look, "You'll find out soon enough. Some guys can maneuver their way through and work in there much easier than others."

His indirect reference of my small stature did not give me a very good feeling.

We reversed directions and headed forward. After re-passing the mess deck and galley, we came to a stairway. It led us down to the operations compartment lower level.

Only nuclear submarines had stairways. Conventional boats were too small to have this luxury, and passage between levels was strictly via vertical metal ladders. Even in the *Clay*, vertical ladders were the predominant means of access from one deck to another.

After descending the stairs, we faced the main berthing area. It accommodated about 80 sailors. Bunks were recessed into the walls and stacked three high, each with its own privacy curtain.

I noticed that the area was devoid of occupants and asked Davis about the circumstance.

He told me the crew was living in barrack until after the overhaul.

Turning around, he led me to the head, which contained toilets, sinks, and showers. A small lounge had shelves crammed with books. The first-class petty officer quarters, a room with two washers and dryers, and missile system's fire control center were also in this area.

Davis showed me the deck hatch into the *Clay*'s 126-cell battery well. The battery was the FBM's emergency electrical power supply. Whenever the reactor was shut down and the emergency diesel generator or shore power was unavailable, the crew pressed it into service.

Electrician's mates spent an abundance of quality time in the space. We usually called it jumping the well. It was no fun. The overhead was too close to the working deck to stand up or even kneel. Men had to either duck-walk scrunched over or crawl to move around. There was no way to avoid getting battery acid on yourself and your clothes.

After cleaning the battery, some electricians asked the cooks to make up a bowl of water and baking soda. Then they used it to neutralize the acid on their hands and arms, which minimized burns. The worst reaction was some redness and a slight stinging sensation. I had so much acid on my hands, the bowl foamed over when I stuck them into it. It sure felt good.

Since acid eventually disintegrates clothing, Davis recommended I designate one set of dungarees for those duties. That way I would only ruin one work uniform.

Next, we went up two sets of stairs to upper level operations compartment.

The forward portion housed the captain and executive officer's staterooms, radio room, sonar, and the *Clay*'s office. Aft of these, the Control Room occupied the majority of the level.

I recalled submarine school teaching other monikers for this area, such as conn and attack center. Officers directed all aspects of the submarine from here.

My head was swimming from all the information Davis spewed: navigational equipment, tables for charts, controls for firing missiles and torpedoes, periscopes, communication equipment, alarm consoles, and so on.

We moved to the ballast control panel (BCP). The chief of the watch (COW) manned it under direction of the diving officer. The diving officer was in charge of main ballast tank vents, emergency-blow chicken switches, and maintaining the submarine's overall trim, which meant keeping the boat at a specific fore and aft angle.

Every so often, men played games with the diving officer, especially if he was new. A group of the crew, called a trim party, moved from one end of the boat to the other. This made the submarine tilt off the desired angle. Pumping water from one tank to another re-established the proper trim. Then the trim party raced to the other end of the submarine. They kept it up until the diving officer figured out what was happening.

Davis pointed toward two seats forward of the periscope stand. They faced an indication panel.

A helmsman and planesman physically controlled the submarine's depth and direction. Each used a control yoke, a device that looks like a small steering wheel. It was similar to that used by an airplane pilot. The helm and planesman took direction from the diving officer. The planesman sat in the outboard seat and operated his yoke to control the stern-planes. These planes have the most influence on a submarine's depth. The helmsman controlled the rudder and sailplanes. He also manipulated the engine order telegraph. It relayed how fast the officer of the deck (OOD) wanted the submarine to go. When he turned the engine order telegraph's knob, a similar device in maneuvering, the control station for the reactor and propulsion turbines, mirrored the signal.

At that point, my mind was a convoluted mass of disjointed facts. I refused to tell him I had had enough. This was what being a submariner was about. He must intimately know his boat from end to end and understand how everything worked and interfaced. That was why it took so long to qualify in submarines and why men had so much pride in earning their Dolphins. Although I felt overwhelmed, it spurred my desire to become the best submariner possible.

My mind refocused when I heard Davis say, "That watertight hatch leads you to upper level missile compartment."

He turned and walked forward. We went down some stairs to the next level. To my amazement, I recognized where we were.

We were a bit forward of the galley and ventilation room. We walked aft to the watertight door separating the operations and missile compartment.

I awkwardly passed through the opening and congratulated myself for not inflicting any pain to my body.

Davis continued with his guided tour.

The missile compartment had three levels. Crewmen fondly called it Sherwood Forest. That was because the two rows of eight missile tubes each were like tree trunks. Other than access to parts of the missile tubes, there was not much in either the upper or the lower levels. The upper level didn't have a real deck, just deck grating. On patrol, the crew stored supplies in the lower level.

It was almost breathtaking the way the missile tubes virtually filled the entire space. Knowing the tube's purpose made me shudder. To calm my nerves, I reminded myself that the weapons' purpose was deterrence, not as an offensive strike.

Feeling a bit better, and still in the middle level, we walked to the starboard side. On the outboard and forward end of the compartment was the missile launching control panel. Knobs, switches, and indicators covered it. I saw Davis's mouth moving as he described the complex station, but he might as well have been talking to a wall. My mind flashed back to the question on the psychological test at submarine school: "Would you launch nuclear weapons?"

As he rambled on, I scanned the panel for the terrible launch mechanism.

It should stand out somehow. Warning signs should flank something that important, and it should have a huge lock. On the contrary, every switch, button, and knob appeared benign. As hard as I tried, I couldn't find it and was too shy to ask.

We moved to the compartment's port side and walked down the passageway.

The double row of missile tubes in the compartment's center was to our left. Several rooms were on the outboard edge. There was a laboratory for performing chemical and radiological analysis by the engineering laboratory technician (ELTs); it was called the Nucleonics Lab. Next was the doctor's office, office space for the engineering department called the logroom, a lavatory, and another berthing area.

At the aft end of the passageway, we turned left, walked to the starboard side, and came upon another set of stairs.

I was grateful for the short respite from technical jargon and felt ready for him to bombard me with more information.

We climbed the stairs and passed through a doorway.

He explained we were in upper level machinery 1. Even though a wall separated the area from the missile compartment, it was not watertight. Machinery 1 was technically part of the missile compartment.

The area contained the navigation system 400-cycle motor-generators and their control panels. A chrome vertical ladder led to another access hatch. There was an air manifold in the forward port corner. A storage locker held engineering clerical supplies, such as the daily watch stander logs.

Next, we climbed down a ladder to middle level machinery 1. Equipment almost completely filled the area.

The first thing I encountered was the 30/10 KW M/G set. Beside it were the carbon dioxide (CO_2) scrubbers. They removed CO_2 from the submarine's atmosphere. Davis informed me that they barely held their own. The high CO_2 level gave crewmen headaches and cuts took forever to heal.

The most significant pieces of equipment were two oxygen (O_2) generators. They used very high temperatures to transform seawater into oxygen and hydrogen gas. The O_2 generators discharged the hydrogen overboard. The submarine stored the oxygen in tanks. Sailors periodically bled oxygen into the submarine's atmosphere to replace what breathing consumed. The O_2 generators were essential to prolonged submergence. An inexhaustible source of seawater and properly functioning O_2 generators meant submariners never ran out of air. The O_2 generators were nicknamed the bombs. The crew feared them even more than the torpedoes or missiles. As dangerous as the O_2 generators were, the *Clay* never had a problem. Joel McCann was a master at their upkeep and operation.

I got down on my hands and knees. The position allowed me to peek through the deck hatch. Crammed against the forward bulkhead was a small supply office.

The hovering tanks were under lower level's deck. They held the submarine at a stable depth for missile launches.

Davis and I returned to machinery 1 upper level. At the aft end of the compartment was a watertight door. Below it was an ominous yellow and magenta sign: PERSONNEL DOSIMETRY REQUIRED FOR ENTRY DURING REACTOR OPERATION. NO BUNKING OR LOITERING IN MACHINERY SPACES. The middle of the sign had the radiation symbol. Unlike the other hatches, this one was closed. The sign on the door created an imposing warning. I felt as if they were saying: Beware, all ye who pass this portal.

Davis said, "Now it's going to get interesting. The other side of that hatch is the nuclear engineering spaces."

Chapter 8

The Forbidden Zone: The Engineering Spaces

As hard as it was to gain access to a nuclear-powered submarine, it was even more difficult to enter its engineering spaces. I acknowledged the honor bestowed upon me. Not only was I permitted to enter the area, the Navy trusted me to operate the equipment. Graduates of Nuclear Power School manned the watch stations in the engineering spaces.

I preceded Davis to the hatch. Recalling my previous difficulties with similar openings, I hesitated. Then I mustered enough bravado to appear confident. I opened the door and awkwardly passed through without injury. I secretly congratulated myself on applying hard-earned lessons.

We were in the reactor compartment tunnel. It had shielded bulkheads and deck. The shielding provided safe passage over the reactor compartment.

The tunnel was about twenty feet long. The forward end was roughly ten feet wide, with flat bulkheads up to the curved hull. Low to the deck and on opposite bulkheads were oval yellowish lead glass windows for monitoring steam generator water level sight glasses and inspecting the reactor compartment. There was a four-foot-diameter circle in the center of the deck. Under it was the reactor's refueling hatch. At about the tunnel's halfway point, it necked down to six feet wide. There was a watertight door on the port side of the narrower portion for entering the reactor compartment. Securing the hatch was a chain and padlock. At the aft end of the tunnel, three steps descended to the watertight door to machinery 2.

I peered through the port lead glass window. A steam generator filled my view. The window's nearly opaque yellow and the reactor compartment's dim lights prevented me from discerning other components. The

47

nuclear reactor sat in the middle. Large pipes carried the reactor's heated water to the bottom of two steam generators. Pumps transported the cooled water exiting the other side of the steam generators back into the reactor. Steam pipes from the tops of the generators sent steam to the propulsion turbines, turbo-generators, and support auxiliaries.

Davis descended the stairs at the aft end of the tunnel, stopped, turned, and said, "Directly below me is the pressurizer."

I recalled learning about the pressurizer at Nuclear Power School. Using embedded electrical heaters, it maintained a high pressure in the reactor coolant system. The elevated pressure kept the reactor coolant from boiling.

We entered upper level auxiliary machinery 2 and went down three steps to the main deck. Straight ahead was a passageway. Electrical distribution panels running fore and aft flanked the walkway's sides.

I saw they were two-sided. The panels contained the *Clay*'s major circuit breakers. Electricians operated and worked on them. That was a downside of being a submarine electrician. We maintained all of the electrical equipment throughout the boat—lighting, receptacles, distribution panels, breakers, and all the electrical generators. If it was 120 volt AC and above or 125 volt DC, it belonged to the electricians.

The reactor control instrument panels were on the starboard forward corner. At their bottom were the SCRAM breakers. When any one of the breakers opened, the associated control rods dropped into the reactor and stopped the fission process. Legend had it that SCRAM was an acronym for Safety Control Rod Axe Man. The original reactor supposedly had one control rod suspended by a rope. If the scientists wanted to stop the nuclear chain reaction, a person with an axe cut the rope, and the rod dropped into the reactor.

Although the *Clay*'s reactor safety system was much more sophisticated than that, it still used gravity, a constant of the universe.

The forward port corner held a sample sink for sampling the steam generators and the reactor coolant system.

We walked to the back of upper level machinery 2 and stopped. Stretching across the starboard half of the aft bulkhead was a workbench with a vice. There was an open watertight hatch in the middle of the bulkhead.

Davis leaned on the workbench, pointed towards the compartment's aft port corner, and mentioned it contained the engineering space's most important item. Curious, I walked over and investigated.

It was a "head," containing a toilet, sink, and shower. Its light switch was on the outside of the room. On the inner bulkhead, there was a small latched door below the shower nozzle, about waist high. I twisted the latch and the door folded down, revealing a sink. The toilet was opposite the shower and sink.

The intended purpose of the shower was de-contaminating radiologically contaminated individuals. The sink and shower water shut-off valve was outside the little space. The same was true for the head's light switch. There was a metal loop instead of a doorknob and the door opened into the space.

Davis explained how sailors sometimes closed the outer valve and opened the one for the shower. When someone went in, the prankster quietly inserted a wrench through the loop, trapping the man inside. Then the light was turned off, outer valve opened, and the poor sucker inside received a cold douching.

Davis's eyes were alight with mirth and he emitted a mischievous laugh as he said, "Guys aren't allowed to get mad. It's their fault for not checking the valve before going in."

I wandered back to the workbench and examined a voice tube. It was a simple but effective method for people to talk between different areas having high background noise. The voice tube was a dull brass vertical pipe, roughly two inches in diameter. At either end was a highly polished four-inch-long cone. The opening at the cone's end was approximately three inches in diameter. One person signaled another, by tapping on his end of the voice tube and then positioned his ear at the opening. The person summoned placed his mouth very close to his end and answered. The voice tube I was examining extended into lower level machinery 2.

Davis's eyes twinkled as he pretended to pour something down the tube.

I understood his intent. Because of having to get so close to the tube to speak, the person below was in a vulnerable position. The man in the upper level could dump water down the tube. If the man below wasn't alert, he got a face full. Recognizing the cues that it was about to happen, such as the talker speaking softly or mumbling, could save someone the embarrassment of having his head washed. I learned the person in the upper level was not safe either. Ingenious sailors would rig an air hose to the bottom end and blow water up the tube. It was a bit trickier, but possible.

I had heard that episodes like these were a common practice on submarines, but I'd never really believed it. As I observed the matter-of-fact way Davis related the tales and his apparent enjoyment, it appeared they were all true and then some. I was silently dumbfounded by the gleeful manner Davis dispensed the pranks and wondered if I would evolve into someone with a similar frame of mind. Maybe he was an exception. My gut told me different.

We climbed down the ladder to lower level machinery 2 and stood on a diamond-deck walkway. I re-oriented myself. We were at the back end of the compartment on the starboard side looking forward.

Davis pointed at a large horizontal cylindrical machine next to the starboard hull and told me it was one of the 300-kilowatt (kw) motor generators (M/Gs). The other was on the port side. They were remarkable machines. When the submarine's ships service turbine generator (SSTG) was producing power, the AC end of the M/G was a motor. The other end was a DC generator, which supplied DC loads and sent a trickle charge to the submarine's 126-cell main battery. On a loss of an SSTG, the electrical operator adjusted the M/G controls to reverse the operation of the M/Gs. The DC end transformed into a DC motor, powered from the battery. The AC end, which had been a motor, became an AC generator.

Dominating the middle of the compartment was the emergency diesel and its associated generator. Underway, the crew employed it whenever the reactor was not producing enough steam to operate the ships service turbine generators and there was not much juice left in the 126-cell main battery. The *Clay* would come up to periscope depth and snorkel.

On the aft bulkhead was the steam generator water level control station (SGWLC). Davis informed me the station was usually just called "Squiggle."

We returned to the upper level. Davis deftly slipped through the hatch and entered the upper level engine room. I followed, but not nearly as smoothly.

The engine room's brightness surprised me. I looked up and saw a large hole aft of where we were standing. Shipyard workers needed it for some of their work.

Since the *Clay* was in dry dock, most of the engineering systems were shut down. The engine room was devoid of the oppressive heat, humidity, and loud mechanical noises of ordinary operations. The Navy still required a few watch standers to monitor plant conditions.

The shutdown maneuvering area watch (SMAW) was in maneuvering. He maintained oversight of the reactor. The SMAW was also the senior watch station. The shutdown roving watch (SRW) was a machinist's mate and had responsibility for monitoring the mechanical equipment. The shutdown electrical operator (SEO) tended to the electrical gear. Unlike the other two watches, the SEO did not have to remain in the engineering spaces.

Maneuvering, the control room for the engineering spaces, was a few feet aft of us, on the *Clay*'s starboard side, and segregated from the engine room by having its own air-conditioned enclosure. The reactor, electrical equipment, and steam plant were controlled from maneuvering, making it the nerve center of the nuclear-related machinery. It was even more significant to me. I had spent the past two years training and gaining experience, preparing myself for duty in maneuvering. An open doorway existed on the enclosure's inboard side facing the passageway. A chain stretched across the opening. From my angle, I could see only a small portion of maneuvering. I was itching for Davis to show and tell me about the control panels for operating the electric plant, reactor, and the main propulsion turbines. It was almost as if he could sense my anticipation and was withholding going over there on purpose.

I stifled my eagerness as Davis started again, "Those tall tanks with the sight glasses on either side of the hatch are the feedwater surge tanks."

His eyes moved from my head down to my feet and back up. Then he ominously said, "Wow! You're the perfect size to fit inside them and work on the level indicators."

I looked at the tank. It was not more than two feet square and eight feet tall. At the bottom, about six inches from the deck, as a manway for entry. I hoped he was pulling my leg.

Next to the starboard tank was a chrome ladder leading to the after escape trunk. The lower hatch was open. I could see the three large black shore power cables. They attached to connections in the escape trunk. The forward port corner held the lithium-bromide air conditioning unit and the 8,000-gallon-per-day distillation unit. The still processed seawater and made the *Clay*'s fresh water. Engineering plant operating water usage had the highest priority. Personal showers were lowest on the list.

After what seemed to be an eternity, we walked a few feet aft. We were finally at maneuvering. I felt like a kid at Christmas, busting at the seams to open presents. I was about to get my first exposure to the control room of the USS *Henry Clay*'s S5W nuclear plant, the fifth generation of Westinghouse's submarine design. Although I suppressed any outward signs, I could feel the excitement surging through me like an electric current.

Submarine school had briefly covered the S5W control room. I learned the *Clay*'s power plant was worlds apart from S1C, where I received my initial nuclear practical training.

As I peered into the enclosure, I saw a dungaree-clad individual standing and facing the middle control panel. He was intently scanning the dials and recording readings.

After putting his clipboard down, he turned in our direction. He had "Horne" stenciled above his dungaree shirt pocket. Davis explained I was a baby nuc electrician fresh out of school, another non-qual puke he would have to lead by the hand for a while. Then he introduced us. Horne reached over the chain, shook my hand, and told me I could call him Jim. Davis remarked that they called him Horney Toad or just Toad.

Then Davis told Horne to check my profile and said, "We should call him Eaglebeak."

I tried not to show any reaction to the comment. My face felt warm and I was sure a blush was providing evidence of my embarrassment. Neither appeared to notice, or they were showing kindness by not rubbing it in.

Horne mentioned needing to use the head. He suggested Davis relieve him. It would kill two birds with one stone. Horne would get his needed break and Davis could familiarize me with maneuvering.

Davis agreed.

I unhooked the chain across maneuvering's doorway. Davis and I entered.

Horne provided the typical SMAW turnover report, "Air in the banks. Shit in the tanks. Two-slow/two-slow. Rods on the bottom."

After Horne left, Davis filled me in on the protocol for entering maneuvering. Everybody must request permission. It didn't matter who you were, your rank or status. The only exceptions were the captain, executive officer, engineer, and the engineering officer of the watch (EOOW). They had blanket permission.

Maneuvering was markedly cooler than the engine room. Davis related how engineering roving watch standers occasionally stood in the doorway for a respite from the engine room's oppressive environment. I could only imagine the difference when there was steam in the engine room.

While Davis reviewed the logs and indications, I familiarized myself with maneuvering.

I estimated that maneuvering was ten feet deep, from the doorway to its terminus at the submarine's curved hull. It was about six feet wide. Control and monitoring panels occupied most of the area. There were three main consoles, which filled the entire forward edge of maneuvering. Each had a sloped bench section, a vertical portion, and another aft-sloped upper section. The steam plant control panel was on the inboard end, by the doorway. The reactor plant control panel was in the middle, and the electric plant control panel was outermost. Directly aft of the reactor plant control panel and electric plant control panel were elevated chairs that swiveled and allowed watch standers to operate their controls without standing.

I was standing in an open space by the doorway facing forward. In front of me was the steam plant control panel. To my rear was a footlocker with a cushion on top of it.

Electrician's mates usually manned the steam plant control panel and was called a throttleman. Designers provided a round eight-inch seat for the throttleman. Because operating the throttle wheels required standing, it could be swiveled out of the way. I swung the seat away from maneuvering's port bulkhead and sat. Being too small and unstable, and not having back support, it was uncomfortable. Then I sat on the footlocker. I could lean back against the after bulkhead. It certainly wasn't as comfy as an easy chair, but it was much better than the round seat. After all, this was not a home; it was the control room of the *Clay*'s engineering spaces.

Directly in front of me was the steam plant control panel. Its most notable feature was two chrome wheels. A large one, about two feet in diameter, was closest to the panel. The smaller one, about 18 inches in diameter, was several inches farther aft. Both wheels shared the same pivot point and protruded from the top of the lower portion of the panel. They looked like steering wheels. They controlled steam to the main propulsion turbines, which in turn determined how fast the submarine moved. The big one was for ahead bells. The little one admitted steam to the astern throttles, for backing. A loud bell rang if both were open at the same time.

An engine order telegraph was in the lower right hand corner of the sloped bench section. The right half of the dial had the ahead bells—⅓, ⅔, Standard, Full, and Flank. The left had astern bells—⅓, ⅔, Back Full, and Back Emergency. Speed changes were called bells because a bell dinged when the officer of the deck ordered a speed change.

Covering the center of the bench section were alarms and associated cutout switches. There was an array of dials and meters scattered on the remainder of the panel. With my head swimming, I stood. I squeezed by Davis and sat in the seat for the electric plant control panel, with hands clasped behind me. I figured this posture would give Davis peace of mind that I would keep my hands off the panel. It must have accomplished the desired effect, because he did not reprimand me. I did notice that his general body posture implied a readiness to prevent me from touching anything.

Electricians operated the *Clay's* major electrical equipment from this panel. The bench portion had an excellent one-line representation of the submarine's electrical system. There were two complete redundant trains. The left side was a mirror image of the right.

Davis described the icons, at the top of the mimic, going from left to right. The symbol furthest left represented the port ships service turbine generator (SSTG). Next were the emergency diesel generator (E D/G), the shore power connection, and the starboard SSTG. When the reactor produced enough power, two SSTGs were in service and the electric plant was in a full-power lineup.

I mentally traced the left portion of the plastic representation. The line went left and then down towards me. Then it proceeded to an icon for the 300 kw motor-generator. I recalled seeing it in auxiliary machinery 2 lower level. To the representation's right were two large black control knobs. They controlled the M/G's mode of operation. Exiting the M/G symbol, the plastic line continued down a short distance and took a ninety-degree angle towards the center of the panel. In the middle was a representation of the *Clay's* 126-cell battery. I looked at the right half of the panel. It was a mirror image of the left. Embedded at strategic places in both sides of the mimic were circuit breaker control switches.

The *Clay's* normal electrical configuration consisted of two electrically separated SSTGs. Each generator supplied its half of the electrical system, also called a train. The SSTG provided power to electrical busses, which supplied individual loads. The SSTG also drove the motor end of the M/G. The M/G's generator end produced DC power to various loads and kept the 126-cell battery charged. This was a normal full-power lineup.

Sometimes, one SSTG was unavailable. In this situation, the electrical operator paralleled the two electrical trains and powered both halves of the electrical system from one SSTG. This was a half-power lineup.

If both turbine generators were lost, usually because of a reactor SCRAM, the electrical operator used the M/G's black knobs to swap the AC and DC ends of the motor-generators. The DC end transformed from a generator to a motor and the AC end became a generator. The battery then provided all the power to the submarine. In order to conserve the battery, the crew rigged the submarine for reduced electrical power by turning off all nonessential electrical equipment. Designated compartment individuals aligned equipment according to bulkhead checklists. That extended the time the battery could supply power.

Various reasons required using the emergency diesel generator. When it is in service, sailors call it snorkeling. On patrol, the diesel was only used as the last resort. Even though it had special mounts to prevent transmitting noise outside the boat, it was still too noisy. The last thing an FBM wanted to do was give away its position to the enemy.

In port, shore power supplied electricity to the *Clay*. If there was a loss of shore power, the crew did not hesitate using the diesel.

I shifted my attention to the reactor plant control panel. I surveyed the bench portion of the panel. It had a representation of the reactor coolant system. There were icons for the reactor, main coolant pumps, pressurizer, and the coolant-loop isolation valves. I spied a pistol-grip switch in the middle of the reactor panel. There was a label below it that read, "In-Hold-Out."

Davis saw me staring at the switch and said, "We simply call it the In-Hold-Out switch. It operates the reactor control rods."

Later in her career, the *Clay*'s reactor gained the nickname "Ralph." A reactor operator was performing a reactor startup. He had spent the previous evening imbibing in too much liquid refreshment and was really hung over. He controlled his queasy stomach until the reactor was critical. While the EOOW made the 2MC announcement that the reactor was critical, the broadcast included the sounds of the reactor operator puking his guts out. From that day on, the nucs called the reactor Ralph.

Davis pointed out a temperature meter on the vertical section. It was the T_{ave} indicator. T_{ave} is nuclear jargon for the average temperature of the water transferring the heat from the nuclear reactor. As the water passes over the fuel, it picks up heat. The hot water exiting the reactor is called T_{hot} or T_h. The liquid then passes through tubes in steam generators and produces steam for driving the propulsion turbines and electrical turbine generators. The water leaving the steam generators is relatively cold and is termed T_{cold}. Nuclear reactors have strict design operating parameters. Keeping the water temperature within limits is crucial to safe reactor operation. Therefore, the T_{ave} meter is very important.

Nestled in a myriad of indicators, the middle portion of the meter's indicating range was green. The left edge of the green section was the low limit of the reactor coolant system's average operating temperature. The right was the highest. The amount of steam sent to the propulsion turbines varied according to the bell the throttleman was answering. As bells changed, the throttleman had to respond quickly. That changed how much heat was drawn from the reactor coolant system. The reactor operator had to match the heat demanded by the turbines with the heat generated by the reactor, by raising or lowering power. If heat demanded was more than what the reactor produced, the temperature of the reactor coolant system could go below the lower limit of the green band and vice versa.

The chain across the door to maneuvering rattled. Horne was back.

After entering maneuvering, he asked if there were any changes in plant status. Davis told him everything was the same.

As Horne settled into the reactor plant control panel's chair, he commented, "OK, I got it. By the way, Eaglebeak, it was nice meeting you. Don't make yourself a stranger in these parts."

Davis and I exited maneuvering and headed aft on the diamond deck plates paving the walkway. Immediately behind maneuvering was an electrical distribution panel, with rows and rows of 480-volt breakers. Filling the compartment's overhead was a maze of wires and pipes.

The smooth curvature of the sub's hull formed the overhead and sides. We were standing on the centerline of the boat. To our left and right were the port and starboard 2000-kw ships service turbine generators. The walkway extended aft and up two steps between the generators.

Davis grinned and remarked that the coffee pot just inboard of the forward portion of the port generator was the first piece of gear I would learn to operate. Junior nucs had to make and deliver coffee, especially to the guys stuck in maneuvering.

At the aft end of the diamond-deck walkway were throttle wheels identical to the ones on the steam plant control panel. These were for use in emergencies. Left and right of them were the main propulsion turbines, normally called the main engines.

I was about to go up the steps, when he indicated we use the walkway on the outboard side of the port turbine generator. It led us past the port main engine.

I gawked at the plethora of pipes, valves, emergency air breathing (EAB) manifolds, and battle lanterns. The true shape of the FBM's round pressure hull was clearly visible. As it continued aft, I could see it tapered down smaller and smaller. I became transfixed with the image of the *Clay* as a sleek cigar-shaped projectile smoothly slipping though the ocean carrying out its secret missions.

We stopped just aft of the propulsion turbines. The shaft of each main engine extended into a large housing. It contained the reduction gears. They combined the power from the two propulsion turbines and transmitted it to the *Clay's* single main shaft. Embedded in the shaft was the DC emergency propulsion motor (EPM). It was mainly used when the main engines were unavailable, such as after a reactor SCRAM.

The area also housed the aft signal ejector and the 2000-gallon-per-day distillation unit. The still was difficult to operate, but Mike Pavlov eventually mastered it.

We had finally gone as far aft as possible. I could see the pressure hull tapering down. The inside of the boat terminated at a flat bulkhead. Although we had plenty of headroom, the diameter of the space was significantly smaller here than anywhere else in the submarine. Just beyond the bulkhead were the stern planes, rudder, and the screw. Crossing over to the starboard side, he pointed out the main hydraulic pumps. They supplied the hydraulic fluid for operating the planes, rudder, masts, and periscopes. Davis slipped down a vertical ladder to engine room lower level (ERLL). I followed.

Another cramped area greeted me. It was easy to see how a claustrophobic person could have problems. There were no easy exits.

The main propulsion shaft exited the submarine through the aft bulkhead. A scary thought flashed in my brain. There had to be enough clearance between the shaft and the hull such that there was not any rubbing. That meant there was an open conduit from inside the submarine to the surrounding water. To ensure the ocean stayed on the correct side of the submarine's hull, engineers designed shaft seals with a very tortuous path between inside and outside. I hoped the engineers did a good job. Every foot of water adds 0.433 pounds per square inch (psi) of pressure. At 400 feet, the pressure increased to 172 psi. That amount of pressure could cut a man in half. There was an even more disconcerting fact. As the pressure increased, the number of gallons a minute from any leak increased proportionately. That is what doomed the USS *Thresher.*

We turned and headed forward to the condenser bay. The aft end of it had an opening the size and shape of a watertight hatch. On the other end of the condenser bay, about ten feet forward of us, was a similar one. Unlike the others, these had half doors and were made of thin metal.

The condensers on either side of the bay converted the steam from the turbines to water. Seawater passed through one side of the heat exchanger. It condensed the steam. Condensate pumps sent the water back to the steam generators.

Davis showed me a salinity cell. It monitored the conductivity of the water returning to the steam generators. Normally, this liquid was very pure and would not conduct electricity. If seawater leaked into the condensate side of the main condenser, it made the water conduct electricity. Salinity cells detected the current. If it went high enough, the cell sent an alarm to a panel on the back edge of maneuvering. Ninety-nine percent of the alarms were false. The remedy was simply cleaning the salinity cell.

Exiting the condenser bay brought us into the forward part of engine room lower level. This section was about the same size as the lube oil and condenser bays combined. My head swam, trying to drink in everything I saw—condensate pumps, main seawater pumps, auxiliary water pumps, chill water pumps, trim and drain pumps, air conditioning units, et cetera, et cetera. There was double of everything.

Davis tapped me on the shoulder, pointed up, laughed, and cryptically stated, "See those three can-looking things? They're for the bottom posts of maneuvering's chairs."

We climbed up a ladder. To my surprise, we were just port of the *Clay*'s centerline and a little aft of maneuvering. A glance revealed Horne sitting and scanning the RPCP. I quickly checked the base of the chair. A single metal pole extended down from the seat. About eight inches from the deck was a foot-ring. The pole disappeared into the deck.

Davis left the engine room. I followed him through the opening. Much to my relief, we silently retraced our path through machinery 2 upper level, the tunnel, and into machinery 1 upper level. I scanned the compartment one final time before climbing the ladder and exiting the submarine.

My first encounter with life on the *Henry Clay* was complete. The demands of submarine duty caused questions to whirl through my mind. Prior to joining the Navy, outside activities dominated my life. How would I react to confinement in a submarine for months on end? Could I adapt to submarine culture? Even though prototype had exposed me to casualty conditions, would I maintain my composure in actual life-and-death situations when over a hundred other men were depending on me? The *Henry Clay* was capable of annihilating millions of people. How would this awesome level of involvement in the Cold War affect me?

Any doubts of my ability to make it as a submariner were tempered. I was 20 years old with unbridled confidence and determination. My previous prototype success was also comforting. With regards to the dangers, the "can't happen to me" attitude of "indestructible youth" was strong within me and did not allow me to fully comprehend the actual dangers involved. I made a promise to myself that I would measure up and become a top-notch submariner.

Managing to pass through the rigorous gauntlet of qualifying for submarine duty was only the first step of becoming a true submariner. Graduating from Submarine School had earned me the designation of submarine unqualified (SU). Qualified submariners called SUs non-quals. We were considered the next to lowest level in the Navy. In a submariner's eye, the only Navy people lower than submarine unqualified sailors were skimmers. In order to lose the moniker of SU, I needed to learn all of the USS *Henry Clay*'s systems and pass extensive examinations.

I developed a plan. The first step was getting a concept of the general layout of the major equipment. Qualifying would be like prototype: I would learn one system at a time. The *Clay*'s piping tab, a pocket-sized booklet with one-line drawings of all of the FBM's systems, would be my guide through the journey.

I knew the quest of receiving a submariner's Holy Grail, my Dolphins, would not be easy. When aboard the *Clay*, I'd have to devote all of my spare time towards qualifying.

In spite of the arduous task ahead, pride welled within me. I could visualize Dolphins on my chest and being a member of the elite submarine force.

Since I was still technically a fireman, I spent the first part of the *Clay*'s overhaul as a shipyard mess cook. The lowly duty only lasted a few months. When the official results of my third-class electrician's mate test arrived, mess cooking ended and I began performing electrical work.

The promotion to petty officer third-class was effective from the date of the exam. I received the back pay in a lump sum. Southerland, Souder, and I used some of it for a nice celebration at a notorious local establishment.

The overhaul would convert the *Clay*'s missile system from the shorter-range Polaris A-2 to the much longer-range A-3. I found one modification comforting. Workers were repairing a design flaw in the emergency blow system. The same flaw had prevented the USS *Thresher* from reaching the surface and condemned her to doom.

Chapter 9

Test Depth

As the overhaul progressed, I gained the ancillary assignment of logroom yeoman. I was responsible for all the engineering department paperwork and technical manuals.

Just as Davis suspected, he became my mentor. I was happy with the arrangement. The man was a wealth of knowledge, a patient teacher, and a good friend. As workers slowly reassembled the *Clay* and in between my logroom tasks, there were more opportunities for him to impart his experience.

By the end of the overhaul, I was performing electrical duties on my own, such as taking battery gravities, operating and monitoring equipment, cleaning salinity cells, and making minor repairs. I also became an expert on the lube oil sumps' electrostatic precipitators.

Davis encouraged Lewis and me to join him on the *Henry Clay* flag football team. We went undefeated, won the Charleston area championship, and played in the Naval District playoffs in Memphis, Tennessee. True to traditional submarine camaraderie, the team unanimously voted to stay intact and not replace anyone with stars from other teams. We did not advance far, but we were competitive against Naval Air Base teams, which had more than 50,000 potential players. The team unity made me proud of being in the submarine service.

In August of 1969, I took and passed the rating advancement test for second-class electrician's mate. The result surprised me, because 75 percent of the test was on electrical elevators, an item foreign to submarines.

In March 1970, the *Clay*'s overhaul was complete. The officers and men assigned to the *Clay* during her refurbishment were divided into the Blue and Gold Crews. I became a member of the Gold Crew, under the command of Commander Robert Montross.

The Gold Crew's first evolution was performing a fast cruise. The name is a misnomer; the submarine didn't travel anywhere. Fast had nothing to do with speed. The submarine remained tied fast to a pier.

Under these conditions, we could safely test almost all of the *Clay*'s systems. If something went wrong, plenty of assistance was readily available and the boat could only sink a few feet before settling to the bottom.

It was a grueling test of the crew and submarine. The *Clay*'s complement had to react to normal and casualty situations. Not meeting established standards required repeating the evolution until we were judged satisfactory.

The fast cruise revealed a problem with one feedwater surge tank's level indicator. With a smile on his face and reminding me of his prediction, Davis assigned me to make the repair. After giving me some pointers, he obtained the new level column, a wrench, a drop light, and an air hose. I shoved the wrench into my pocket. We walked to the tank, which was located forward of maneuvering. The tank's manway was near the bottom. Davis put the hose into the tank and initiated ventilation. Feeling nervous, I lay on my back and stuck my head into the opening. Davis handed me the drop light and level column. My feet pushed against the back of the SPCP and propelled me into the tank. As soon as my head touched the side of the tank, I angled it up, until my back was against the side. With feet continuing to push, my back slid up the tank, until I was standing. There was barely enough room to move my arms. I told Davis to push the hose further into the tank so it was close to my face. I took a couple of deep breaths and let the butterflies in my stomach settle. Feeling secure about my air supply calmed me and I quickly replaced the level detector. Exiting was the reverse of entering, although gravity assisted my descent. My feet exited first and I hoped they were not going to slip and make my back slide down too fast. Leaving the tank went smoothly, and other than being covered in black corrosion products, which took weeks to disappear, I suffered no ill effects. The task proved I was not the least bit claustrophobic.

The Gold Crew completed fast cruise with flying colors. I felt good about my contribution to the success.

Next were sea trials. The most serious test was actually submerging the submarine.

Submerging a submarine is always dangerous. Due to the comprehensive work completed during her two-year overhaul, the *Clay*'s first dive involved additional risk. We employed several safety precautions. For one, the first dive took place over the continental shelf, where the water depth was only about 500 feet. As an added safeguard, the submarine rescue vessel USS *Falcon* escorted us. If we sank, the *Falcon* could extract us with a rescue bell. Knowing the rescue vessel could save us provided some relief from apprehensions.

A submariner's first dive is a significant event. Mine was no exception, although for a different reason: I was sleeping. The diving klaxon sounding its mournful ah-oooo-gahs and the 1MC blaring, "Dive! Dive!" brought me to the edge of consciousness. I was barely aware of the boat's diminishing sporadic reaction to the surface conditions and the subsiding sound of the sea swishing over the hull. When I awoke, we were uneventfully submerged. During my next watch, I checked the status of the main propulsion shaft seal. It had a small steady trickle. Machinist's Mate Rusty Wishon happened by and saw me staring at the leak. He adjusted the packing and assured me that it would not be a problem. The remaining testing went without incident.

A few days later, the *Clay* headed out to sea for her next major event—diving to test depth.

Beyond the continental shelf, the ocean is deep enough to accommodate diving to test depth. It is also far deeper than *Clay*'s crush depth, a potentially negative aspect. At the appointed time, we rendezvoused with the submarine rescue vessel USS *Falcon*. She would monitor our dangerous excursion.

I checked the newly posted watch, quarter, and station bill. My station was the reactor compartment tunnel. I was responsible for monitoring the tunnel and poorly lit reactor compartment. Unlike my first tour of the *Clay*, I was very familiar with these areas and was trusted to detect the slightest problem.

Before manning the station, I decided to check the shaft seal. Verbal reports of its status hadn't relieved my fears and I wanted to see it for myself. A quick trip to lower level engine room revealed it was merely a trickle, just as Wishon predicted. Although it made me feel better, I wondered how it would behave during our descent to test depth. I shuddered at the thought of it catastrophically failing.

As I turned to head back to the tunnel, Southerland arrived and donned an engineering communications headset, designated the 2JV. Because of engine room noise, he nodded at me, winked, and gave a thumbs-up. Seeing his calmness had a comforting effect.

Everybody monitoring for leaks, including myself, would wear a 2JV headset. The device permitted quick communication when reporting status and abnormal conditions. The 2JV circuit also allowed anyone wearing a headset to hear everybody else. There was also a special loudspeaker in maneuvering. We called it the White Rat. It repeated all 2JV communications.

I climbed the ladder from shaft alley to upper level engine room and walked forward,

While passing through machinery 2 upper level, I saw Schweikert sitting on the after workbench and talking to Lewis.

I heard Lewis say, "*Thresher* sank doing the same thing."

Schweikert scrunched his face. "Thanks for reminding me. I was already nervous about going so deep."

I reminded myself of the facts. Many submarines had done such a dive. It was a once-in-a-lifetime experience that I could brag about to my grandchildren. Our shipyard overhaul corrected the problem with the emergency blow system.

I continued to the tunnel. Once there I donned my headset and established communications. Rushing was a waste of time. Metzgus, the maneuvering phone talker, informed us the test's start would not begin for at least half an hour. It was typical Navy protocol—hurry up and wait.

I sat on the linoleum deck and leaned against the bulkhead. Waiting with nothing to keep me occupied was not good for my psyche. Things better suppressed swirled through my mind.

During the overhaul, workers had cut two large holes in the *Clay*'s High Yield 80 (HY-80) hull—a special grade of steel. Since the hull protected us from the crushing pressure of the sea, only specially qualified welders could repair the openings.

One of the holes was directly above where I was sitting. Workers had used it to refuel the nuclear reactor. The other was larger and above maneuvering. Perfect repairs were crucial. Inspectors had checked the welders' work with the most sophisticated methods available. There wasn't any room for error. Our lives depended on their soundness.

Even though the welds had passed all examinations, the ultimate test was subjecting them to actual conditions.

So far, they proved their soundness. I prayed they would withstand test depth.

Additionally, the realization that any component exposed to the sea can fail under the unrelenting pressure of the ocean's depths created consternation.

Lewis's reminder that the *Thresher* was lost during her post-overhaul dive to test depth fueled my concerns.

Similar to our situation, the *Thresher* was beyond the continental shelf. She sank in 8400 feet of water. The ocean at our location was not quite as deep. Unfortunately, it was much more than the *Henry Clay*'s crush depth. Crush depth is a calculated value. It is 30 to 35 percent greater than test depth. If something went wrong, it would not matter if we were only one foot below the FBM's limit. We would be just as dead.

The most likely initiator of the *Thresher*'s demise was the failure of a small seawater pipe. The highly pressurized water sprayed electrical equipment and caused a reactor SCRAM. With the reactor shutdown, the propulsion system became disabled and lost the ability to drive the *Thresher* to the surface. With the influx of water giving her negative buoyancy, the submarine sank even farther. Her captain resorted to his last option. He ordered an emergency blow to the surface. Unfortunately, a design flaw in the blow system allowed the air-lines to become clogged with ice. Unable to lighten enough to reach the surface, the submarine slipped back deeper and deeper to her doom. When *Thresher* imploded, all 129 men died instantly.

The *Thresher*'s support ship was unable to do anything to save the submarine and crew.

If we developed similar problems, the only thing our escort, the USS *Falcon*, would be able to do was record our death song.

Metzgus's voice in my headphones interrupted my morbid thoughts. He informed all stations we were starting our excursion into the cold, dark depths of the ocean. The submarine confirmed his statement. Her sympathetic reaction to the ocean swells slowly subsided as the submarine went deeper. Soon, the boat's movement through the sea became undetectable.

When we reached 100 feet, the submarine stopped descending and all stations were inspected for leaks. Although I had been continuously watching for problems, I made a more comprehensive inspection of every nook and cranny of the tunnel. Then I peered through each yellow-tinted lead-glass window and inspected the reactor compartment. Poor lighting and a limited range of vision provided an extra level of difficulty. If a leak developed inside the reactor compartment, the best chance of detecting it would be the glint of water spraying or the compartment fogging. At the conclusion of my inspection, I reported that my areas were satisfactory.

When all the other stations reported similar conditions, the submarine descended another 100 feet. The process would repeat until our arrival at test depth or until we had to abort.

While the submarine was passing 75 percent of test depth, I heard the sound of someone clomping up the tunnel stairs.

Schweikert entered the space from machinery 2. He walked to my side, looked at the overhead, and said, "Gee, you can't tell where the hole in the hull used to be. The one above maneuvering is the same way."

Facing forward and looking up, I responded, "Yeah, I've tried to find any evidence of where it was. Those yardbirds did a good job."

Schweikert added, "Let's hope it's as sound as it looks."

Suddenly, cold water struck the back of my neck.

Something was leaking.

A knot formed in my stomach. I was on the verge of panic. Controlling my emotions, I recalled a lesson drummed into me repeatedly: remain calm and assess the situation. It was only a stream and not a huge flood; therefore, the immediate safety of the submarine and her crew was not in jeopardy. First, I needed to discover what was leaking.

As my mind drafted a report to maneuvering, I quickly turned towards the stream.

It did not take more than a moment to determine its source.

Lewis was standing in front of me. He started laughing hysterically. In his meaty upraised hand was a partially filled plastic bottle. The spray was coming from it. He directed the flow onto my face and chest until the bottle was empty.

Lewis finally contained himself, "I wish we had a camera. The expression on your face was priceless."

"You guys got me good. I'll say this, though: I'd rather it be a prank than a real leak."

As they left the tunnel, Schweikert wondered aloud if they could get anyone else. I scolded myself for falling for such an obvious stunt. There wasn't any reason to doubt the hull's integrity.

Once again, the submarine moaned disconcertingly as we took the next step towards test depth. The sounds made me wonder what the crews of *Thresher* and *Scorpion* had heard as they headed towards destruction. The thought was too morbid to dwell on. I hoped their crews believed they could save their boats and fought valiantly to the end.

The *Thresher*'s and the *Scorpion*'s hulls were HY-80, just like the *Clay*'s. What did I know about the substance?

During Nuclear Power School, we had a course on metallurgy. It mostly delved into the metals involving reactor components, but a small portion taught us about this material.

Its yield strength was 80,000 pounds per square inch (psi). This incredibly large value gives a false impression about how deep a submarine can dive without collapsing. Water exerted 0.433 psi for every foot we descended. The deepest spot in the ocean is 35,810 feet below the surface. That means the maximum sea pressure is 15,505.73 psi.

What does the 80,000 psi really mean?

Yield strength is a measure of how much pulling force a substance can endure and still spring back to its original shape. Highly ductile materials can change shape quite a bit and return to their original form after the stress is gone. Rubber bands are ductile but icicles are not. Our hull, being ductile, would constrict the deeper we went, as sea pressure increased, and then return to its original configuration when the pressure lessened.

More important than its strength was HY-80's ductility.

HY-80 had its limits, as demonstrated by the *Thresher*'s hull collapsing. Contrary to what most people imagine, a submarine's hull telescopes in and does not flatten like a pancake. Although the *Clay* could safely dive deeper than *Thresher*, both submarines had to perform their dive to test depth, in waters far deeper than crush depth. A rhetorical question bantered about by submariners: When a submarine sinks, what actually kills the crew? Is it the wall of water or the wall of flame? Either way, it happens too fast for those on board to know what hit them.

Suddenly, I heard several loud bangs in my headphones. Quickly following the unsettling noises was a panic-stricken voice yelling, "Emergency in the galley!"

I expected the *Clay* to rise and escape the crushing sea pressure. Instead, she remained stationary and the headphones were silent. A few minutes later, much to my chagrin, the submarine descended to the next step of the test.

The deeper we went, the more stressed I became. Having water sprayed on me and the mysterious report of an emergency in the galley added to my anxiety. The probability of a leak and the resulting negative consequences vastly increased the deeper we descended. With every level change, the *Henry Clay*'s hull complained about the unrelenting sea pressure surrounding her. Random unnerving pops and groans emanated throughout the boat as she reacted to going deeper and deeper. The noises kept the danger of our situation in the forefront of my mind. A submarine operates on the edge of survivability. Our excursion to test depth challenged those limits even further.

Feeling the pressure of my responsibility to the rest of the crew, I constantly checked my spaces for problems.

Finally, the submarine achieved test depth.

I could hardly wait for the *Clay* to escape from the clutches of test depth's unrelenting sea pressure.

It seemed as if we remained at test depth for an eternity. The reports trickled in. The *Clay's* crew were taking their time making comprehensive inspections.

Southerland was the first to report. He had good news. The worrisome shaft seal leakage had only increased a little from what it was at 100 feet. The packing gland was working as designed. A sense of relief washed over me.

My report of no leaks and no problems was similar to the others.

We were still missing one report. As I waited for Mike Pavlov to make his report from lower level auxiliary machinery room 2, my idle mind had time to imagine all sorts of possible troubles.

Pavlov was one of our most diligent crewmen. No matter what he did, he did it perfectly. His reports were always one of the last.

Finally, we heard Pavlov say over the 2JV, "Maneuvering. Lower level AMR 2. All conditions normal. No leaks or problems."

Metzgus made his required response: "Lower level AMR 2, maneuvering aye."

Once again, the butterflies in my stomach settled. I exhaled and felt relieved.

Despite test depth's unrelenting sea pressure, the *Henry Clay* had survived.

Like before, the submarine announced the start of our ascent by moaning, popping and creaking, as the merciless sea relaxed its deadly grip.

Before long, I heard a welcome announcement to secure from deep submergence.

I stuffed the 2JV headset into its storage locker and headed aft.

When at the bottom of the steps in AMR2, I saw Southerland. He was having a conversation with Marchbanks and Lewis. Curious, I wandered over.

Marchbanks was describing the mysterious emergency in the galley report. "It really wasn't an emergency. Just some sheet-metal rivets popping. A piece of sheet metal wasn't the right size. It flexed too much as the hull shrunk. The mess cook had every reason to be scared. The rivets were ricocheting like crazy."

After sea trials, the *Clay* returned to Charleston and we turned over the boat to the Blue Crew.

Our stay in Charleston went by quickly. As with all nuclear submarine crews, training filled our days. Southerland and I managed to squeeze in stimulating the local economy and playing basketball while hung over.

Before we knew it, it was time to take control of the *Clay* from the Blue Crew. We would be conducting sound trials out of Roosevelt Roads, Puerto Rico. The *Clay* and the Blue Crew were waiting for us.

First, the Gold Crew had to get to Puerto Rico. We flew in a propeller-driven troop transport from Charleston. The 1000-mile journey was the worst flight I had ever experienced. The plane did not have a bathroom. If someone had to urinate, there was a hole on the port side of the plane. The trip was over the ocean, so people below were safe. Anyone needing to do "number two" had to use a bag and dispose it when we landed. The seating accommodations were not much better. There were four rows of web seats, running parallel to the sides of the aircraft. The middle two rows were back to back. The backs of the outside rows were against the sides of the plane. To make matters worse, the facing seats were so close the people in the middle and outer rows had to interlock their legs. That even included me, in spite of my short legs. Tall men like Southerland were worse off. If someone wanted to move forward or aft, he had to walk along the backs of the seats in the middle of the aircraft. Submariners are used to close quarters, but this was ridiculous.

Things did not get much better after we landed. Our transportation was tractor-trailer trucks with wooden benches. It was a miserable trip from the airport to the barrack at the Roosevelt Roads Naval Base. The heat and humidity of Florida did not hold a candle to the climate of Puerto Rico, especially while we were stuffed in unventilated sweatboxes. By the end of the trip, my dress white uniform was soaked with sweat. The barrack was not bad, but we were grateful to move back into the submarine.

That evening we discovered an enlisted man's club within walking distance of the *Clay*. Being good submariners, the Gold Crew paid it a visit. It turned out to be our last. A shot of rum was ten cents and we capitalized on the deal. I was sitting on the club's outside patio with Southerland, Souder, and several other crewmates. Our waiter would take drink orders, but he would not pick up the empty glasses. This turned into a problem, because the bartender was running out of glasses. We in turn, due to our inebriated state, refused to get up and take the glasses back. I cannot remember who threw the first empty glass off the patio onto an asphalt parking area fifteen feet below us, but we all joined in, whenever there was an empty glass. It wasn't long before the shore patrol showed up and banned us from the club. We were lucky to escape the brig. I think it was because there were so many of us and we had to begin sound trials the next morning.

As scheduled, the *Clay* and her hung-over crew left for sound trials the next morning.

Sound trials determined the *Clay*'s noise level. A stationary barge packed with sophisticated listening devices recorded our sounds, as the submerged submarine sailed past it. Each pass was carefully scripted. Hundreds of cards delineated every imaginable combination of equipment and speed of the submarine. We aligned the equipment as required and then sailed past the barge. When the sensors captured an adequate recording, we made the next alignment. The process was repeated over and over.

After experts analyzed each recording, we would know which combination was best for certain situations. One of the more significant conditions was ultra quiet. It was the *Clay*'s absolute quietest combination. The analysis also determined the *Clay*'s signature. A signature is like a fingerprint. Every vessel has one; each is unique and is used for identification.

During sound trials, a strange sensation disturbed my sleep. The submarine was experiencing periodic concussions. They were violent enough to awaken me from a deep sleep. I was groggily aware of each, but could not figure out the cause. Before my mind could clear from its fog, I heard the 1MC announcement to surface. The shuddering ceased. I quickly fell back to sleep. Port and starboard auxiliary electrician aft watches (six hours on watch, six off, then six hours of watch), plus working on submarine qualifications had left me exhausted.

When I entered the crew's mess, a loud din of animated conversations filled the area. I sat with Southerland and Lewis.

They were excitedly talking about depth charges.

Southerland was performing an equipment shift in the lower level engine room when the first shock wave struck. The EOOW passed the word to cease realigning equipment and determine what was happening. The lower level watch and Southerland inspected everything. Southerland checked the forward end and the LLER did the same back aft. Both determined the source was external to the boat. The shocks continued and increased in intensity. They could not find any abnormalities, so Southerland went to the upper level engine room. Then the boat surfaced.

Southerland went to maneuvering. He figured the EOOW, Mr. Murphy, might know what was going on. Murphy was the most experienced person in engineering. He was an enlisted man before becoming a limited duty officer (LDO) and had a lot of knowledge. Murphy said he was not positive, but if he did not know better, he would bet they were depth charges.

My heart skipped a beat at the thought. Without saying anything, I recalled seeing the torpedo coming at the *Fulton* and remembered how that incident scared me. Fear again permeated my psyche. I was silently grateful for being in a stupor during this incident.

At the end of the watch, Mr. Murphy came through with the answer. They *were* live depth charges! He told us an American destroyer was the culprit. It was conducting its own testing. They somehow got out of their sector and into ours. Our captain realized what was happening. Unfortunately, he was sleeping when the action started, and that delayed evasive action. Even though there was enough time to take safety measures before being in immediate danger, it was too close for comfort.

Captain Montross was furious and we surfaced. He then royally chewed out the destroyer's commanding officer. I wish I'd been there to hear our captain's tirade. I heard it left the destroyer's captain very concerned about his career.

Luckily, we emerged unscathed and the rest of sound trials were uneventful.

The Gold Crew's next assignment was testing our upgraded missile system. The *Clay* pulled into Port Canaveral, Florida, to conduct the testing.

To qualify in submarines, submarine sailors study and understand every system and component on a submarine. The *Clay*'s missile system was the first I mastered. Maybe it was because the "Would you launch nuclear weapons?" question on the psychological test had been haunting my subconscious. In submarine school, the real significance of possessing the knowledge to launch a missile had not sunk in. Now that I was about to participate in an actual launch, the nagging question resurfaced. I reassessed my original answer. As before, it still stood. I'd rather not actuate the launch. On the other hand, given an attack on our nation, there wasn't any doubt I could carry out the act.

For our missile launch, the *Clay*'s crew members were permitted to have guests ride an escort destroyer and view the event. My dad's brother Harry and his wife Vicky lived not far from Port Canaveral. I invited them. They appreciated the opportunity, especially since Uncle Harry served in submarines during World War II. Harry inspired me to volunteer for submarine duty.

As a side note, when I was mess cooking on the USS *Fulton*, a chief petty officer asked if my father was Harry Dubay. I told him he wasn't, but I had an uncle by that name. It turned out they served on the same submarine during World War II. I put him in touch with my uncle, and he exchanged correspondence with Harry until my uncle passed away. It was gratifying to know I was instrumental in reuniting old buddies.

On May 22, 1970, the *Clay* left Port Canaveral early in the morning. Uncle Harry and Aunt Vicky were aboard the escorting destroyer, USS *Cone*. The surface ship shadowed the *Clay* and provided the perfect vantage point from which to observe us submerging and firing our missile.

I was in the engine room as the countdown neared zero. I braced myself. The deck dropped from under my feet when the missile blasted away from the *Clay*. I grabbed the after-signal ejector to keep my balance. My unbalance was short-lived as the *Clay*'s hovering system quickly stabilized the FBM. It was a perfect test and our missile struck its intended target.

Next on the agenda was a simulation of firing all 16 missiles, called a salvo. The *Clay* did not launch any projectiles. The test only ejected the equivalent of the weight of a missile out of each tube. I was in shaft alley when the shuddering of the submarine announced the event. The *Clay*'s ability to dispatch more destruction than that deployed by all sides during World War II, and in such a short time, left me shaken. I hoped and prayed our nation never needed to order such an act. There wasn't much opportunity to dwell on that thought. Work assignments and watch station duties demanded my time and attention.

After we returned to port, I was in the group of nucs who could leave the FBM for the evening. Uncle Harry, Aunt Vicky, and I made plans for dinner.

The non-nuclear trained crewmembers could go on liberty as soon as the boat tied up to the dock. Nucs had to remain onboard until the engineering plant was shut down. Although difficult and time-consuming, shutdown of the plant allowed some of us to have a few hours of free time. Early the next morning, we nucs would awaken before everyone else and

Test missile launched by USS *Henry Clay*. U.S. Navy file photograph (May 1970).

start the plant back up again. It was a pain in the butt, although it had advantages.

When my tasks were complete, I changed into a set of rumpled civilian clothes, hoping they did not reek too badly.

Emerging from the *Clay*'s hatch, I glanced around. Harry and Vicky were on the far end of the pier. They spied me.

I apologized for being late and hoped they hadn't been bored.

Harry had kept Vicky entertained by telling her some of his submarine service experiences. Harry shook my hand and Vicky gave me a hug. If my submarine smell offended them, they were polite enough to keep it to themselves. I did not press the issue.

Harry, an ex–World War II submariner, rubbed his chin and said, "I can't believe how long it took your submarine to submerge. In my day, if we were that slow, you wouldn't be talking to me right now."

I suspected his World War II–era submarine had larger ballast tank vent valves. There was another difference. Nuclear-powered boats operated completely opposite of his submarine. His submarine ran on the surface most of the time and needed to dive in order to escape from sudden attacks. Nuclear submarines mostly operate undersea and do not surface until returning to port. The *Clay* was also a lot bigger than his submarine. That made it take longer to get under. Size makes a difference. Nuclear attack submarines are smaller than an FBM. If an attack boat and the *Clay* started diving at the same time, the fast attack would be waiting at 150 feet by the time the *Clay* was at periscope depth.

As we traveled to the restaurant, Vicky wanted to know what made a submarine dive. I provided the basics. When the *Clay* is on the surface, it has large ballast tanks full of air. They give the submarine positive buoyancy and she floats. The tanks are open at the bottom and there are valves on top to let the air out. This is similar to submerging an inverted drinking glass in water. The glass stays full of air, making the combination of glass and air less dense than the surrounding water. In other words, it has positive buoyancy and it pops to the surface, when released. Making a hole in the bottom of the inverted submerged glass allows the air to escape as the water pushes it out. Releasing the glass in this condition will let it stay submerged, because it has negative buoyancy. The same things happen in a submarine's ballast tanks. Opening the tanks' vent valves allows water to rush in and displace the air. The sub develops negative buoyancy and submerges. Submarines have other tanks to control the amount of negative buoyancy, so it maintains the proper depth. Submarines surface by replacing the water in a ballast tank with air. Submariners do this by blowing air from special bottles into the ballast tanks with the tank's vent valves closed. The air flows in, water flows out openings at the tank bottoms, the submarine becomes buoyant, and it comes to the surface.

Submariners sound the diving alarm twice when submerging and three times for surfacing.

While enjoying a delicious fresh seafood supper, they caught me up on recent family news.

After dinner, Harry and Vicky dropped me off at the pier. We waved goodbye. It was the last I saw of them until I got out of the Navy.

While walking back to the *Clay*, I realized I had missed an opportunity to compare the *Clay*'s diving procedure with that of Harry's submarine.

The *Clay*'s initial rigging for dive preparations take an hour to an hour and a half.

She has several positions dedicated to the diving evolution.

In the control room are the chief of the watch (COW), the diving officer, and the helmsman who controls the rudder, along with a radar operator and the *Clay*'s executive officer. The XO is in charge of diving.

There are four men stationed on the bridge at the top of the sail. The officer of the deck guides the surfaced submarine. With him are a junior officer of the deck (JOOD), a lookout, and quartermaster.

Because the submarine will remain submerged for two months, keeping navigation and communications exposed to the elements is unwise. Modern submarines employ portable equipment to carry out those functions. They are in a special piece of equipment called a suitcase. It's portable and looks like a silver clothes suitcase.

When the *Clay* is rigged for dive, with the exception of the bridge, the officer of the deck ensures the boat is answering ahead one-third—about five knots. Then he formally transfers the deck and the conn to the new officer of the deck—the XO—inside the submarine. When the XO orders, "Rig the bridge for dive and lay below," the officer in the bridge has the quartermaster disconnect the suitcase. In parallel, the new officer of the deck has the helmsman prepare to take control of the sailplanes, the chief of the watch shifts hydraulic pumps to run, and the forward auxillaryman secures ventilating the submarine with the low pressure blower.

The lookout takes the suitcase below, becomes the planesman, and controls the stern planes.

The quartermaster installs watertight caps on the suitcase cable connections in the bridge. The officer in the sail orders: "Clear the bridge." Everybody goes below. The officer is the last to leave the bridge. While descending, he shuts and dogs the upper bridge watertight hatch. When the officer is in the control room, the quartermaster shuts and dogs the lower hatch. Next, the officer on the bridge says: "Last man down; hatch secured."

The chief of the watch and diving officer verify a green board. That is a special panel for showing major hull penetration's status. A lit red circle means open. A green bar indicates closed. When all the green indicators are lit, it's called a green board.

The officer of the deck orders: "Submerge the ship; make your depth 60 feet." Then he sounds the diving alarm twice. For each ah-oooo-gah, simultaneous pre-set actions happen. On the first, the diving officer has the planesman place the stern planes to full dive and maintain a five-degrees-down bubble. The radar operator lowers the radar mast and becomes the sonar operator. Termination of all radio transmissions occurs at this time and the men checking for leaks increase their diligence.

The officer of the deck sounds the diving alarm a second time and makes a shipwide announcement: "Dive! Dive!" This initiates more scripted actions. The helmsman rings up ahead two-thirds, about ten knots, places the rudder amidships, and operates the sailplanes. He coordinates with the planesman to maintain the five-degrees-down bubble. The chief of the watch opens the forward and then the after ballast tank vents, which makes the submarine gain negative buoyancy.

As the submarine submerges, the diving officer reports the boat's depth at ten-foot intervals. When the boat is at 50 feet, the chief of the watch shuts the ballast tank vents. Several things happen at 60 feet, the ordered depth. The helmsman and planesman manipulate their planes to maintain 60 feet. The chief of the watch opens and shuts the ballast tank vents to ensure the tanks are completely full of water. Then he shifts the hydraulic pumps to standby. After trimming the boat for ahead one-third, the diving officer adjusts the boat's buoyancy for ahead one-third and 60 feet.

Other than the suitcase, I wondered how much different it was diving a submarine during World War II.

I did not dwell on it. When back in the *Clay*, I immediately hit the rack. In four hours, I had another long day ahead of me.

After returning to Charleston, the *Clay* headed up the Cooper River to the Naval Weapons Station.

Once there, the *Clay*'s sixteen missile tubes became hosts to war-shot nuclear-tipped ICBMs.

Shortly after the event, the yeoman gave me bad news. I was not eligible to have the government pay for shipping my belongings to Hawaii.

I said, "Wait a minute. Everybody second-class and above is eligible."

"There's another requirement. You have to be stationed in Hawaii for twelve months. You're supposed to transfer off the *Clay* after her first patrol."

I was ticked off and requested a meeting with the executive officer. My argument that the Navy would most likely transfer me to another boat in Hawaii fell on deaf ears. He agreed with the probability of staying in the Pacific Fleet, but there was no guarantee.

I consoled myself by focusing on my immediate future. Transiting from Charleston to Hawaii through the Panama Canal by submarine was an extraordinary event. Then I would be living in Hawaii for an undetermined time. The experience was something to savor. I was determined to make the most of it. I shoved the disappointment aside and was ready to begin my next adventure.

On an unusually cold, rainy, blustery June 1970 morning, the USS *Henry Clay* embarked on her 8,000-mile transit to Hawaii via the Panama Canal. The Blue Crew would be waiting for us.

This was perfect weather to begin a trip to the tropical paradise.

Chapter 10

Transit to Hawaii

After leaving the Cooper River, the USS *Henry Clay* entered the Atlantic Ocean, passing through a portion of the Bermuda Triangle. Speculation of an unfortunate fate befalling the *Clay* in that notorious area circulated throughout the boat. I doubt if anyone really believed the superstitions. As expected, we passed through the Triangle without incident and proceeded southwest, skirting the east coast of Cuba.

Since I was not qualified in submarines or all of my watch stations, I had no spare time. Connell's long-ago prophecy had come true. The *Clay*'s Gold Crew strictly enforced the regulation banning non-quals from enjoying any entertainment, such as movies. My days were an endless series of standing port and starboard watches, performing work, qualifying and trying to get some rest.

Each day rolled into the next, without reprieve. Tasks kept me so busy, I was not aware we were getting close to the Panama Canal.

One day when awakened by the duty messenger, I sensed the gentle rolling of the FBM. I surmised that the boat was at periscope depth. When entering the mess deck, I spied real milk on the tables. There was a buzz of excitement in the air. I sat with Southerland. He told me the submarine was in the Panama Canal. We received a supply of fresh stores, which explained the milk. My exhaustion had kept me in such a deep sleep, I was oblivious to it all. The klaxon sounding three times and the announcement to surface had not awakened me.

I even slept through the *Clay* almost having a collision.

It did not take long to learn the details. The *Clay* was approaching a stopped ship. The OOD signaled for all-stop, but the port and starboard propulsion turbine ahead control valves were stuck. A back one-third, back two-thirds, and finally a back emergency quickly followed all-stop.

Wishon had to bang on the poppets with a sledgehammer to free them. When the turbines responded, the prop's wash sent a wave over the turtle-back and the after portion of the missile deck. Several crewmen got their feet wet.

After eating lunch, I went back aft and relieved Davis as throttleman. He was still smiling like the Cheshire cat and cackling his typical mischievous laugh.

Everybody liked the man. His infectious good humor, his extreme technical competence, and his excellent athleticism made him one of the more popular members of the crew.

Having recently qualified as throttleman, I hoped my watch went by without a similar near-miss. Luckily, other than some benign speed changes, it did.

Not long afterwards, Southerland stopped by maneuvering to deliver some good news. The captain declared holiday routine while we were in the Canal. This meant the crew did not have to perform any work other than standing watch, unless it was absolutely necessary. Southerland and I decided to spend as much time topside as possible.

Dick Treptow, one of our nuc interior communications technicians (IC-men), relieved me as throttleman. IC-men and electricians were in the electrical division. As such, we shared a special bond. Regardless, it did not stop either group from pinging on the other.

As I was exiting maneuvering and knowing Treptow always checked the condition of the after lighting ground detector, I razzed him about a ground on phase-C, from a main seawater valve's position indicator.

He took it good-naturedly and commented about electricians having their own issues with lighting system grounds. Then he would have the last laugh, while electricians tried to find and fix it.

After leaving maneuvering, I quickly passed through the engine room, machinery 2 upper level and the tunnel, and paused in machinery 1 to gaze out the open hatch to the outside. The faster I ate, the more time I could be topside. I continued through the middle level missile compartment to the mess deck in the operations compartment.

After wolfing down lunch, I hurried through the operations and missile compartments to machinery 1. As I stood at the bottom of the ladder, the welcome odor of our proximity to land permeated my nose. While I was looking up through the hatch, the brilliant sunshine hurt my eyes. I climbed the ladder slowly, allowing my eyes to adapt to the brightness. Nearing the top, I could feel the confined space of the submarine releasing

USS *Henry Clay* **passing through the Panama Canal, during her transit from Charleston, South Carolina, to Pearl Harbor, Hawaii. Individuals are unidentifiable. From the archives of Ted E. Dubay (June 1970).**

its grip. In its place was a feeling of freedom, and my soul seemed to stretch to infinity. I saw something my consciousness was not aware of having missed. It was distance—space between me and other objects—something most people take for granted.

Technicolor replaced the *Clay*'s drab interior. The submarine was in the muddy brown Chagares River. I relished the lush jungle, of every imaginable shade of green punctuated by an abundance of multicolored flowers. It was such a contrast to the black exterior of the *Clay*. The cloudless sky was a perfect shade of blue.

I noted safety lines along the sides of the missile deck and the edges of the fairwater planes. They were not substantial, but someone had to be very careless to fall overboard. Tempering the freedom and natural beauty was the intensely hot and humid air. Underneath a long-sleeved poopie suit, underclothing, and ball cap, a layer of sweat quickly coated my body. The other crewmen who escaped the confines of the *Clay* were in the same state and did not seem to care. Being outside the boat, I felt temporarily paroled from my submarine prison. Everyone was enjoying his brief period of freedom. Some were sitting and quietly talking. Others were lost in absorbing the atmosphere. I saw that Southerland was sleeping. There were a number on the fairwater planes enjoying an elevated view. I decided to observe the scenery from the missile deck and snap a few pictures. My Kodak Instamatic camera was not the best, but serviceable and compact. Not long after arriving topside, we passed a waterfall, off the starboard side. It was so beautiful I could not resist capturing the image.

During my time topside, the natural environment fascinated me. The marvelous technologically advanced equipment inside the *Clay* failed to inspire the same awe. It was probably a subconscious attempt to escape the stark interior of the submarine.

Birds flitted amongst the foliage. Brilliant butterflies fluttered everywhere. Puffs of wind twisted and turned leaves in every direction. I bathed in the wonderful rays of the sun. Even the foam kicked up by the *Clay*'s wake, as she slowly churned through the muddy water, enthralled me.

Although I marveled at the monumental effort of wresting the canal from the primitive and hostile environment, the result paled in the face of the surrounding natural beauty. It was a shame that the locks replaced such beautiful scenery.

One of the major obstacles the canal builders overcame was malaria-infected mosquitoes. Even my dad had contracted the disease when stationed here during World War II. He suffered all through the war in Europe and several years afterward. On the day the war in Europe ended, he was delirious in a hospital in Germany. Dad did not find out about the declaration of peace for several days.

The lack of mosquitoes while transiting the canal surprised me. Maybe our submarine smell was acting as a repellant.

As the submarine approached the Bridge of the Americas, an ocean liner was to our left and entering the canal from the Pacific. There were so many people lining our side of their ship, waving and taking pictures, it was actually listing. The *Clay*'s sailors moved to the port side and enthusiastically returned the gestures. Southerland and I spied several especially attractive young women and tried to get their attention.

Suddenly Southerland shouted, "Snakes!"

He tapped me on the shoulder and pointed at the hundreds of sea snakes swimming beside the *Clay*. Almost as one, we retreated from the safety rail to the center of the missile deck. I am not sure about my fellow crewmembers, but even non-venomous snakes give me the heebie-jeebies. Knowing sea snakes are one of the most poisonous species in the world sent a shiver up my spine. In spite of these critters' surrounding the *Clay*, it was not enough to drive me back into the confines of the submarine. The feeling of freedom overshadowed all other factors and I did not want to go below until there was no longer a choice.

That moment was not long in coming. The water was deep enough for the *Clay* to dive. Reluctantly, after giving a final glance around, I entered the boat's dreary interior. A metal tube of artificial light, navy gray equipment, Formica that barely simulated wood, and cramped quarters replaced the limitless, vibrant-hued and alive world, which for most of my life I had taken for granted.

Although Hawaii lies to the northeast and 4500 miles from the western exit of the Panama Canal, the *Clay* did not head in that direction. Instead, our course paralleled the coast of Mexico. Prior to arriving in Pearl Harbor, we were going to have a port of call. The crew unanimously voted on stopping in Acapulco. Somehow, that didn't happen, and we headed to Long Beach, California. Captain Montross was from the area.

Our change in liberty port disappointed us, but we quickly settled into the underway routine. For me, I was condemned to port and starboard throttleman watches, on watch for six hours, off for six, etc. There was one upside. We were not conducting any drills. This allowed me to remain rested, work on qualifications, and stay caught up on my work. Since we were in transit and expected in Long Beach on a certain day, the submarine ran fast and deep.

One day our watch section in maneuvering was talked-out. We had no interest in intellectual discussions about girls, food, or anything that could take minds off our encapsulation in a metal cylinder. After an hour of silence, the numbing atmosphere affected the engineering officer of the watch. His eyes began to droop. Soon his head was nodding as he ineffectively tried to fight off falling asleep. Davis, the electrical operator, noticed the officer's demeanor.

Wishon, the engine room supervisor, appeared in the door to maneuvering. After a few subtle hand signals from Davis, Wishon left without speaking. Davis placed a forefinger on his lips. The reactor operator and I did not understand, but we got the message to remain quiet. Davis turned around and tied the officer's shoelaces together.

A few minutes later, we heard a loud crack from beneath the officer. I quickly looked in his direction. Suspended about a foot above his chair, the man had a wide-eyed expression of terror. When settled back in his seat, he realized the state of his shoes. He glared as we erupted in laughter. The man could not reprimand us. If he did, he had to admit to a lapse of attention, which was severe enough to allow someone to violate his footwear and send him flying. Wishon emerged from lower level engine room and walked aft of maneuvering. In his hand was Bruce, the short-handled 12-pound sledgehammer.

The sledge and the officer's flight made me understand Davis's amusement during my initial tour of the engine room when he said, "See those three can-looking things? They're for the bottom posts of maneuvering's chairs."

Wishon joined us in having a good laugh at the officer's expense.

Our levity ceased when the submarine abruptly developed a severe down-bubble. I quickly grabbed the ahead throttle wheel and kept from falling. Thinking that the captain was executing unannounced angles and dangles, I formed a string of expletives on my tongue. Before I had a chance to utter them, the engine order telegraph demanded a back emergency, and "Jam dive" blasted from the 1MC. Due to the submarine's initial high speed and depth, I realized our dire situation. Survival depended on ending the descent.

My job was stopping the submarine's forward motion. I instinctively acknowledged the bell with my right hand. The left began shutting the ahead throttles by turning its control wheel clockwise.

At the same time, I sang out, "Back emergency!"

In parallel, the reactor operator shifted the reactor coolant pumps to high speed.

Without skipping a beat, my right hand relieved the left and furiously continued shutting the ahead throttles. To save a few seconds, my left shifted to the astern control wheel and simultaneously whipped it in the counterclockwise direction. Although this saved time, it was a dangerous action. Admitting steam through the propulsion turbine's reverse poppets, while the ahead throttles were still open, would catastrophically damage the turbines. The *Clay* needed them to stop her downward momentum and prevent our destruction. Luckily, my experience had taught me exactly how far to turn the astern wheel. After a momentary verification that the shaft was at zero RPM, I rapidly opened the astern throttles. The sudden massive steam demand sucked heat from the nuclear reactor. The reactor operator wore a grim face as he adjusted control rods. Matching reactor power with steam demand without causing a SCRAM was critical for survival.

I tersely barked, "Answering back emergency."

The boat's down-bubble had gotten worse, and the hull was noisily complaining about the extreme pressure as we went deeper. My hands were locked onto the astern throttle wheel in a death grip. I realized I was fruitlessly pulling on the wheel trying to end our descent, but couldn't resist the urge. Accentuating everything, the throttle wheel was violently moving fore and aft, matching the submarine's throbbing.

My heart pounded while waiting for a sign that my actions were improving our situation.

Then I succumbed to temptation. A check of maneuvering's depth gauge made my heart shudder.

Although the submarine was rising, we were still far below test depth.

The submarine had flirted with crush depth.

After what seemed an eternity, the engine order telegraph signaled all-stop. With the throttles closed, our return to the surface was at the mercy the *Clay*'s positive buoyancy. I breathed a sigh of relief as the submarine continued rising and its rate accelerated.

With the submarine finally wallowing on the surface, I felt drained and had to sit. I recalled wondering about my performance during a real crisis. My chest swelled with pride. I had been a major contributor to saving the USS *Henry Clay* and her 125 officers and men.

It did not take long to find out what happened. A hydraulic pipe blew apart. The component supplied the controlling fluid to the planes. It may sound strange, but planes fail full dive on a loss of pressure.

Our incessant training paid off. The crew functioned as a highly skilled team or I would not be here telling this story. Our captain personally awarded each man who carried out corrective actions a much-deserved "Well done."

Following the event, I recalled how I wondered about my ability to meet the challenge of becoming a submariner and maintaining my poise in a real crisis. The incident proved to me that I had a healthy future in the submarine service.

Although the *Clay* was safe, repairing the broken pipe posed another challenge. We were essentially out in the middle of nowhere and on our own. Submarines carried limited spare parts. Extra pipes and valves were definitely not in the *Clay*'s tiny storeroom. This is the sort of risk that had been faced by all submarines since they came into existence. It is one reason why the submarine force only takes volunteers and then selects the best. The crew of the *Clay* was no exception to this tradition.

Our talented and ingenious crewmen quickly repaired the damage.

After the near catastrophe, no one in the crew displayed any outward signs that the event affected him. Maybe it was a form of denial. Regardless of the reason, levity was running rampant.

During this period, someone overheard a greenhorn torpedoman stating he would do anything for a letter from his girlfriend. She had promised to write every day.

Later that day, word spread throughout the FBM that we needed a person to retrieve a bag of letters from a mail buoy. The rookie torpedoman readily volunteered.

When all arrangements for the ruse were complete, the captain surfaced the *Clay*. As the torpedoman was about to climb the ladder to go topside and retrieve the mail, catcalls and laughter erupted from the perpetrators in the attack center. The victim's face turned beet-red when he realized it was only a mischievous prank.

All levels of the crew, even the captain, masterfully planned and executed the hoax. Although it was sophomoric, I'm sure it helped relieve any residual tensions from the jam dive.

The remaining trip to Long Beach was uneventful, and we all looked forward to three days in sunny California.

Even though Long Beach was the home of a large naval base, very few submarines visited. The city considered our captain a hometown hero and they rolled out the red carpet.

City officials requested we make a dramatic and grand entrance by performing a super-surface. Prior to emerging from the depths, we were supposed to fire a smoke bomb out of the signal ejector so a helicopter could capture the moment.

At the scripted time, men launched the projectile.

Shortly after we'd surfaced, the captain's angry voice blared over maneuvering's intercom, "What the hell did you shoot?"

Prior to this, the engineering officer of the watch, Lieutenant Robert Hawthorne, one of our more talented young officers, had been relaxed and casual. He was youthful, good-looking, intelligent, hard-working, and personable. In anticipation of getting off the boat as soon as we docked, he was wearing, contrary to regulations, his white dress uniform with a short-sleeved shirt. We good-naturedly chided him about wearing short sleeves in the engineering spaces. In response, he donned paper sleeves, complete with lieutenant bars.

In almost a panic, Hawthorne ripped off the false sleeves and had a very concerned demeanor.

In a more controlled communication, the conn informed us that we had launched a flare instead of a smoke bomb. It detonated very close to the helicopter. The pilot instinctively executed evasive maneuvers, but missed taking photos of our surface. The helicopter's pilot was upset and expressed his displeasure.

From the tone of his voice, we could tell that our captain wasn't happy with the incident either.

Mr. Hawthorne was despondent. There was the potential that the captain would rescind his much-anticipated liberty. Even worse, the captain could document the incident in Hawthorne's service record. Had his promising career come to a screeching halt? It had not, because he went on to an illustrious career and retired as a captain.

He looked so forlorn that we tried to console him. Somehow, our comments about having a future as a junior anti-aircraft gunnery officer on a surface ship did not alleviate his dejected mood.

Because no one was hurt or any real damage inflicted, the crew reveled in the fact we almost shot down a helicopter. It didn't take long before a cartoon of the *Clay* appeared on the maneuvering status board. It depicted an FBM submarine with a helicopter icon on the sail, mimicking how World War II submarines painted symbols on their sails when they sank enemy ships. An added touch to the cartoon was a broom affixed to the periscope, signifying a clean sweep.

Much to the credit of the helicopter pilot, he managed to regain his composure and took pictures of us entering the harbor.

Just after docking, I was still the throttleman. Suddenly, all hell broke loose in maneuvering. The horn for the steam plant control panel, the siren of the reactor plant control panel, and the salinity panel bell started sounding randomly and intermittently. The White Rat emitted a series of clicking noises. Screech. Click. Ding. Ding. Click. Click. Screech. Honk. Ding. Honk. Click. Ding. Screech.

I scanned the alarm section of the steam plant control panel and no alarms were flashing. A check of all other indications showed everything was normal.

Nobody in maneuvering could discover a reason for the noises.

Then they stopped.

Everyone in maneuvering looked at each other with confused expressions.

Before we were able to relax, the commotion began again. Honk. Ding. Click. Screech. Ding.

Again, the cause couldn't be determined, and we expanded our investigation.

Before long, Treptow reported something strange going on with the after lighting ground detector. The lights for all three phases were blinking in a random pattern.

Treptow appeared in the doorway with a devilish grin. His previous curse had befallen us electricians. There was a ground in our equipment.

Electricians worked around the clock trying to discover the culprit. It did not take long to determine that the ground was in the engine room lighting. Finding which fixture was the actual problem proved more difficult. It was a miserable job. The engine room was very hot and humid at deck level. Lights and their wiring were in the overhead, where the conditions were even worse. Adding to our discomfort, machinist's mates hurled complaints when the lights above where they were working went out. Even Southerland became irritated with me.

Sweating profusely, we disconnected circuits and performed megger checks. Sometimes we thought we found the offending fixture. Then the demon ground raised its ugly head and dashed our hopes.

After we had searched in vain, the problem disappeared without our having found the culprit. Disappointment permeated the electricians. Nevertheless, we were happy it was gone. At least Treptow enjoyed the show.

Of the three days in Long Beach, every crewman got at least one day away from the boat. I spent mine at Disneyland. Because no one had room for civilian clothes, I was condemned to parade around the amusement park in my dress white uniform. Following the excursion, I contributed to the local economy by imbibing excessive liquid refreshments. Other than wearing Mickey Mouse ears instead of my Dixie cup white hat when returning to the *Clay*, I did not remember my evening.

In the middle of the night, a clamor awakened me. Southerland and Souder were returning from another of their legendary escapades.

The public made out. The captain opened the submarine for tours.

Visitors came in droves. A continuous stream paraded through the boat. They entered through the hatch in ARM 1 and traveled through the missile compartment, the operations compartment, and the torpedo room. At the end of each day, we turned away hundreds of disappointed people.

The naval base in Long Beach was full of surface warships. Many took advantage of having a submarine so close. The *Clay* was a perfect target for their sonar operators and they pinged us unmercifully. Unlike sonar noises heard on TV or the movies, a real ping is more like a high-pitched two-syllable bird's song. They almost drove us crazy with their incessant pinging. Although it was nerve-wracking, at least they were friendly vessels not bent on our destruction. It made me wonder how Uncle Harry had felt.

We elicited some revenge on the surface armada. One of our torpedomen was showing his father how to fire a torpedo. Someone inaccurately labeled the tube as empty. He aligned the torpedo tube to fire a water-slug. When he triggered the firing mechanism, it ejected the projectile, which slammed into the aft end of the destroyer in front of us. As far as I was ever able to determine, the responsible torpedoman never suffered any consequences. Maybe our captain figured this evened the score, after the pinging and our being nearly depth-charged during sea trials.

While we are preparing to get underway, Treptow's curse emerged again. Ding. Screech. Honk. Click. Screech. Honk. Ding. Click.

All available electricians mustered in the engine room as we tried to resolve the issue. The condition lasted a few hours and mysteriously disappeared.

My best hypothesis was a temperature- and humidity-sensitive floating ground. It never returned and I could never figure out why.

Other than a flotilla of small pleasure craft escorting us out the harbor, our exit was without fanfare. Determined to arrive on schedule, the captain had the FBM run fast and deep on the 2,700-mile journey from Long Beach to Pearl.

After the submarine surfaced off the coast of Oahu, I was itching to climb up to the bridge and get my first glimpse of Hawaii. First, I had to complete a couple of tasks. Another hurdle was mustering up enough courage to request permission. I was still transitioning from a quiet, shy bumpkin from Hickory Township to a confident submariner.

I approached the OOD, swallowed hard and tried not to appear nervous. Holding out my Instamatic camera, I said, "Request permission to go to the bridge and take some pictures."

The OOD replied matter-of-factly, "Sure Dubay, permission granted."

I placed the camera in a pocket of my poopie suit, grabbed the cold chrome ladder, and started up. While I was climbing the narrow tube leading to the bridge, the sweet smell of the sea replaced the rank odor of the submarine. Every few rungs of the ladder, I had to shove the camera back into my pocket, because it kept threatening to fall.

At the top of the sail, a picture-perfect Hawaiian day greeted me. It was nicer than I imagined. Off the starboard quarter was Diamond Head, one of the most famous landmarks in Hawaii. Shielding the camera from the wind-driven salt spray, I snapped pictures of Diamond Head and Honolulu. I remained on the bridge about 20 minutes, enjoying the soft undulating motion of the submarine as it cut through the crystal-clear water. The submarine forged toward Pearl Harbor, gliding by the beaches of Waikiki, off our starboard side. Breathing in the fresh sea air was like an elixir, cleansing my soul. A glance at my watch told me my time topside was at an end, and I unenthusiastically re-entered the confines of the submarine.

When we arrived in Pearl Harbor, the *Clay* became a member of the Pacific Fleet's Submarine Squadron 15. Although the *Clay*'s home port was Hawaii, she would actually operate out of Guam.

Chapter 11

The Eve of My First Patrol

Apra Harbor, Guam. Late November 1970. The *Henry Clay* was moored on the port side of the submarine tender USS *Proteus*. My first deterrent patrol would begin when the *Clay* got underway the next morning.

I was the 0600 to 1200 shutdown electrical operator. Although a roving watch, the job kept me confined to the submarine's engineering spaces. While in machinery 2 lower level, I heard tapping emanating from the feed station's voice tube. Curiosity overcame me and without thinking, I spoke into the tube's opening. Suddenly, a gusher of cold water hit me in the face.

The voice tube delivered the source. I heard Southerland laughing and saying, "Now we're even."

He was paying me back for what I had done to him the previous week. Southerland and I were part of an all-hands working party. We were loading a 90-day supply of food and necessary patrol items. Only chiefs and officers were exempt, although some occasionally lent a hand. The *Clay*'s sailors formed a human chain stretching from the tender, across a brow aft of the sail, over the missile deck, down the machinery 1 hatch, and through the submarine to the supply's storage locations. Southerland and I were in the middle of the shoulder-to-shoulder men on the missile deck. We passed the items hand to hand. It was tedious hard work, especially in Guam's hot and humid climate. I was handing off to Southerland. While passing heavy boxes of batteries, I noticed a similar-sized but much lighter box of light bulbs coming my way. I gradually drifted away from Southerland, increasing the distance between us. When I received the box of bulbs, I pretended it was heavy and threw it to Southerland. He expected to catch a box of batteries and adjusted his catching technique accordingly.

When the super-light box landed in his arms, he flipped it over his head into the water. Very embarrassed, Southerland managed to summon some nearby divers, who rescued the package.

That was the last time I had been outside the submarine.

A need to escape the submarine's confines smoldered inside me. Fueling it was what the next day would bring. Early in the morning, the USS *Henry Clay* would depart Guam and submerge for at least two months.

A two-month submerged patrol. How long was it? Sixty days. One thousand, four hundred forty hours. Eighty-six thousand, four hundred minutes. Five million, one hundred eighty four thousand seconds.

The theory of relativity applies to patrols. Albert Einstein said, "When a man sits with a pretty girl for an hour, it seems like a minute. But let him sit on a hot stove for a minute and it's longer than any hour. That's relativity"[1]

For me, patrol was more like the hot stove than being with the pretty girl.

Additionally, two months was just an approximation. They were normally scheduled to last 60 days, although unforeseen circumstances usually extended them longer. In spite of this, we always considered them two months.

With respect to accumulated time submerged, a Coast Guard admiral told me, "Before being confined to a desk job, I used to fly helicopters. You know, us pilots tend to stick our chests out and brag about how many flight hours we have. You submarine guys measure your time under water in *years*!"

It is true.

Schweikert relieved me as the shutdown electrical operator. I glanced at my watch. There was enough time to go topside without missing lunch. Before I had a chance to escape, a salinity cell caused an alarm. Since I was the nearest qualified electrician, it fell upon me to take initial actions. I gathered the necessary items, went to engine room lower level, and cleaned the cell. This solved the problem. By the time I was done, there was barely enough time to grab lunch before the cooks secured the mess deck. Not being able to go topside was a disappointment, but the day was only half over. There was still time for another opportunity.

After lunch, I had to perform a repair in the battery well. With part and tools in hand, I went to my rack to change into battery well diving dungarees. Battery acid had riddled them with holes. If I had not heeded the advice Davis gave me during my initial tour of the *Clay*, all of my uniforms would be in the same condition. The work went well. As hoped, there was time to make good on my desire to relax topside before supper.

After I exited the battery well, something in the crew's lounge caught my eye. A glance in its overhead, crowded with wires, piping, and fluorescent lights, revealed what was amiss. One of the lights had a greenish-blue tint and did not match the slight yellow glow of the others. Our captain had an idiosyncrasy with the *Clay's* lighting. Every fixture in each compartment had to be functional and the same hue. The color did not matter, as long as all the lights in the compartment matched.

Being a junior electrician, I spent countless hours correcting the issue. The captain of the other crew apparently did not share this opinion. When we assumed possession of the *Clay* from the Blue Crew, there were always many broken, burned-out, and mismatched bulbs. I suspected the Blue Crew left them in that condition on purpose.

There had always been competition between the Blue and Gold Crews of FBMs. The *Clay* was no exception.

The best story I ever read about submarine hi-jinks was "Purdum's Pirates," John Dudas's submission to *Submarine Skullduggery*. The book is a compilation of pranks, gags, jokes, and tricks, edited by the Submarine Research Center. "Purdum's Pirates" documented how two FBM crews took turns mischievously planting a noisy horn. During several boat turnovers, each crew came up with an unusual place to hide the object and a devious way for it to activate. One crew finally mounted it in the ventilation room across from the mess deck. Whenever the electrical operator, at the other end of the submarine, turned the ground detector switch, noise blasted through the ventilation. Because it seemed to activate at random times and did not stay on long enough, no one could locate the horn. The victimized crew declared the other the winner and a truce ensued.[2]

While standing in the crew's lounge, I hoped finding the correct colored bulb would not take too long. Sometimes matching the fluorescent bulb's hue was as simple as swapping a bulb from one compartment to another. The task became more difficult when I needed a new bulb. It was impossible to tell if the replacement matched until it was installed, which could be very time-consuming. This bulb was probably not going to be easy. I did not have any spares marked with their associated shade.

I took a leak in the head and then retrieved a handful of new bulbs. After several attempts, I found a spare of the correct color.

I paused for a moment to assess the crew's lounge ambiance. The small area had the same linoleum deck and tan simulated wood-grained

Formica bulkheads as the rest of the submarine. The yellow-hued fixtures provided ample light for anyone sitting at the table in the center of the lounge. There were shelves packed with an assortment of books. Mounted on a bulkhead was a fold-down ironing board. Other than stewards ironing officer uniforms, I never saw anyone use it. The *Clay*'s designers had attempted to create a homey atmosphere in the lounge, but to me it felt sterile and impersonal.

I examined the old light. It was not only the wrong hue; the bulb was nearing the end of its life. There was severe discoloration on both ends. I deposited the spent 12-inch bulb in the lounge trash can. Before going too far, I returned to the trash can and smashed the bulb to smithereens. There was a chance that the lounge's garbage would not make it off the submarine before the *Clay* left on patrol. If that happened, the unbroken light bulb would be discharged out of the trash disposal unit (TDU). Then, as the weighted garbage sank to the sea floor, the bulb would implode, causing a distinct pop. The noise was a transient, made only by a submarine. Transients travel great distances. Other submarine-generated transients were items falling to the deck and doors slamming.

Although submarines have weapons to protect themselves, being able to remain as quiet as possible is their first line of defense. Silence was a major aspect of American FBM design. While on patrol, it was the crew's responsibility to prevent compromising the designers' efforts. The last thing an FBM needed while sneaking around the ocean was a careless act causing a transient. Russian hunter-killer submarines were constantly on the prowl searching for American missile boats. There were a few documented instances of Soviet Fast Attacks trailing FBMs for short periods. These did not last long. The quiet nature of the FBM allowed it to slip away into the ocean's shadows, leaving the Soviet skipper exasperated. There were probably many other occasions when a Russian submarine was near the *Clay* and not even aware of our presence. Minimizing extraneous noises was crucial. A transient could totally negate the *Clay*'s silent design. The Soviets' detecting one of these from the *Clay* would allow them to pinpoint our position. An FBM's mission was dangerous enough without being in the cross hairs of an enemy hunter-killer attack boat. Giving away our location had the potential of jeopardizing not only our lives, but also national security. If the Russians could destroy the *Clay*, her counterattack deterrence no longer existed. The Soviets' gaining the upper hand was one of the major fears of the Western nations.

Resolving the lounge's bulb problem had erased another chance to escape the confines of the metal cylinder. My hoped-for respite outside the submarine would have to wait until after supper. I rationalized away the disappointment. The only things left on my agenda were rearranging my locker and a few logroom yeoman activities. They would not take long. The evening was a better time to go topside. It would be cooler and more peaceful.

I went back to my rack to change into non-tattered clothes, and then scurried to the mess deck for a quick supper.

After dinner, I decided to rearrange my locker and then perform my final logroom chores. The plan provided ample opportunity for a leisurely topside sojourn.

The locker was directly aft of my rack. It had two shelves, and was 24" tall by 18" wide and 24" deep. Other than a small storage compartment attached to the overhead of my rack, the locker was the sole storage space for my belongings. Not only did the locker contain everything needed for the next two months, it had to store items not needed until after patrol. Already stowed in the back was the canvas duffle bag I used as luggage. It took up a significant portion of the locker. Crammed on top of the bag was my dress white uniform. These articles were only needed when arriving and departing Guam. The uniform ended up a dingy yellow and very wrinkled after three months of not seeing the light of day. When it was needed for the trip back to Hawaii, I would retrieve the uniform and wear it as-is. In front of these items were my poopie suits. They got their name from the original version, which had a flap in their seat. I removed the coveralls and replaced them with my dungarees. In the morning, the uniform of the day shifted to poopie suits. They were lint-free, which helped maintain the cleanliness of the *Clay*'s atmosphere.

After the locker was ready for patrol, I headed to the logroom. I climbed the stairs and entered middle level operations. A short walk brought me to the open watertight hatch into the missile compartment. Marchbanks was exiting the opening from back aft.

He said, "Oh, there you are. I've been looking for you. The below decks watch overflowed the potable water tanks. The water grounded a motor in the valve pit. We have to dry it out."

I suppressed the urge to protest the task and tell him how it was jeopardizing the sating of my urge to escape the boat. Realizing he was in the same situation helped quell my frustration.

Marchbanks and I arrived at the stairs to lower level operations. He was ahead of me. Upon reaching them, he placed one hand on each of the chrome handrails and deftly slid down, without his feet touching any of the steps. I followed in the same manner. This worked well, as long as one rail or hand was not wet. The moisture created a much lower coefficient of friction and the individual had all he could do to avoid crashing. As long as the out-of-control slide was happening to someone else, it was very entertaining.

It took several hours to dry the motor and reinstall it. The task had eaten a big chunk out of my spare time. I climbed the stairs to middle level operations, walked aft to middle level missile compartment, went halfway down the port passageway, and arrived at the logroom.

After making the transit, I noted that not more than an hour ago, the submarine was a beehive of activity. Now, most of the crew was sleeping, in an effort to get some extra rest prior to commencing patrol routine. The few still awake moved slowly and talked in muffled tones.

One of my ancillary duties was logroom yeoman. I was responsible for all the engineering department paperwork. Being logroom yeoman, like any other assignment, had its positives and negatives. A plus was having a workspace I could call my own, a submarine rarity.

The logroom's condition was my responsibility. I was making sure everything was secured for sea.

My experience as logroom yeoman taught me to stow things properly as soon as they entered the closet-sized space. This evening, I was making a final inspection to ensure everything was in order. Even though the check delayed my going topside, I was determined the logroom would not be the source of a transient.

The room contained several bookshelves. Each had a restraining device, a metal bar that kept materials from falling onto the deck. One was ajar. A quick tug seated it. I checked each, one more time.

Confident that the space was properly secured for sea, I grabbed an army-green hardbound legal ledger. Emblazoned on the front cover was *Engineer's Night Order Book*. Book in hand, I stepped into the passageway and headed to maneuvering.

While passing through machinery 1, I could not resist glancing up through the open hatch. The sight of the evening twilit sky transformed my previous desire to go topside into an obsession. The fixation gripped me like a vise. The need to escape the confines of the submarine one final time, to relax and enjoy the world outside, if only briefly, had to be satisfied. There was no way I could to get to sleep unless I quelled the desire. The brief escape had to wait until I delivered the *Night Order Book*.

Davis was the shutdown maneuvering area watch. When I delivered the ledger, he was taking his readings. His pen was almost out of ink and he requested I bring a whole box of them because there were not any spares in the engineering spaces.

I sighed in resignation. One more task to accomplish before I could quench my need to relax outside of the *Clay*. I placed the book on the EOOW desk.

With teeth clenched in annoyance, I hurried to the logroom. The task was consuming valuable moments of my time out of the submarine.

When I returned with the pens, Davis had his back towards the door. He was talking to the shutdown electrical operator on the 2JV. I placed the box on maneuvering's footlocker and walked away unnoticed. I was grateful he was busy. By this time, I had calmed down a lot, although if we had spoken, I'd have said something regrettable.

My brief sojourn out of the submarine was almost at hand. I hurried to machinery 1. While climbing the ladder, my tension evaporated.

Once topside, I slowly made my way forward over the flat missile deck. At the aft end of the sail, my body suddenly felt drained and I slumped to the deck. I summoned the effort to move to the harbor side of the superstructure and sat.

Even at this hour, it was hot and humid. The temperature and humidity were both in the low nineties. Sweat was flowing freely. The moisture could not evaporate and quickly dampened my clothing. The harbor's water looked so inviting I contemplated jumping in. It required a lot of willpower, but I exercised better judgment and diverted my attention to the sky. A low-hanging, waning moon in a cloudless sky barely lit the harbor and landscape. Millions of stars punctuated the darkened heavens.

The scene reminded me of similar sweltering evenings in rural Hickory Township. Back then, my brother Frank and I would politely excuse ourselves, go outside, and lie in the damp grass. Sometimes we would talk. On other occasions, we lay quietly listening to crickets, whippoorwills and far-off train whistles, and stared at the Milky Way. The sharp contrast between then and being a crew member of the most powerful weapon on Earth made my heart ache for those simple carefree times.

I reminded myself why I was sitting topside and redirected thoughts to my temporary freedom from a steel container crammed with equipment and smelly people. I refused to try to identify the components of the *Clay*'s interior odor. When in the submarine, I knew it was there and simply got used to it. Outside, the smell was gone and quickly forgotten.

As I sat on the metal deck, man-made noises quickly faded into oblivion, and I became engrossed in the island's serenity. Compared to the din of the *Clay*'s confines, it was almost like being in a vacuum. I inhaled deeply and savored the fragrance of the night air. Wafting into my nose were the jungle's distinct scent, a sweet perfume of tropical flowers, and the salt mist of the sea. I felt weightless. It almost seemed as if I could float away. I closed my eyes and savored the sensation. Amid the relative silence, the rustling of the wind through palm tree fronds and small wavelets softly lapping the sides of the hull soothed me. Off in the distance, huge Pacific Ocean waves roared like continuous far-off thunder. Every once in a while, the silhouette of a Guam fruit bat crossed in front of the sliver of the crescent moon. Somewhere along the dark shoreline, I heard the dull thump of a falling coconut. Quickly following the noise was the loud scolding of a cardinal honeyeater. I delighted in the magic of the exotic setting. My escape from the inside of the *Clay* was better than anything I could have imagined.

The sound of the topside watch turning over to the next shift signaled that my time outside the FBM was over. I grudgingly went below. As I entered the submarine's interior, colors evaporated, reminding me of Dorothy's return to Kansas from Oz.

All of my preparations for leaving in the morning were complete. I went to the mess deck for something to eat. Since it was midnight, the meal was mid–rats, short for midnight rations. The fare was typical. There was a selection of cold cuts, peanut butter and jelly, bread, milk, and bug juice. I made myself a small baloney sandwich. A glass of milk from the dispenser, nicknamed the Cow, completed the snack. I chose milk over bug juice, because the transit had taught me how fast we used up our limited supply of the commodity. After running out of the real thing, there was only powdered milk. I did not care for that type; to me, it was watery and tasted like plastic.

I sat with Ron O'Heiren. He was a fire control technician. Like me, he was making his first patrol. We did not broach this subject. Instead, we talked about his recently broken watch. He was one of those people who could hardly do without one. O'Heiren had the misfortune of breaking his watch without any chance of getting a replacement. He was dejected.

The *Clay*, unlike surface ships, did not have a ship's store where small personal items were available for sale. Once we left port, crewmen must do without anything they ran out of or forgot. It didn't matter what it was.

The only possible relief was finding someone willing to share his supply. The same went for items that broke, as in the case of the watch; O'Heiren had to accept his fate.

Once finished eating, we headed to berthing to get some shuteye. O'Heiren, a non-nuclear trained sailor, could sleep until 0600. I had to awake at 0400 to disconnect the shore power cables, the *Clay's* electrical umbilical cord when she was not making her own electricity.

I stripped off my dungarees and slid open my rack's curtain. I stuffed the clothes into the laundry bag, which was hanging off the back bulkhead of my rack.

A surprise was waiting for me. Lying on my pillow was a letter from my brother Frank, written in his typical cramped scrawl. I was very tired, so it was difficult translating the script. I deduced that his wife Marcia had their baby and they named him Seth. I composed a quick letter expressing my congratulations and expounded on how they picked a wonderful name. I hurried to the attack center and placed the letter in the mailbag. As I scurried back to berthing, a good feeling swept through me. Taking the time and effort was worth it. Frank and Marcia would not have to wait until I returned from patrol to know how proud I was to have a nephew named Seth.

Lying down with the privacy curtain closed, I surveyed my six-foot-long, two-foot-wide, and 18"-high sanctuary. It was the only space on the submarine I could truly call my own. The sides and overhead had the same style of Formica as the rest of the *Clay*. A fluorescent light, a small ventilation supply, the little locker, and hooks for hanging a towel and laundry bag were there for my use. Amenities issued by the Navy were a two-inch-thick plastic-covered mattress, a pillow, two sheets, a navy-gray wool blanket, and a thin tan bedspread. To make my haven less stark, I had two quasi-companions. Taped to the space's overhead was a poster of Raquel Welch. Lying beside me was a small teddy bear. The doll served no purpose other than irritating officers during weekly inspections. Gazing at my Spartan surroundings, I took it in. Although tight quarters, it was surprisingly comfortable and essentially a smaller version of the submarine. The *Clay's* hull isolated me from the sea. My rack's coffin-like enclosure and curtain separated me from the rest of the submarine. I felt serene and protected.

After turning off my light, I rolled over onto my stomach. My arms were pinned under me. I had them fully extended, with palms against my thighs. This may sound like a strange position, but it was the only pose which allowed me to fall asleep when on the submarine. Sleep quickly and mercifully overcame me. My three and a half hours of slumber would be over too soon.

Notes

1. Fred R. Shapiro, ed., *The Yale Book of Quotations* (London: Yale University Press, 2006), 230.
2. Submarine Research Center, *Submarine Skullduggery* (Silverdale, WA: Submarine Research Center), 2004, 31–3.

Chapter 12

Getting Underway

The messenger of the watch jarred me awake by jerking my curtain open and shining a flashlight in my face. While pointing the light at my eyes, he half-shouted, "Hey, Dubay. Wake up. Boy, I love getting nucs up two hours before everybody else."

I tried to shield my eyes. Looking past the light, I recognized him. It was one of the sailors fresh from submarine school. So far, he had an over-inflated opinion of himself and tried to take liberties not yet earned. Nuclear-trained personnel were his favorite targets.

I did not appreciate his actions and said, "Get that light out of my face, you non-qual puke. Keep harassing us nucs and your engineering checkouts will be pure hell."

He left, although his demeanor did not show he took my warning seriously. If his attitude did not change, he would soon discover the consequences.

Giving every unqualified crewmember a fair chance was the normal submarine culture. They were volunteers and had made it through submarine school. As long as the non-quals had a good attitude, the qualified men would bend over backwards helping them with their quals. On the other hand, the wrong approach brought about a miserable time. It was their choice.

I rolled out of my rack, irritated by the combination of too little sleep and the treatment of the messenger. Shaking my head cleared the cobwebs. I slowly counted to ten. At seven, the irritation was subsiding. By the number ten, I felt much better.

A few moments of bewilderment ensued. I could not find my dungarees. Then I remembered the uniform of the day was poopie suits.

I chuckled at my confusion. From now on, we did everything in our power to preserve the *Clay*'s atmosphere as clean as possible although, the submarine produced various contaminants and crewmen could smoke. The FBM had an atmosphere analyzer. It sampled every compartment and analyzed them for freon, carbon monoxide, oxygen, carbon dioxide, and hydrogen concentration. As precious as we considered our air, its potential to become foul was far from being the limiting factor of how long we could stay submerged. Filters in the ventilation systems and the carbon dioxide scrubbers purified the atmosphere. Oxygen generators produced more O_2 than we consumed. Even so, our equipment could not remove some pollutants. We either minimized their production or restricted potential sources. Personal items such as radium dial watches that emitted radioactive isotopes and aerosol cans were of particular concern.

While I was asleep, another group of nucs had started up the reactor and the *Clay* was self-sustaining on nuclear power. Our boat no longer needed electricity from the shore power cables and my job was disconnecting them. Detaching the cables was not a difficult task. My main concern was making sure things were de-energized before sticking my grubby mitts on them. Coming in contact with an energized shore power cable meant certain death. My electrical training had ingrained a deep respect for electricity and I refused to take any shortcuts. I located the tagout log and checked the proper sheet. The paperwork was in order. Even so, I physically checked each component. The verification revealed that the electrical breakers were in the correct position and associated safety tags were in place. Not leaving anything to chance, I entered maneuvering and confirmed the proper meters on the electrical plant control panel indicated zero volts and no amps.

When connecting the cables, I used a multimeter to verify no electricity was present. During the disconnecting process, this was not possible. With the cables connected, the situation was similar to a household extension cord plugged into a wall socket. The prongs of the plug were not accessible. That was why I took the extra safety precautions.

I obtained a spanner wrench and climbed the ladder just forward of maneuvering leading to the after-escape trunk.

Although designed to hold several sailors for an emergency escape, the cavity was not large. In my situation, the cables nestled on the side of the trunk occupied much of the void. They severely limited the available working room. My miniature stature was an advantage in the confined space.

Each end of the three shore power cables had a bronze female threaded connector with a rubber gasket. I used the spanner to loosen the female end from the male connection at the side of the escape trunk and unscrewed them by hand. When they were disconnected, I placed the cables on the FBM's hull. Once there, workers from the sub tender hauled the heavy wires to their ship. I was sweating liberally due to a combination of exertion and Guam's climate. Next, I attached threaded watertight caps onto each connection inside the trunk. Lastly, I removed the safety tags. The engineering spaces of the USS *Henry Clay* were ready to go to sea.

In parallel, topside preparations were in their final stages. Anything which may rattle was tack-welded. These included covers for the anchor and our emergency buoy. This may sound unsafe but it really was not. We never used the anchor during my time on the *Clay*. The emergency buoy deployed and emitted a signal if the submarine sank. Because the portion of the ocean in which we operated was so deep, the buoy's cable was not long enough to reach the surface in case the worst happened.

Getting underway was a carefully orchestrated production involving all hands.

Unlike surface ships, submarines did not adhere to an 0800-to-1600 workday routine and we never heard reveille or taps.

Once everybody had a chance to eat, the crew manned the maneuvering watch. Submarines station it whenever the boat was leaving or entering port. Akin to battle stations, each sailor had a particular role for which he demonstrated special expertise. I was the throttleman.

While final preparations for casting off all lines were occurring topside, not much action occurred in the engineering spaces. We nucs enjoyed the lull while it lasted. Once the *Clay* started moving, most of the engineering folks were busy operating or monitoring equipment. The throttleman position was no exception. It was one reason I enjoyed the assignment. I liked the challenge.

Along with me in maneuvering were four others. Lewis was at the electric plant control panel. The responsibility for the reactor plant control panel belonged to Dick Love. Love was the consummate professional. Nothing fazed him. Sitting at his elevated chair and desk was the EOOW, Mr. Hawthorne.

The fourth person was Schweikert.

Schweikert had one function. He recorded every speed change, called "bells" (all-stop, ahead one-third, ahead two-thirds, ahead full, ahead flank, back one-third, back two-thirds, back full, and the dreaded back emergency), on the engineer's bell book. Its name was a misnomer. The bell book was really a single sheet of paper with three sets of columns, with 27 rows per column. Each major column had four sub-columns, for recording: the time the bell was received, the bell ordered, the shaft RPMs corresponding to the bell, and shaft counter reading. Schweikert retrieved the shaft counter reading from an indicator, much like the odometer of a car. It tracked the total number of revolutions made by the propeller. During the maneuvering watch, there were so many rapid-succession entries that Charlie initially recorded only the bell, the last three digits of the counter, and the minute. He filled in the remaining data when the action slowed. Every mistake on the log required adding the new correct number, crossing out the error, and initialing the modification. The *Clay* had an unusual rule regarding the bell book, which added another degree of stress to the task. If there were more than three cross-outs on the sheet, the person making the last error had to recopy the data onto another sheet. Consequently, we became masters of the write-over. This was an attempt to disguise the error and make the mistake appear as if it never happened. The EOOW inspected and signed the bell log when he was relieved. On many occasions, the EOOW commented that he knew there were many write-overs, but they were so skillfully done he could not prove it.

After securing the maneuvering watch, there were few speed changes and the throttleman maintained the bell book himself. If there were no bell changes, he logged the current bell, shaft turns, and counter once an hour on the hour.

The officer of the deck stood in the bridge. He was in charge of guiding the *Clay*.

He shouted, "Take in all lines."

Our life-jacketed line handlers detached the two-inch-diameter nylon lines from the submarine's cleats and threw them into the water. Boatswain's mates on the tender hauled them in.

Without needing orders, our men topside unpinned and rotated the horn-shaped cleats one hundred eighty degrees. The cleat was now upside down and inside the hull. The bottom side of the device was smooth and matched the contours of the hull. This kept the submarine as sleek and quiet as possible.

There were plenty of volunteers for the line handler and lookout positions. I was not sure who chose these men, but they considered themselves lucky. These sailors enjoyed the freedom, sensations, and sights outside the confines of the submarine the longest. Most non-submariners take fresh air, trees, the smell of land, sky and clouds, the feel of wind blowing through their hair, being able to see farther than 50 feet, and most important, sunlight, for granted. Because of our experiences, submariners developed a deep appreciation of these for the rest of our lives. Even to this day, I would rather have car windows open versus using the vehicle's air conditioner.

Each individual had his own emotions about leaving on patrol. For me, I was departing on an adventure, a test of my mental, physical, and psychological capabilities.

When topside preparations were complete, the OOD issued the command, "Back one-third."

In response, a crewmember with him in the conn repeated the direction, "Back one-third, aye."

The sailor turned his knob on the engine order telegraph. The action made an arrow point to the back one-third position. An indicator on my panel responded likewise and rang a bell.

The ding of the engine order telegraph bell broke the tranquility in maneuvering. I reached over and matched my arrow with the other pointer.

Simultaneously, I opened the astern throttles, admitting steam to the main turbines, which made the propeller turn in reverse.

I sang out, "Back one-third."

We were underway.

Mr. Hawthorn responded, "Back one-third, aye."

The boat shuddered as it began to move.

Love increased his vigilance on the reactor plant control panel's indications. Because I was demanding more steam from the steam generators, the temperature of the reactor coolant system decreased. The temperature dropped and some complex nuclear physics caused the reactor to produce more power. To minimize how low the temperature went and to speed up the increase in power, Love withdrew the reactor's control rods. The fission rate became faster. When I closed the throttles and sent less steam to the turbines, the result was the opposite. Due to these effects, the throttleman and the reactor operator (RO) work in concert.

A flurry of bell changes quickly followed the back one-third.

The large number of bell changes made it clear who was manning the conn. It was Lt. Fudd. He was legendary for the number of course and, especially, speed changes ordered.

Fudd became a rapid-fire machine of directions. He dispersed almost nonstop course and speed alterations: all-stop, ahead one-third, ahead two-thirds, left full rudder, ahead one-third, all-stop, right full rudder, back one-third, all-stop, ahead one-third. Schweikert furiously recorded his data error-free, which was why he was picked for the task.

In Mr. Fudd's defense, getting underway required complex maneuvers to avoid collisions and running aground, although there was a noticeable difference between him and other officers manning the maneuvering watch officer of the deck.

Every bell required a response by the reactor operator and me, with Schweikert keeping the bell book. I could not see where we were going or what was in our path. Therefore, I had to respond quickly and accurately to the demanded orders. It was much like driving your car with the windows painted black and having someone sitting on the roof giving you directions. Making my job even more difficult was the fact that the throttle wheels did not have indicators, corresponding to the various speeds. It had taken much experience to attain my present level of expertise.

As Love reacted to my actions, he had to keep certain nuclear parameters within predetermined bands. One of the most important was the average temperature of the water transferring the heat from the reactor. The temperature indicator displaying this value contained the green band. The span encompassed only a small portion of the dial's full range. His job was to keep the temperature within that part of the indicator.

It was traditional for throttleman and RO to play a good-natured game of rapid recognition, reflexes, and pride, regarding the temperature band. My goal was to drive him out of the green band. He tried to stay within in it, by manipulating the reactor's control rods. In defense of my actions, I had to have the submarine moving at the proper speed as quickly as possible, and I took great pride in my ability to accomplish the feat. If my actions drove his temperature out of the green band, so be it.

The engine order telegraph signaled ahead two-thirds. I announced the bell and rapidly whipped the throttle wheel in the open direction. A quick glance at Love told me he was struggling to keep pace. With a determined look, his fingers were tense from holding the In-Hold-Out switch hard into the out stop. This made the control rods withdraw from the reactor and raise power. He intently monitored the fission rate. Once he achieved the proper indication, Love made other adjustments and kept parameters from overshooting. These actions tested our proficiency to the maximum. Who had honed his skills the finest? In this instance, the temperature dropped, but he had kept it within the band and breathed a sigh of relief. The round was a draw.

I matched actual propeller RPM with those desired and announced, "Answering ahead two-thirds."

In addition to testing our abilities, these exertions provided a genuine sense of accomplishment, as we felt the boat react in response to our actions.

Their jobs completed, topside line handlers went below. Before descending into the fluorescent-lit depths of the boat, already filled with stale, foul-smelling air, they took a final glimpse at the sea, sky, horizon, and the island of Guam. Their concluding acts were inhaling deeply and savoring the last breath of fresh air for the next two months.

When the men on the bridge descended the ladder and closed the hatch, the submarine was hermetically sealed. Anybody with claustrophobia was long gone.

"Ah-oooo-gah! Ah-oooo-gah! Dive! Dive!" Then the bell of the engine order telegraph sang its tinny "ding," as the needle sprang to ahead two-thirds. In concert, I instinctively acknowledged the speed change. With my left hand twirling the ahead throttle-wheel, I increased the steam flow to the propulsion turbines.

I cried out, "Ahead two-thirds."

The gentle roll of the submarine diminished as we gently slid under the water. Those in areas with low background noise could hear the swishing sound of the sea on the hull slowly disappearing. We reached our predetermined depth and leveled off. There were no leaks. Although we did not expect any, I was always relieved when we confirmed the condition.

The submarine was rigged for ultra quiet. It was the *Clay*'s quietest designed equipment configuration. There was a very good reason for operating in that condition. We had to sneak through a gauntlet of Soviet vessels stationed at Apra Harbor's opening to the Pacific Ocean. One was a surface ship thinly disguised as a fishing trawler. It was bristling with electronic listening gear. Accompanying the trawler was at least one Russian fast-attack submarine. The trawler, using its array of sensitive sensing gear, attempted to determine the *Clay*'s course and relay the information to the enemy submarine. The attack boat was also listening for the *Clay*. If either vessel detected us, the submarine would attempt to follow.

The Soviets' task was daunting. In addition to rigging for ultra quiet, we employed a few other tactics to elude detection. I will not reveal any, as I am sure the United States Navy still uses some to this day. In spite of these, each crew member felt the pressure of maintaining our silent state and the gravity of the consequences. An inadvertent noise, such as dropping a tool, could compromise efforts by giving away our position.

The effect on the crew was noticeable. My hands were moist from tension-induced sweat. Love had his hands clasped together behind his back. Upon close inspection, his fingers were white from squeezing them tightly. Lewis seemed outwardly unaffected. Then I noticed he was nervously tapping his foot. Grim-faced Southerland silently walked by maneuverfing. The crew's acts were deliberate; a no-nonsense, businesslike expression adorned faces. No one wanted to be the person revealing our location to any Soviet submarine trying to tail us.

Before long, we secured the maneuvering watch. Schweikert relieved me as throttleman. This gave me a few hours before I had to relieve the auxiliary electrician aft. Patrol routine had begun.

I decided to work on my submarine qualifications. In order to perform the task, I needed the *Henry Clay* piping tab. It was in my locker. The book had a one-line drawing and other information of the system I was studying.

I found a pleasant surprise in my rack. It was a letter from Mom, Leona Gus Dubay and Dad, Frank Dubay, Sr.

Some last-minute mail had arrived before the submarine got underway. This also confirmed that my letter to Frank had actually made it off the boat. The patrol was starting out on a good note. I carefully opened the letter. It was my last contact from home for the next two months. My Mom's dainty, smooth script emphasized the loving nature of the composition. As with all last letters, I intended to read it throughout patrol.

My melancholy mood abruptly changed to horror when I read that Frank and Marcia's baby's name was Scott. The thought of my letter, mailed the previous evening, left me aghast.

Scott? Scott? Not Seth?

My letter to Frank and Marcia was unrecoverable, and I could not make a phone call or even write a quick follow-up note to apologize until we returned. Any communication with the outside world from me was on hold for over two months. I had no way of knowing their reaction. Would they think it was funny and chalk it up to Ted being Ted or be insulted? Wasn't patrol bad enough without having something like this in the back of my mind? As with other situations over which I had no control, I resolved to take whatever lumps I deserved and not worry about it until then.

With piping tab in hand, working on the difficult task of qualifying in submarines helped relieve my agony.

Chapter 13

Christmas on Patrol

I was perched face-down atop an air mattress floating on my parents' pond. The float was gently rocking back and forth. Warm sunshine bathed me. Faint wisps of a cool breeze tickled my head and shoulders.

The sound of something sliding combined with a clicking noise, disrupted the peaceful setting.

My brain tried to connect these particular noises with a summertime foray on the small body of water.

I opened my eyes. Darkness surrounded me. Confusion swirled in my mind. A perplexing dim light was nearby.

I heard someone softly saying, "Dubay, Dubay. Hey, Ted."

My fog-enshrouded head turned towards the sound. With eyes slowly focusing, I tried to comprehend the source.

They encountered the kind face of Third-Class Sonar Technician E.K. Lingle, the messenger of the watch. I checked my watch. He had let me sleep as long as possible. If I wanted breakfast before relieving the watch, I had to hurry.

Reality gradually dawned on me.

I had been dreaming.

In actuality, I was aboard the nuclear-powered submarine USS *Henry Clay*. She was somewhere in the Pacific. It was several weeks into my first patrol. Her slow rolling motion told me she was at periscope depth. Connections evolved between my dream and present situation. Both involved an association with water. The cool air emanating from my rack's air conditioning vent equated to the wisps of a cool breeze. Sun-warmed air surrounding me matched the tepid atmosphere in the submarine. We were still cruising in tropical water and the *Clay*'s air conditioning system barely kept the inside of the boat cool. While getting dressed, I assessed the disparities of the conditions between my actual circumstance and those in the dream. I was not surprised about having such an apparition; it was wishful thinking.

I found no novelty in my first patrol, having already experienced extended time submerged during shipyard testing and the transit to Hawaii. Like the other two occurrences, electrical maintenance and pursuing qualification in submarines and nuclear watch stations filled my off-watch time.

My current circumstance had a difference: the end of my qualification process was in sight.

I had one more under-instruction (UI) electric plant control panel watch. I would be standing it under the tutelage of Davis. His presence was a mere formality. After many hours of study and practice, I knew all of the necessary procedures and was proficient at operating the electric plant control panel's touchy controls.

In a few weeks, I would complete the progression through submarine qualification and earn my coveted set of Dolphins.

These tasks helped suppress the agony of not knowing Frank's reaction to my unrecoverable letter.

I entered crew's mess. It was breakfast time. Eggs were not rotten yet, so I ordered two over-easy, bacon, and toast. A glass of tomato juice completed the meal.

Davis was already eating and I sat with him. Between mouthfuls of steak, scrambled eggs, hash browns, and grits, he asked if I was well rested.

I told him I was and wondered why he asked.

He put on his most innocent expression and explained that it was my last Under Instruction (UI) watch and he would not be surprised if the engineer threw some interesting casualties at me. He'd want to make sure I was ready to go solo as electrical operator.

He saw my crestfallen reaction. "Don't worry. You know how to handle anything they can come up with. After all, *I* trained you!"

He erupted with his typical good-natured laugh.

After eating, we headed aft to maneuvering.

On the way, thoughts of drills (responding to planned plant casualties and abnormal transients) swirled through my mind.

Being able to handle all aspects of the operation of the submarine, both good and bad, was paramount. Drills kept the crew trained to the highest levels.

Nucs maintained their expertise several ways. For an FBM, when one crew was on patrol, the other underwent countless hours of instruction. Unfortunately, the nuclear-trained sailors could not receive practical training on equipment associated with the nuclear reactor. We could only practice when on the submarine, via drills.

Ninety percent of the time, submarines operated where the ocean bottom was well below crush depth, a precarious position. Even though conducted in a controlled environment, drills put a submarine in an even more perilous situation. If the nuclear-trained operators did not take the proper measures, it would spell doom.

We initiated most engineering drills by physically operating a component. Sometimes it was a valve. On other occasions, someone manipulated an electrical switch. In either case, they negatively affected actual equipment. Even though I was competent and had confidence in the abilities of my shipmates, drills made me uncomfortable. Unfortunately, they were a necessary evil. There was no other way the Navy could train us to react to real problems.

Upon reaching the watertight door between machinery 2 and the engine room, I deftly passed through the opening. The performance was a far cry from my first futile attempt many months ago. The hot, humid air of the space made me catch my breath. Sweat quickly coated my body. Standing between the ships service turbine generators were Southerland and Souder. Southerland was relieving Souder as the upper level engine room watch. Both their faces had rivulets of sweat. I was grateful my watch station was in maneuvering, where it was much cooler.

Davis and I stopped at the doorway to the control room.

I said to the engineering officer of the watch, Mr. Jakucyk, who had already relieved his predecessor, "Permission to enter maneuvering and relieve the electrical operator."

"Permission granted."

Soon eight people filled the tiny space. Joining the three original watch standers (throttleman, reactor operator, and electrical operator) were their reliefs, plus the EOOW and me.

Davis and I were relieving Marchbanks. He gave Davis a quizzical look.

Davis said, "Pretend I'm not here. This is Eaglebeak's final UI."

Marchbanks provided an update on the electric plant's status. "The electric plant is in a normal full-power lineup, with a trickle charge on the battery."

A quick glance at the panel verified his statement.

He informed me about a small electrical ground. After he checked the usual culprits—galley range, deep sink, and clothes dryer—it went away on its own.

"I relieve you."

Davis nodded in agreement.

Marchbanks turned to Jakucyk and said, "Davis, with Dubay as UI, has relieved me as the electrical operator."

"Very well."

It did not take long before all engineering spaces reported that the new section was on duty.

Davis settled into the space between the electric plant control panel and the *Clay*'s curved hull. I sat on the panel's designated stool. Vince Dainotto was the reactor operator. Schweikert was the throttleman.

Anticipating the drills, I intently scanned the panel's indications. Dainotto and Schweikert were nonchalant, lapsing into a conversation about Dainotto's pet dog, Dino.

I was not paying attention to their discussion, until Dainotto said, "Dino acts almost human."

While turning my head to comment on the statement, my eyes passed over the electric plant panel's instruments.

A slight deviation on one of the meters for the port ships service turbine generator caught my attention.

My body stiffened and senses sprang to full alert. The load carried by the #1 SSTG had decreased slightly. I held my tongue and performed a meticulous inspection of the rest of the panel. The initially identified parameter was the only one amiss.

Trying to maintain my most composed intonation, I reported to the EOOW, "Load on number one SSTG is decreasing. I suspect a loss of vacuum in the starboard condenser. All other indications are normal."

The report caused everyone in maneuvering to focus more intently on the operation of the engineering plant.

Jakucyk contacted the engineering watch supervisor to investigate the condition locally.

He had barely completed directing the needed instructions when the effects of the loss of vacuum suddenly became more severe. It had worsened to the point where the change was noticeable on the steam plant control panel's indications.

Schweikert reported, "Vacuum getting worse in the starboard condenser. Shaft turns are decreasing."

While the EOOW was responding to Schweikert's statement, I rose from the seat, preparing to take action.

I stated, "Recommend shifting the electric plant to a half-power lineup, on the number two turbine generator."

Mr. Jakucyk responded, "Shift the electric plant to a half-power lineup on the number two TG."

As soon as my steps were completed, the reactor plant control panel siren wailed and the steam plant control panel's horn honked.

Dainotto immediately flicked the required switches and simultaneously announced, "Reactor SCRAM."

The reactor was now shut down and not producing enough heat to make the needed steam for driving the propulsion turbines. Schweikert shut the throttles and rang up all-stop on the engine order telegraph.

As Charlie had done with the propulsion turbines, I had to secure the remaining turbine generator to keep from removing too much heat from the reactor. I twisted the proper knobs and operated switches. This shifted the source of the *Clay's* electrical power from the remaining turbine generator to the *Clay's* main storage battery.

In parallel, the EOOW selected the 1MC microphone from an array hanging in the overhead. It allowed him to make an announcement throughout the submarine.

Jakucyk cleared his throat. He calmly spoke into the microphone, "Reactor SCRAM. Rig ship for reduced electrical."

His announcement alerted the entire crew of the casualty. It also set into motion actions to turn off non-essential electrical equipment.

By the time he finished speaking, I had completed the electrical transition. Until the reactor operator restarted the reactor, my main job was monitoring how long the battery would last. Minimizing the drain on the battery was essential for maintaining the *Clay's* silent mode of operation. The submarine's storage battery was very large but could only last so long. If depleted, it forced us to start our emergency diesel generator. Because the diesel was an internal combustion engine, it needed an air supply to run. To accomplish this, the submarine had to rise to periscope depth. When the snorkel mast was above the surface of the water, it drew in the required air. Although the diesel provided electrical power much longer than the battery, it had its limits. The USS *Henry Clay*, like her sisters, did not have an inexhaustible supply of fuel oil. Minimizing its use conserved fuel for real emergencies. Additionally, it was very noisy and compromised the silent nature of an FBM.

By monitoring the amp-hour meter, I saw the drain on the battery slowing down. It told me that rigging the ship for reduced electrical was in progress. Others in maneuvering were aware of the same fact, without being able to see the meter. The temperature in the little space was rising rapidly. The cooling was a non-essential load. Soon we were sweating as much as Southerland and Souder, at the beginning of the watch.

The condition would continue until the reactor produced enough power to support operation of at least one SSTG. In order to accomplish that, sailors had to find and correct the cause of the SCRAM and loss of vacuum. Watch standers outside maneuvering frantically worked to accomplish this, with the assistance of the casualty assistance team (CAT). One of the CAT members, Marchbanks, was in maneuvering wearing a 2JV headset. It was his job to relay communications between maneuvering and the rest of those in the engineering spaces.

Before long, we received good news. Southerland had corrected the loss of vacuum.

The cause of the SCRAM was still unresolved. The amp-hour meter was steadily clicking, as the battery continued to drain. If it depleted much more, we had to commence snorkeling and relieve the battery with the diesel generator. Just in time, sailors corrected the problem that was preventing us from restarting the reactor.

Mr. Jakucyk ordered, "Dainotto. Commence a fast SCRAM recovery."

"Commence fast SCRAM recovery, aye."

Before long, the reactor was critical and producing enough heat to support the propulsion turbines and the SSTGs.

The EOOW ordered me to place the electric plant in a half-power lineup on the #2 turbine generator.

In parallel, Schweikert answered bells on the main engines.

When I completed the ordered electrical alignment, Mr. Jakucyk directed restoring to a full-power lineup.

After I performed the needed actions, the engineer appeared in maneuvering's doorway. He nodded, smiled, and told me to report to the wardroom for an electrical operator board.

Davis said, "Good job. Hand me your qual card. I'll sign it off. Like I said before, you know everything needed to pass with flying colors. Don't let them rattle you."

He was correct. At the completion of the qualification board, the captain deemed me qualified on my last nuclear watch station.

One milestone completed and one to go. My next goal was earning my Dolphins. Up to this point, I'd been maintaining the minimum allowed progress towards submarine qualification. With qualifying as electrical operator behind me, I no longer had to split my limited spare time between two time-consuming tasks. Becoming a fully accepted submariner was right around the corner.

About a week later, I walked by the mess deck. Bingo night had just ended. Because I was not qualified in submarines, I couldn't participate. O'Heiren, the man whose watch broke the evening before we left on patrol, stepped out of crew's mess. He had a huge grin.

Spying me, he held up his left arm and showed me the watch he had won playing bingo. He was elated.

Before I had a chance to respond, he disappeared down the passageway so he could show others.

When I saw O'Heiren the next day, he was wearing a dejected expression.

His current mood was a puzzle. The last time I'd seen him, he was in a great mood, so I asked what was wrong.

He pulled up his sleeve and exposed a bare wrist. His new watch was not there.

"Where's your watch?"

"I'm too ticked-off to talk about it. Not sure how, but I know the nucs are messing with me."

I headed back aft and relieved Ballard as the auxiliary electrician aft. Because it was a roving watch, I'd be able to pass through all of the engineering spaces and see if anybody could provide insight about O'Heiren's missing watch. All encountered watch standers disavowed any knowledge, until I came upon the engineering lab technician (ELT), Walt Pottenger. He was at the sample sink in auxiliary machinery 2 upper level.

At first, he claimed no knowledge about the subject. A sheepish grin told me otherwise. When pressed, he made me promise not to repeat anything he said, especially to O'Heiren.

I readily agreed and shook his hand to seal the deal.

He described how O'Heiren was showing his new watch to some nucs, when one of the ELTs noticed it had a luminous dial. The ELT asked if anyone had checked it for radium, a banned substance. That was O'Heiren's first clue something was up. Whoever bought the watch would have considered that. When the ELT realized O'Heiren did not know the watch couldn't contain radium, he saw an opportunity to string him along. They went to the ELT lab to check the watch in the radiation counter.

After putting the watch in, the ELT placed the rad monitor's switch in TEST. It became O'Heiren's second hint the ELT was up to something. When the switch was in TEST, it inserted a *false* high radiation signal. O'Heiren was horrified when the indicator needle flew past the alarm set-point and stopped near the top of the scale.

At that point, the unnamed ELT knew the ruse could turn into something special. He turned off the counter so the alarm stopped and summoned Dr. Smyth. Somehow, the ELT clued in the doctor, who decided to play along. The doc showed up with a straight face and solemnly confiscated the watch. When he told O'Heiren it had to be kept in the locked medical safe for the rest of the patrol, O'Heiren was crestfallen.

I recalled hearing him say he knew the nucs were screwing with him. He just could not figure out how.

It did not matter how long the deception lasted. The nucs were having a lot of fun with it. Every additional day was icing on the cake. The patrol was not even half over. I doubted that any nuc would reveal the truth. There was no reason to feel sorry for him. If there is one subject somebody stationed on a nuclear submarine carrying atomic weapons should understand, it was how a radiation monitor worked. My lips were sealed. It was up to O'Heiren at that point. The material for him to gain the necessary information was easily available. Submariners had no sympathy for anyone not having the proper level of knowledge. This was especially true in this case. O'Heiren was qualified in submarines.

One day, I was standing throttleman. Metzgus was the electrical operator. Dainotto had responsibility for the reactor plant. Lt. Ward watched over the lot of us as EOOW. Manning the upper level engine room was Souder.

As always, the engine room was miserably hot. In an effort to get a reprieve from the heat, Souder was standing in maneuvering's doorway and facing forward, with half his body in maneuvering's cool air. He suddenly sneezed violently. His forehead smashed into the stainless steel doorframe, generating a loud THUNK.

Metzgus exclaimed, "What are you trying to do, give away our position to the Russians? That was enough noise to wake the dead. I'll bet we're going to hear from sonar any second. They'll be asking what the heck happened." Others added their own sarcastic comments.

Rubbing the red mark on his noggin, Souder was in no mood for our lack of sympathy. Glaring at us, he snapped, "Normal people would ask if I'm okay."

I countered, "Hey. What about all the psychological testing we've been through? We musta passed or we wouldn't have made it into the submarine service. Therefore, we *have* to be normal."

Without skipping a beat, he replied, "Not true. The testing just found sailors who are a special kind of crazy and eligible for submarine duty. What's bizarre is submariners are proud of it!"

The next week, a few days before Christmas, one of the *Clay*'s two clothes dryers developed a mechanical problem and emitted a terrible noise. The laundry queen immediately stopped it before any lurking Russians could locate the *Clay*.

The captain wanted the dryer returned to operation promptly. He was a stickler for trying to keep the crew as comfortable as possible. This was especially important to the nucs. We could almost wring sweat out of our garments after spending time in the engine room.

The electricians had to perform the repairs. We quickly determined the problem. A snap spring, holding the dryer's fan on its shaft, was broken. The repair proved to be more difficult. We did not have a spare in our limited supply of replacement parts.

Every available electrician worked on the issue. The situation was especially arduous on me. I had to spend all of my six hours after watch working on repairing the dryer. That only left my rest period to make progress on submarine qualifications. I was down to two and a half hours of sleep in the 18-hour workday. Being able to earn my Dolphins in the next few weeks made the sacrifice worth it.

On Christmas Eve, in a state of exhaustion, I descended the stairs to berthing. A mixture of an off-key rendition of "Jingle Bells" and a plethora of foul language greeted my ears. The normally dark area was alit with the overhead fluorescent lights. In spite of my diminished senses, I realized what was happening. A group of crew members filled with the Christmas spirit was serenading those occupying the berthing area. The sleeping individuals failed to appreciate the carolers' efforts, hence the verbal intensifiers flung unmercifully. Threats of severe bodily harm convinced the revelers to retreat and find a more appreciative audience. I was secretly glad they had not disturbed *my* abbreviated sleep. If I had been sleeping, Mom would not have been proud of my behavior.

Late Christmas eve, I suggested an innovative repair of the dryer. The baling-wire jury-rig worked like a charm. E-Div considered it the best Christmas gift ever.

Because of missing so much rest, I decided to celebrate the success by catching up on sleep. Hitting the rack as soon as possible allowed me to snooze for seven glorious hours.

I quickly fell into a deep dreamless sleep.

The next thing I knew, the curtain to my lair opened and someone softly called my name. I saw Metzgus.

"Are you getting up for Christmas dinner? There're serving turkey, prime rib and lobster." Responding in a drowsy stupor, I said, "No, man. I'm too tired. Thanks anyway."

Gratefully, he did not persist and was kind enough to slide the curtain shut. I rolled over onto my stomach and dropped off into slumberland. The curtain reopened. This time it was Souder. He asked the same question. Again, I politely refused the invitation. Before I had a chance to fall asleep, Lewis appeared. Like the other two, he did not want me to miss the best meal of the patrol. Once more, I declined the offer, although my response was less courteous.

A few minutes after he departed, Mike Pavlov repeated the scenario. When he asked if I was going to get up for Christmas dinner, I couldn't contain myself and snapped, "Yeah I'm gitt'n up. Damn it. Nobody's going to leave me alone anyway. Geez. Too many people disturbed me. It doesn't matter how tired I am. There isn't any way I can fall back to sleep now. Geez."

Pavlov was startled by my tirade. I realized he was not aware of the others' efforts and apologized.

"Aw, don't worry about it. I've been that tired myself. Just go, enjoy the meal, and hit the skid again."

I sat with Southerland. He told me he had initially refused to get up for the meal, also. We agreed the food was excellent and worth the loss of sleep. I departed the mess deck resolved to apologize for my rude behavior to Metzgus, Lewis, and Souder. It would also be good practice for apologizing to Frank.

My head hardly hit the pillow and sleep engulfed me.

Before I knew it, the messenger of the watch woke me along with the rest of the oncoming watch section. Supper consisted of Christmas dinner leftovers and hamburgers cooked to order. It was another great meal.

While my section was standing watch, the remainder of the crew celebrated Christmas in the mess deck. In an effort to generate the holiday spirit, one of the more rotund members of the crew dressed as Santa. A small artificial tree resided by the bug juice machine. Although my watch section wasn't there to witness the festivities, reports trickled in. Santa handed out gifts. Most were from the sailors' families and friends. Some were gag gifts between crew members. Our section had presents waiting under the tree.

After watch, our section enjoyed the holiday festivities. Chief Cochran, *sans* the red suit, aptly filled in for the original Santa. The presents were small simple items, because they arrived prior to the *Clay*'s embarking on patrol and we had limited storage space. Two of my gifts were a Swingline Tot Stapler and a pocket dictionary. What the actual presents were did not matter. Knowing that someone outside the confines of our metal cylinder sent them was comforting.

Two days later, I received another treat. It was the third of my five allotted family-grams. Like the others, there was no mention of Frank's reaction to my letter, but that was normal. Three officers screened each family-gram to ensure it did not contain coded expressions, riddles, profanity, risqué items, or sad or depressing news. Another restriction was a family-gram could be no longer than 40 words, which included the recipient's and senders' names. Given those limitations, the messages did not contain much information. They were no less valued—family-grams were our only conduit from our loved ones. I kept mine under the mattress at the head of my rack, where they were easily accessible.

The next week, New Year's Eve came and went without any fanfare. It was a moot point. Our timepieces were set to Greenwich Mean Time. When the *Clay*'s clocks said midnight and we rolled into a new year, the sun was shining brightly above our portion of the ocean.

A few weeks later, I earned the last signature on my submarine qualification card. There was only one more hurdle to overcome. I had to pass a final oral examination by a group of senior qualified submariners. The board was led by the navigation officer and COB Cochran. Three other qualified submariners assisted. They grilled me for over three hours. I was well prepared. They commended me on my performance and the officer signed my qualification card.

The next day, January 15, 1971, the captain designated me qualified in submarines. He conducted a ceremony in the passageway outside of his stateroom. It happened in front of our original oil painting of Henry Clay, the statesman. Also in attendance was the yeoman. The captain pinned the Dolphins on my poopie suit and presented me with a "Qualified in Submarines" certificate. After saying a few words about the significance of being qualified, he had the yeoman take a Polaroid picture of us in front of the painting.

When the ritual was over, I walked down the narrow passageway clutching the picture and certificate. After letting out a sigh of relief, I rubbed the coveted silver Dolphins. My quest for the Holy Grail of submarines was finally over. I was accepted into an elite group of individuals. I vowed to uphold the traditions of previous generations of that select society. Pride flowed through my soul. While heading to my locker to stow the newly acquired prizes, I saw First-Class Missile Technician Earl Lusaini. He saw the Dolphins on my chest and gave me a thumbs-up. His right hand moved towards me. I thought he was going to shake my hand and started raising mine in return. Suddenly, pain shot through my chest as his fist slammed into my Dolphins. My eyes shut in reaction to the throbbing. They reopened to his grinning face. His arm came up again and I flinched. This time he grabbed my hand and shook it enthusiastically.

"Congratulations, Dubay."

He slapped me on the back and nonchalantly continued down the passageway.

Tacking on my Dolphins continued for the next several days. Some sailors gave a little tap. Others were less gentle. After the rite, I wore the bruises as proudly as the silver Dolphins.

When someone on the *Clay* qualified in submarines, he could purchase a special chrome buckle for his web belt. A set of Dolphins adorned it along with the inscription: USS *Henry Clay*, SSBN 625. I gladly paid the five dollars and like most of the qualified submariners on the *Clay*, wore it instead of the pin.

It took less than a week before the novelty of being fully qualified wore off. Before earning Dolphins, I never had a moment to spare. Working on electrical tasks, logroom duties, studying, and sleeping filled every bit of my off-watch time. Afterward, I was amazed about how much spare time I had, and boredom set in.

Helping to fill the void was hanging out in the sonar shack with E.K. Lingle. Every so often, we heard the songs of porpoises and whales. Mostly the chatter of shrimp permeated the earphones. Every so often, a civilian ship passed by with its propellers going whomp—whomp—whomp. Sometimes Lingle played tapes of Russian attack submarines. Although he heard numerous enemy boats, I was happy my only encounters were via recordings.

I began helping with the crew's newspaper. Being logroom yeoman, I had access to clerical supplies and a typewriter.

Some books in the *Clay*'s small library stirred my interest. Reading them in the solitude of my rack also helped pass the time.

Watching movies was another diversion. They happened once a day at 1900 (7:00 p.m.), in the crew's mess. Even so, I did not have many opportunities see them. Living an 18-hour cycle allowed me to be coordinated with the movie schedule once every three days. Most were second-rate and just helped pass time, so it wasn't a big deal to miss one. Each evening two movies were on the agenda. A majority vote determined the selection. Sometimes neither movie met the viewers' interest and the men picked another flick.

One day, I made an offhand statement about missing the movie *MASH*. I had a burning desire to see it and made a pessimistic remark about never having an opportunity.

That evening, I settled in the mess deck for the daily movie. Something strange occurred. Crew's mess began filling with nucs. As I looked around, some who were supposed to be sleeping, including Southerland, were present. It did not take long before the small space was overflowing with nucs. There weren't enough seats and many stood. When it came time to vote on the regularly scheduled movie, it was voted down. Then, much to my surprise, Lewis nominated *MASH*. The nucs, as one, voted it in. Metzgus already had the three cans of film ready. He winked at me and placed the first reel on the projector. Not long into the flick, men began trickling out. Soon, the place was devoid of anyone except Metzgus and me. A warm feeling flowed through my body. I recalled what Pottenger said about nucs sticking together. He was right. I had many people to thank.

Another tactic used to keep boredom from setting in was standing different watches when on duty. My watch section had that luxury because all three of the E-Div sailors assigned were qualified on every position— auxiliary electrician aft, throttleman, and electrical operator.

One day, I was the roving electrician during a drill requiring us to wear emergency air breathing (EAB) masks. Making matters worse, the *Clay* was at periscope depth in rough seas. While I was running forward and outboard of the port main engine, the *Clay* took a vicious roll. In spite of the deck dropping from under my feet, my momentum kept me moving forward through the air. A collision between my head and something in the overhead ensued. I continued heading forward, unaware of a gash in my scalp. Southerland noticed the blood running down my neck. It took five stitches to close the cut. The injury had an upside. I did not have to wear a breathing mask for drills until the cut healed.

While the stitches were in, I only stood the throttleman and electrical operator watches. The strategy protected my injured noggin from additional damage.

Not long afterwards, one of our shipmates developed a serious medical problem. Although the man's condition did not warrant aborting our mission, Dr. Smyth kept the sailor comatose in the man's rack until we returned to Guam. The doctor and corpsman took turns continuously monitoring him. Because the man's rack was near mine, a solemn mood permeated our portion of berthing for the patrol's remainder.

While relieving Schweikert as throttleman, I realized the propeller revolution counter would indicate all nines and roll over to zeros during my six hours of watch.

I kept the information to myself. The *Henry Clay* Gold Crew had a tradition. The person standing throttleman the particular moment the counter rolled over and it registered all zeros had to buy sodas for the watch section.

As the counter clicked higher and higher, I was able to estimate when the rollover would happen. Shortly before the event, I feigned a need for a bathroom break. Since all stations in maneuvering must have a qualified individual on station at all times, Mr. Hawthorne summoned the auxiliary electrician aft. The roving electrician and I would swap duties, allowing me to leave maneuvering and take care of my business.

I provided an abbreviated synopsis of the watch station's condition and assured him that I would be right back. I purposely did not mention the counter.

After leaving, and knowing everybody in maneuvering could hear me on the White Rat, I picked up a 2JV handset, "Maneuvering, upper level machinery 2. This is Dubay. What is the value on the shaft counter?"

Metzgus answered, "Upper level machinery 2, maneuvering. We'll check." It did not take long for a response.

Metzgus was stifling a laugh as he said, "Upper level machinery 2, maneuvering. It is 47 turns from rolling over. Your relief wants to know how much longer you're going to be."

"Maneuvering, upper level machinery 2. About five minutes."

The counter would roll over before I returned. In the background, the man who relieved me was cussing up a storm. He knew I got him.

After the requisite time elapsed, I returned to maneuvering. My conscience got the better of me. Feeling bad about tricking him, I offered to pay for the sodas.

To his credit, he decided to ante up. He had the watch when it rolled over and should've checked the counter. Initially, the trick ticked him off. Then he realized if I were not injured, he would have been standing the throttleman and I the AEA. Given those circumstances, he would have tried to suck *me* in. It was his fault. I got him fair and square.

Still feeling a bit guilty, I suggested he serve himself first and leave it with me in maneuvering. It assured him of having a cup and prevented anyone from messing with it. The soda machine was dispensing Sprite. There was an occasion when someone did a soda run and missed the lower level machinery 2 watch. The guy serving left his full cup on the AMR-2 workbench. While he was gone, the ticked-off man in lower level drank the Sprite on the bench. Then he refilled the cup with the soap solution used for checking air leaks. When the man came back to enjoy his cold drink, all he got was a mouthful of soapy ice. Since the man I tricked was springing for the cold drinks, the least I could do was make sure his stayed safe.

He turned to the EOOW and said, "Mr. Hawthorne, I'm going forward to pay my penitence and bring back a pitcher of soda."

Hawthorne smiled and said, "Going forward, aye. Hey, since the soda machine only gives out six ounces of soda for every nickel, do you have enough? I have a stash in case you need some."

"No thanks, I have plenty."

When the electrician arrived back at maneuvering, he was holding a stainless steel pitcher filled nearly to the brim with Sprite and chipped ice. Condensation coated the container. After filling his white-with-blue-stripes Navy regulation coffee cup, he placed it in the cup-holder on the wall to the left of the steam plant control panel. I took a long draught of my drink. It tasted especially delicious, because I was able to trick my buddy into having him treat us.

The remainder of the run passed by uneventfully. Watches, electrical work, logroom duties, reading, movies, and drills kept me occupied.

Our sixty days of patrol was almost over. I was looking forward to seeing the sky and green grass, when bad news circulated throughout the boat. Extenuating circumstances were delaying the end of patrol. It initially disheartened the crew. The depressed mood did not last long. The resolute attitude of the *Clay*'s Gold Crew came through and extinguished our dispirited disposition. After having survived this far, the extension was a mere bump in the road compared to what we've already endured.

The extra days slowly rolled along. The thought of seeing the sun and something outside the confines of the submarine consumed me. I tried to imagine what fresh air smelled like and could not. Somehow, I pushed the thought from my mind before frustration affected my sanity.

At long last, our time on-station expired. The *Clay*'s speed increased from patrol's three-knot pace and we began making going-home turns. It was a joyous occasion.

The next milestone happened at 0700. We stationed the maneuvering watch. I assumed the throttleman. Fifteen minutes later, like music to my ears, the diving alarm sounded three times.

"Surface! Surface! Surface!" blared the 1MC.

The engine order telegraph rang up ahead-two-thirds. I answered the bell. It was not with the same vigor as when we left on patrol. Love, the reactor operator, was easily able to keep the temperature within the green band. Our good-natured game of recognition and reaction was more subdued than it was over two months ago. We did not have the energy to pursue it.

I heard air blowing the water out of the main ballast tanks. Following closely was the submarine's gentle roll on the surface.

My mind was numb from the cumulative effects of spending over two months submerged in a hermetically sealed container. Before I knew it, the Blue Crew relieved us and we were back in Hawaii.

My first act was phoning my brother Frank to apologize about my misreading his son's name. I explained how fatigue contributed to my misunderstanding. He told me not to worry about it. Agonizing about his reaction for the whole patrol was baseless.

Then, I phoned my mom telling her that I'd be leaving the next day for a well-deserved rest in Hickory.

Chapter 14

Dolphins and Patrol Pins

I arrived at the Honolulu airport wearing my Navy dress white uniform. Although I would rather travel in civilian clothes, the attire allowed me to fly "military standby," which was half the normal fare.

The trip terminated at a small airport in Vienna, Ohio.

As I emerged from the airliner, an unusually warm late winter Saturday afternoon greeted me. The sun's rays comforted my body. Crocuses were sprouting near the terminal. I inhaled deeply. Even though the air had the lingering scent of jet fumes, it was boundless and refreshing.

Mom, Dad, and my sister were waiting. In an effort to portray a self-imposed stoic submariner demeanor, I fought back tears of happiness. Trying to disguise my emotion-filled voice was more difficult. It cracked a bit. I had to clear my throat several times before getting it under control.

My younger brother Curt was not there.

Mom saw my confusion and told me that Curt was at a trombone lesson.

Dad dropped us off at home and went to pick up Curt.

Mom went into the house to fix dinner. My sister, Sweetie, walked with me. John Wilson, my best friend since junior high, was on the back porch sitting in a folding lawn chair. He stood.

"Hey, Ted. Welcome home."

As we shook hands, the contrast between our shades of skin was stark. Even though it was late winter, his minimal sun exposure since last summer maintained some of the previous year's tan. Prior to leaving for Guam, I had a deep Hawaiian tan. My tone had faded severely.

"Whoa. You're as white as an albino. How can someone stationed in Hawaii not get any sun?"

"Ha, ha. You know I was stuck underwater on patrol for over sixty days."

He wrinkled his nose and asked, "What *is* that smell?"

I explained that it was common to all submariners. It was the product of living in a hermitically sealed container. Whatever air was in her when she submerged was the same as when she finally surfaced, plus built-up contaminants.

"If you're sealed in, how come you don't suffocate?"

I gave him the basics. The submarine had equipment to remove CO_2 and carbon monoxide. The real key was the ability to make oxygen from seawater and store it in high-pressure tanks. As the sub's oxygen depleted, matches barely burned. When it was too low, sailors manually bled O_2 into a submarine's atmosphere. Then, a match's flame was several inches high and cigarettes burned at a frantic pace.

John's comment about my obnoxious odor made me want to change out of the reeking uniform as soon as possible. I excused myself and told them I'd be right back.

My sister followed me inside. She related her admiration because I was a submariner, even though I stunk. Mom and Dad were also very proud. Dad would brag about it to anyone who would listen.

After hurrying upstairs to my old bedroom, I removed my shirt. Pride welled within me as I carefully unpinned my Dolphins from above the shirt's left pocket. I recalled the effort required to earn them.

Life on a submarine isn't the safest job on the planet. Having a highly qualified crew reduces the risk. Every crewman must be on the alert for potential problems. Understanding how a system works and any nuances is critical to protecting the submarine from destruction. Is that drip of water from condensation or the beginning of a leak? If not sure, crewmen have to figure it out. A submarine hiding in the depths of a huge ocean has no one but her crew to solve problems. That is why there is a comprehensive qualification process. It ensures submarine sailors have the proper level of knowledge.

Besides having shipmates capable of taking the proper actions during emergencies, there are other motivators to become qualified in submarines. When a sailor initially reports to a submarine, his official designation is submarine unqualified (SU). Another term given these individuals is NUB. It is an acronym for non-useful body. The most commonly used phrase is non-qual puke. These men must spend all their spare time devoted to working on submarine qualifications. Non-quals are not allowed to watch movies or play games, like cards, bingo, etc.

Sometimes guys take that protocol to the extreme. There have been occasions when qualified sailors denied access to the mess deck when a movie was showing, even if the non-qual only wanted a drink of bug juice. It doesn't matter if the man outranks the guy who made him leave; Dolphins trump military rank.

A non-qual's first phase of qualifying is demonstrating a basic understanding of every system on the submarine. He studies one system at a time. Then a system expert administers an oral exam. If he is satisfied the man knows enough, the system expert signs the qual card. The process continues until the non-qual masters every system.

If properly prepared, the exams are not hard. It may sound weird, but an easy test is a disservice. The whole idea of the qualification process is to ensure the examinees are proficient. The crushing sea pressure surrounding a submarine is relentless and never takes a day off. If something goes wrong, the crew needs to act correctly and quickly.

Not maintaining the proper pace of qualification advancement turns the non-qual into a dink. The term is short for delinquent about making the proper progress in qualifying. Crewmen treat dinks even worse than standard non-quals. There is also the humiliation of having one's name publicly posted on the dink list.

Once someone exhibits satisfactory systems expertise, the non-qual must show he has a comprehensive knowledge of all six of the submarine's compartments. They are the torpedo room, operations compartment, missile compartment, reactor compartment, machinery room 2, and the engine room. As with system experts, a designated officer or senior enlisted man, usually a chief petty officer, gives the oral checkouts. These exams are more comprehensive. Damage control, which is the ability to respond to an emergency, is a major focus of these verbal examinations.

The next step is undergoing a final comprehensive oral exam. A board composed of several submarine-qualified sailors—an officer, a chief petty officer, and at least two very experienced submariners—administers it. One of the favorite questions is: How can you get fuel oil out of the ship's whistle? It is a complicated question and entails a very tortuous path. It requires knowing cross-connections between many systems. The answer takes quite a while to draw and explain. There is a good side. If you get that question, it is the only one.

Qual boards last several hours. The examiners can only recommend the man become qualified in submarines. Final approval is the responsibility of the captain.

Becoming qualified in submarines is the first step of becoming a true submariner. It is a never-ending process. Although newly qualified Dolphin wearers demonstrate a high level of proficiency, it is the bare minimum. There is always something new to learn or become even more skillful at performing. Even if someone is not self-motivated, continual classes and retraining are mandatory.

Next, I removed my patrol pin from the shirt's left pocket flap. Its actual name is SSBN Deterrent Patrol Insignia. It is the successor to the Submarine Combat Patrol Insignia, an award for World War II submarine patrols.

I earned my patrol pin by being on the *Clay* when she left on patrol and when she got back. FBM sailors are a trapped audience. After leaving on patrol, no one had the option of saying he wanted to go home. Deterrent patrols are so important, there are very few situations that make an FBM captain abort a patrol. One FBM had a sailor commit suicide. Its crew placed him in a body bag and stored him in their freezer until the boat returned to port, as scheduled. During my patrol, one of our men developed a medical problem. Our doctor kept him sedated in his rack, which was next to mine. The doc and corpsman took turns maintaining a continuous vigil on him. Even though he was oblivious to everything around him, the man got credit for completing a deterrent patrol.

Rifling through my dresser, I found a pair of jeans and a shirt. I had left them behind the last time I was home. Just to be sure, I gave them a quick sniff. They didn't smell musty. Mom must have washed them just before I arrived.

John and Sweetie were waiting on the back porch. He wrinkled his nose, had me bend over, and smelled my head.

"Is that all it takes to be a submariner? Smelling awful?"

His comment made me smile. He could razz me about my military service and not hold it against me. Several of my crewmates from the *Clay* were not so lucky. They had friendships torn apart because of peacenik acquaintances. Antiwar agitators harbored no respect for anyone in the military.

John had his head on straight and really cared about me. I knew he was kidding and did not respond. Then he said, "What's up with your hair? It's ragged, especially above the left ear."

I explained how I cut my head and received stitches.

Sweetie, always the thinker, said, "Since it was a war patrol and you were wounded, will you get a Purple Heart?"

When I was in high school, I found out my dad had refused several Purple Heart medals while serving in Europe during World War II. I researched the subject and found out there are specific qualifying conditions. Conversely, some nonqualifying criteria exist. In my case, it was an accidental wounding not related to or caused by enemy action.

"No, but good question. My own submarine sliced my head open, not the enemy."

I thought back. After getting five stitches, I returned to my watch station. I was simply grateful for a reprieve from wearing a respirator for a while. The main reason I did not miss a watch was the bind it would put the other two men who stood the same watch station, when I was off. There are only three sailors for each watch. If I were unable to stand watch, the other two would have to change their schedule. Instead of being on watch for six hours and off for 12, they would have to be on watch for six, get the next six hours off, and then have to be back on watch. Sailors call it "port and starboard." It really stinks and quickly wears someone out. I could not see putting my buddies through that. A small cut on my head was nothing compared to what happened to my dad during the war. Although my head was sore and I did not sleep well, I was proud that I never missed any of my watches.

We stepped off the porch and headed towards a small pond at the back of my parents' property. Because of the warm weather, Dad mowed the lawn. The odor of freshly cut grass wafted into my nose. Inhaling deeply, I savored the smell. It was almost intoxicating.

We walked slowly, with John upwind. To our left was a pasture. Several white cows grazed peacefully. A two-strand electric fence separated them from us. Compared to a submarine's hull it was not much of a barrier.

We arrived at the edge of the pond. When on patrol, I tried to imagine this view. What my mind conjured did not hold a candle to the real thing. The cry of a red-winged blackbird from a grove of cattails fell on my ears. A slight breeze carrying the sweet scent of cut grass ruffled my hair. It was not strong enough to disturb the mirror-like surface of the water. The water's reflection of the blue sky dotted with a few fluffy clouds was so clear it was almost impossible to detect any distortion. Feeling the warmth of the sun gave me a feeling of freedom. Its rays crossed 93 million miles unimpeded to my body. When I was entombed in the *Clay*, the sun's emissions could not reach me. After the light had traveled all that way, several hundred feet of water and our HY-80 hull stood between the rays and me.

As far as the sunshine was concerned, I might as well be on the edge of the universe.

I did not notice John and Sweetie leaving my side until the perfect inverted picture on the pond's surface was distorted when a rock skipped across the pond. My sister was standing at the water's edge. She was the source of the rings, which were slowly expanding across the water. She was beaming as if she had won an Olympic gold medal.

"Hey Ted. Can you tell that I've been practicing?"

"That was pretty good. Can you do it again?"

"I'll sure try."

John handed her a smooth stone. She carefully positioned it in her hand and gave a few practice swings. Her arm drew all the way back and flew forward, parallel to the pond's surface. The projectile hit the water. After many skips and innumerable pitty-pats, it reached the opposite edge of the small body of water.

"Whoa. Did you see that? I made it to the other side. I'm glad there are witnesses."

John and I joined her in the fun.

Being able to throw rocks was a treat. If I swung my arm only half as far on the *Clay*, I'd smack into something.

When we depleted our supply, we sat on metal milk crates under a maple tree. It was always my favorite spot. When on patrol, I would daydream about sitting there and drinking in the openness and serenity.

After we sat, I realized how being cooped up in a metal container for more time than I cared to think about had affected me. I really missed being outside and having unlimited space around me. Most people take distance for granted. Living in a submarine made me really appreciate it. Skipping stones was a treat. Throwing something on a submarine is also a no-no. It could generate a transient. A transient is a noise from inside a submarine that travels through the surrounding water. They traverse great distances and can give away a submarine's position to lurking Russians. The event could compromise a deterrent patrol.

Sweetie interjected, "That submarine-shaped medal I saw on your pocket—it's a patrol pin. Right? Do all submariners get one?"

"Very good, little sister. You have a good memory. You're as smart as you are cute."

She blushed at the compliment.

I had to admit that even though it wasn't fair, they were only awarded to Fleet Ballistic Missile submarine sailors. My experiences were not any more dangerous or demanding than what any submariner endured, regardless of the type of submarine. Somebody important must have decided FBM crewmen deserved a patrol pin. Who was I to argue?

Curt arrived on his bike. It was brand-new. He greeted me warmly and related how he had bought it with his pay for delivering newspapers. He also brought welcome news. Dinner was ready.

Curt rode proudly away. John raced after him. Sweetie followed.

I dawdled behind. I felt free to be away from the *Clay*'s regimented yet discombobulated schedule.

Life on an FBM submarine is a bizarre experience. A few activities revolve around a 24-hour day. There is a meal every six hours. Breakfast is 5:00 to 6:45 a.m. Lunch is 11:00 a.m. to 12:15 p.m. Supper is 5:00 till 6:45 p.m. Mid-rats, a meal of soup and sandwiches, is between 11:00 p.m. and 12:15 a.m. Movies begin at 7:00 p.m. Sometimes organized activities such as casino or bingo night replaced the daily flick.

To complicate matters, when the *Clay* left Guam, the crew changed the clocks to Zulu Time. That is the time in Greenwich, England. Because the *Clay*'s patrol area was on the opposite side of the world from Greenwich, when her clocks indicated noon, it was midnight. The only way to know when it was really dark outside was when the attack center was rigged-for-red. The space had red tinted lights along with white ones. Red light is special. It allows people to have night vision and still see everything inside the submarine as well as when the normal lights are on. If the conn was rigged-for-red, it was actually night. White lights meant daytime.

Actual day and night is irrelevant on an FBM submarine. On patrol, every day is divided into four six-hour watch periods: Midnight to 0600, 0600 until noon, 1200 through 1800, and 1800 to midnight.

During each watch, nuclear-trained sailors record temperatures, pressures and other necessary equipment parameters on pre-printed sheets called logs. At the end of each day, watch standers turn in the old logs and get new ones.

Even though the boat's basic schedule is based on a 24-hour time frame, the crew lives an eighteen-hour day. Submariners divide the 18 hours into three six-hour segments. If a sailor is on watch 06:00 a.m. to noon, he then has lunch. His next six hours are devoted to completing work and qualifying. If there is time left over, he can do whatever he pleases. Whichever nuclear-trained watch section was on duty the previous six hours becomes the Casualty Assistance Team (CAT). They help the watch standers deal with engineering drills or real emergencies. When this six-hour segment is over, it's suppertime.

The mess deck cannot accommodate the whole crew; each meal has two seatings. The oncoming watch section eats at the first sitting, in this case 5:00 p.m. These men can't loiter over their meal. After they finish eating, they're supposed to relieve the people standing watch at 5:45 p.m. This allows 15 minutes to transfer information between the two groups. Then the section which just got off watch has their meal. That's the second seating. In this example, the section at the end of their non-watch period has to find empty spaces in one of the two seatings. The first is preferable. If someone is stuck with the second, he won't finish eating until 6:45 p.m. My bedtime routine consisted of brushing my teeth, going to the bathroom, and reading a book for a few minutes. By the time I was finally sleeping, it was probably 7:00 p.m. Eating at the first sitting gave me an extra 20 minutes of sleep.

At 10:45 p.m. the duty messenger wakes the sleeping watch section, thus giving them four and a half to five hours of sleep. Then these men begin another 18-hour cycle.

Being tired is a fact of life on a submarine. There is no guaranteed sleep. Battle Station Missile could happen anytime. That meant somebody's sleep was interrupted.

I finally made it to the house and went into the bathroom. The porcelain sink and standard commode were a pleasure to use. They were a far cry from the *Clay*'s facilities.

All of the *Clay*'s wastewater, toilets, showers, and sinks drain into a sanitary tank, which in my mind is an oxymoron. Whenever it was full, we pressurized the tank and blew its contents into the ocean.

The *Clay*'s toilets were not like the ones in a house. At the bottom of the sub's stainless steel toilet bowl there was a valve with a long handle attached. The valve was a ball with a hole through it. When the handle was straight up, the valve was closed. When someone finished his business, he pulled the handle towards the front of the toilet. This aligned the hole in the valve with the tank. As the stuff in the bowl flowed into the sanitary tank, the sailor opened another valve, which rinsed the bowl with seawater. After flushing, he left both valves closed.

Flushing the toilet was benign as long as someone did not open the ball valve with pressure in the tank.

Warnings about a pressured tank were signs on each stall's door stating, "SECURED—BLOWING SANITARY."

The most common cause for someone opening the ball valve while the tank was pressurized was fatigue. Sometimes a sailor could not wait until the tank-blowing process was completed. To remind himself about the pressure in the tank, he held the sign in the same hand he would use to pull the handle. Every once in a while, the sailor's tiredness made him transfer the sign to his other hand and pull the handle. As soon as the valve was open, even a little bit, the contents of the sanitary tank blasted out. The poor smuck got a face full of the tank's stinky contents. Ventilation systems sent the odor all through the *Clay*. Although the smell was disgusting, the crew had fun with it.

When someone opened the valve with pressure in the tank, submarine sailors called it "venting a sanitary inboard." The poor devil who committed the act was a venter. There was no difference between this and the man who did not understand the radiation monitor. Anyone who vented a sanitary tank inboard should've known better. He had to pay the price. In most cases, there was no hiding the infraction. He was covered with the evidence. After discovering who did it, we razzed the culprit unmercifully. He became an official member of the Royal Fraternal Order of the Green Mist and condemned to wear a special red baseball cap, until someone else committed the foul deed. Because several guys performed the vile act each patrol, the crew of the *Clay* developed the Turd League. We published standings in our newspaper, the *Henry Clay Clarion*. At the end of last patrol, the final standings were Shitters—3 and Venters—1. The score meant people vented a sanitary tank inboard four times, and on one occasion, we never found the culprit. That was a win for the Venter. I think it was an officer.

Having finished my business in the bathroom, I went to the kitchen. I opened the refrigerator door and scanned the contents. The first thing that caught my eye was a plate piled high with golden cream puffs oozing with Mom's homemade egg-custard filling. Resisting the urge to eat one then and there, I refocused on what to drink with dinner. A glass of fresh milk with ice cubes was an easy choice.

John had permission to stay and eat with us.

Dinner consisted of fried chicken and potato salad. Mom's homemade cream puffs rounded out the meal. It was John's and my favorite meal.

After supper and polishing off two cream puffs, John walked home in the failing light.

While my dad set up the movie projector and screen, Curt demonstrated his trombone prowess. He had improved greatly and impressed me with his virtuosity. We spent the remainder of the evening watching home movies.

I went to bed. As I snuggled in freshly laundered sweet-smelling sheets, my mind started organizing some of the things I would share with my family about submarine life.

Although everyone in the *Clay's* crew got grumpy now and then, it was hard to stay that way. The submarine's crew was great, especially the nucs. They were bright and witty. Somebody was always joking around. It was hard not to be amused with their antics, although a lot of it was sick and sophomoric.

The secret to survival on a submarine was maintaining the proper attitude. The sooner you learned to take whatever treatment your crewmates dished out, the better. There wasn't any future for someone who was sensitive. A valid reason existed for the madness. The safety of the submarine is dependent on everyone maintaining his composure. Every so often, we found a chink in someone's armor. If the man could not adapt to the grueling life style of a submarine sailor, the individual earned a transfer to the surface fleet.

Regardless of rank, as soon as a new man reported aboard a submarine he was under constant scrutiny. We needed to determine if he was worthy of becoming a submariner. The behavior also diverted our thoughts from the stress of our ominous purpose.

If someone didn't stay alert in the engineering spaces, a nuc would try to fill the man's poopie suit pockets with water. I always had a small plastic bottle filled with warm water. If it wasn't warm, the person getting his pocket filled would feel the coolness. Warm water lets the pourer sneak away before the victim realizes what happened. We also tried to fill as many of the victim's pockets as possible. That really increased the chance of being caught. That almost happened to me once. I was the throttleman and a forward non-qual was in the engine room studying a system. We were able to convince him the electrical operator was very good at teaching the system. The electric plant control panel is the furthest into maneuvering. This allowed me to flank the non-qual under the guise of providing useful information. The electrical operator occupied the man's attention while I did the deed. I had just filled his right back pocket when the non-qual stepped back and bumped into a radiation monitor. He felt the wetness and then saw the radiation sign. The look on his face was sheer terror. We asked him if he touched the radiation monitor and all he could do was nod his head yes. Fortunately for us, he did not understand the monitor could not contaminate him. We had him put on bright yellow anti-contamination clothing. Then we sent him for radiological decontamination.

I laughed to myself. The engineering officer of the watch, Mr. Hawthorne, let us pull off the ruse. He was as amused as we were. Besides, the non-qual was not in jeopardy. Understanding all aspects of the submarine or having to pay the consequence is part of submarine culture. We felt he was taught a valuable lesson.

Mr. Hawthorne's behavior during this bit of fun inspired additional respect for him. Although exceptionally competent, he was very youthful-looking and had earned the nickname of Baby Bobby.

Nicknames were commonplace. Any anomaly associated with body shape, physical characteristics, mannerisms, or attitude would inspire a nickname. Some were benign. Greg Metzgus is from California and good-looking, so we called him Hollywood. My best friend on the boat, Bob Southerland, has red hair. We nicknamed him Red. Another man is Payload, because he is really a hard worker. An additional category is a non-sensical play on a person's name. Rich Treptow became Tree Toad. Some are derogatory. One of our heavier electricians is Hogbody. Another guy, who is Italian and gets easily seasick, earned the moniker Green Ginny.

Anyone acquiring a nickname has to accept it. He does not have a choice in the matter. How someone reacts is the most important. If the sailor embraces the name, there's hope of acceptance. Guys called me Eaglebeak. Up to that point in my life, I'd always been self-conscious about my oversized snout. Initially I really hated the nickname. Regardless of how much it originally hurt, I refused to display my feelings and accepted my fate. There was an upside. I learned that attitude is more important than any self-perceived physical fault.

I rolled over in the bed. The action sent a wave of sweet-scented clean bedding up my nose. I inhaled deeply. Compared to upper level engine room's harsh steamy smell and lower level engine room's distinct lubricating-oil aroma, it was like breathing in Heaven. There was one favorite smell when I was on the submarine. Occasionally, one of our cooks made donuts. They were just like my mom's. Their scent was heavenly. When he cooked them, the *Clay*'s ventilation system distributed their fragrance throughout the boat. The engine room was one of the first places it reached. We were mesmerized by the thought of eating them and couldn't wait to get off watch.

I awoke the next morning refreshed. The rest of the week flew by. I filled it with regaling my family with stories of our submarine exploits, having fun, and mostly relaxing.

The restful visit with my family ended with them seeing me off at the airport. In contrast to the day I arrived, it was cold and overcast. Snowflakes fluttered in the air.

The destination awaiting me tempered the sadness of the emotional farewell. My clothing was a reminder that I was heading to a tropical paradise. The standard Navy dress white uniform with short sleeves did not afford much protection from the bitter winter elements. At least it didn't have that submarine smell. Several trips through the washing machine had removed it. Mom, bless her heart, insisted I wear one of Dad's winter coats, even though it was a couple sizes too large. I was grateful. Without the garment, the walk to the terminal would've been miserable.

When it was time to board the plane, I handed the coat to Mom and winked. We hugged.

Dad and I exchanged a warm hearty handshake.

Curt, in transition between boy and man, acted as if he wanted to hug, but stood awkwardly off to the side, waved, and simply said, "Bye, Ted."

My sister couldn't contain herself and ran to me. She wrapped her arms around my waist like a vise. With a tear-streaked face, she sobbed, "I wish you could stay."

I tousled her hair and reciprocated the hug. Fighting back my emotions, I said, "Hey, if I don't go, how am I going to find exotic sea shells for you in Hawaii and Guam?"

Teary-eyed, she relaxed her grip. I maintained my composure by quickly exiting the building.

A snow squall was in progress. Glancing to my right, I saw the crocuses, which were reaching for the sun when I arrived, were now drooping as flakes accumulated. It was eerie how the flowers mimicked my mood on my arrival and while leaving my family.

Yes, I was continuing my adventure. Unfortunately, the emotions stirring inside me proved what price I had to pay.

As I walked briskly to the plane, goose bumps coated my bare skin. Clouds of condensation formed with every exhalation. I scrunched my shoulders against the chill. At least I would not have to endure these conditions in Hawaii.

My uniform made me stand out like a sore thumb on the plane. A stewardess led me to my seat. To my surprise, it was in first class. That was one of the perks of flying military standby. The airline assigned me whatever seat that was available. The downside of flying at half price was taking the chance that the flight did not have any available seats and I would have to wait for another plane. I was the only one in military attire. Most of the passengers ignored me. Across the aisle were a couple of young men with unkempt shoulder-length hair. They shot me dirty looks.

I wanted to say, "Excuse me, your immaturity is showing."

I refrained. Even though they had to come from well-to-do families, they were not worthy of a retort. I flew military standby because I could not afford to fly full price. My monthly pay was $450. That included $12 of sea pay and $75 for submarine duty. When on patrol, submarine sailors were constantly on duty. Even sleeping crewmen had to wake up and respond to casualties and battle stations. Given those circumstances, my $450 equated to $0.625 an hour, even on Christmas.

Besides, I did not care what these privileged, haughty young men thought. Those who knew and cared about me understood my sacrifices and the dangers I endured. They also realized that I was maintaining the freedoms enjoyed by everyone in the USA. My family and friends were the people who mattered. I hoped the rude fellows would eventually understand. Maybe not. I patted my Dolphins and patrol pin. They were physical reminders of my contribution to maintaining American's freedoms. I felt good about myself.

By the time the plane arrived in Hawaii, the sadness of leaving my family was waning. Replacing it was the excitement of being on the island of Oahu. A view out the aircraft's window revealed a lush green island sprinkled with houses. The mighty metropolis of Honolulu loomed in the distance.

Chapter 15

R & R in Hawaii

While I was exiting the plane at Honolulu International Airport, heat rising from the tarmac engulfed me. I stopped for a moment. Compared to the weather back in Hickory, it felt like an oven. My discomfort quickly passed. This was Hawaii. What was there to complain about? A breeze swept over me. I basked in the warmth. Goldilocks came to mind. The weather in Hickory this time of year was too cold. The engine room of the *Clay* was too hot. This was just right.

After entering the terminal, I located a pay phone. I placed a call to the Honolulu apartment where I would live with Southerland, Tommy Lee Connell, and Joel McCann. They'd already moved in. I didn't have a key and needed to ensure someone could let me in.

Southerland answered the phone. After verifying I knew the directions, he assured me he would be waiting.

A taxi transported me to the building on Atkinson Boulevard. Exiting the vehicle, I retrieved my Navy issue sea bag and small handbag from the trunk. Hefting the larger one onto my shoulder, I excitedly walked to the building's front door.

After a short walk, I was at the elevator. I pushed the button for the tenth floor. When its door opened, apartment 1007 lay ahead. I knocked. After a short wait, the door opened; Southerland greeted me and grabbed my big bag.

I followed him down a short hallway. We entered the living room. I saw a couch directly in front of us. It was facing to my left. On it was Connell. He was lying on his back, fast asleep. An open *Sports Illustrated* was face-down on his slowly heaving chest. He looked too peaceful to disturb.

I gave Southerland a what-is-up-with-him expression.

He explained how they named it the magnetic couch. It was Connell's typical spot. It had a captivating power over him. Just about every time he walked past the couch, it attracted him like a magnet. Once Connell sat down, the progression was inevitable. He would pick up something to read. Then he'd recline, with his feet propped on the couch's back. Finally, gravity exerted its force on his eyelids and what I saw was the result.

We turned left and I followed him past the kitchen, which was to our left.

As we walked, he extolled the virtues of the apartment's location. I looked through the glass door ahead of us, and beyond the dining room table was the Pacific Ocean. Through the sliding glass door on the adjacent wall to my right, I could see a huge building covered with room upon room. It was on the opposite side of the street. Southerland said it was the Ala Moana Hotel.

While I was gawking at the sights, I wondered how long I could stay in this wonderful apartment. The Navy was supposed to transfer me off the *Clay* before the next patrol. I'd live here as long as possible. Maybe the Navy would send me to a submarine home-ported in Pearl and I'd be able to continue living here. The Navy was always looking to cut costs.

He led me to a bedroom on the ocean side of the apartment. The carpeted room had a double bed, two dressers, and one closet. I wandered to the glass door and gazed out.

This was certainly nicer than berthing on the boat.

I slid the door open. We stepped onto the balcony. Southerland informed me that the Hawaiian term for balcony was lanai. Being on the tenth floor gave us an excellent view of the Pacific Ocean and Ala Wai Yacht Harbor. The height muted the sounds of the busy city streets.

We exchanged glances. Filling his face was a wide grin.

"Not bad, huh?" he remarked, and added, "This pad's in a terrific location. The hotel across the street has a great nightclub: the Hawaiian Hut. We can walk there and stagger back."

He filled me in on some other facts. On the other side of the hotel was the Ala Moana Shopping Center. Between the hotel and yacht club was Ala Moana Park. We could walk to the beach in about five minutes. A tall building to the left was the Ilikai Hotel. It was right on Waikiki beach. Jack Lord, the star of the TV show *Hawaii Five-0*, lived in the penthouse.

I could hardly believe a country bumpkin like me was living in a high-rise Waikiki apartment. I wasn't going to think about transferring off the *Clay*. There were still almost three weeks of R & R to enjoy. I'd make the most of it while it lasted.

With my head swimming with good fortune, I went inside. After stripping off my uniform, I hung it in the closet. It was next to one of Southerland's. His was wrinkled and yellowish, and it emanated a distinct submarine odor.

Although mine was creased from traveling, it was pristine compared to his. My mom put considerable effort into making sure mine was thoroughly clean. The deplorable cleanliness standards we maintained on the *Clay* would have driven her crazy.

Rummaging through my bags, I located a pair of cut-off blue jeans and a tee shirt. Barefooted, I stepped out onto the lanai.

The lanai was awash with sunlight. I greedily drank it in and savored the sensation. Looking left provided a view of the mighty Pacific Ocean, all the way to the horizon. Of all the wonderful spectacles surrounding me, the one I most appreciated was the boundless distance. On the *Clay*, we were lucky if there was somewhere that had a 50-foot line of unobstructed sight. I banished the thought. It wasn't something to dwell on until it was time to go to sea again.

Southerland's lanky frame was slouching in a chair. He wasn't sleeping but his eyes were closed. I heard the slow rhythm of air flowing with every breath. His face was alight with a peaceful countenance.

Bob stirred and saw me sitting next to him. I suggested we hang out at the beach. Then we could decide about dinner.

He readily agreed and recommended I wear sneakers instead of flip-flops. There were biting red ants in the park's grass.

Both of us put on Converse canvas basketball shoes. They had served us well in pickup basketball games.

All thoughts of basketball evaporated when we exited the building. Two of the most exquisite members of the opposite sex were standing across the street. I stopped in my tracks and soaked in their beauty.

Bob tapped my shoulder and told me, "Eat your heart out. You better get used to sights like that. Hawaii is loaded with 'em."

After longingly gazing at them, we agreed they were out of our league. The sad truth was, even though we were living in an expensive $400-a-month apartment, we were poor sailors. Not only that, the antiwar attitude of most women their age meant they wouldn't have anything to do with someone in the military. It was their loss if they didn't associate with great guys like us.

I cast a final longing glance in the direction of the two beauties. The sight of them entering a chauffeured limousine confirmed our assessment.

While walking through the park, Southerland squatted. I followed suit. He pointed to some plants with short oval leaves, much like a miniature fern. They were almost flat to the ground.

His finger gently brushed one of the plants. Instantly, the leaves folded inward toward the stem. He was not sure about its real name, but called it sensitive fern. I thought to myself that the only alive green thing in the *Clay* was *mold*. Touching the leaves and watching them react was addictive. Before long, there were not any open fronds in the whole patch.

We continued our trek. A high-pitched sound emanated from beyond a grove of large banyan trees. Altering our path to determine the cause of the commotion, we came across a small pond. Beds of tropical flowers lined its edges. Several high-speed model hydroplane boats skittered across the water, throwing up glistening rooster tails. Two men were on a bridge. Each remotely guided a boat.

Southerland and I watched for a few minutes. It was too much racket for a peaceful park and reminded us of some of the *Clay*'s equipment. We moseyed to the beach, where we could not hear the racket.

Having grown up in a rural setting, I always appreciated the outdoors. On the *Clay*, it was impossible to escape man-made noises. When we were at sea, I missed direct contact with nature, like here in the park. That was why I hung out in sonar. I could hear what was living in the ocean. It helped. Unfortunately, I could not forget there was a degree of separation between the ocean sounds and me. At least I was performing a valuable service to my country.

We walked until all we can hear were waves washing onto the beach and wind rushing through palm trees.

The water drew me towards it. I removed my shoes and waded in. It was comfortably warm, unlike the hot water in Guam. Soft sand coated the bottom. The waves caused my feet to embed when the water rushed out. I had to keep changing position to maintain my balance. It was almost as if the ocean was alive and trying to draw me deeper. The sensation made me think of FBM submarines hiding in the depths of the oceans. They were the guardians, as the *Clay*'s Gold Crew had been several weeks ago. I gazed out over the water and said a silent thank you.

Southerland was sitting in the soft sand beyond the reach of the waves. With closed eyes, he was leaning forward, forearms resting on knees. The sun's rays created golden hues in his red hair as a sea breeze swept over it. I sat beside him and assumed the same pose. The warm rays and wind made me feel free. No wonder he looked so content. Without warning, my stomach emitted a growl. It reminded me that the last thing I had eaten was a crappy, dinky airline meal somewhere between Los Angeles and Hawaii. The type of meat was a mystery and it was camouflaged with gravy. The airline advertisement said an award-winning chef created it. I was glad we did not have him as one of our cooks. If that meal were any testament to his skill, he'd be demoted to mess cook. I asked Southerland if he knew any place where we could get dinner without waiting. Anything would be better than my lunch.

He suggested the Ala Moana Mall's Burger King. We sat outside the establishment and enjoyed watching the female clientele frequenting the stores.

When we got back to the apartment, our other roommate, Second-Class Auxillaryman Joel McCann, was there. He was excited. Second-Class nuc Machinist's Mate Mike "Payload" Pavlov and he were planning a trip to the big island of Hawaii. They were going to stay at the Kilauea Military Camp (KMC), located in Volcano National Park. The cost was reasonably affordable—$4.75 a day per person. This included bus transportation from and to the airport, meals, a guided bus tour, and lodging.

McCann said they were leaving the next Tuesday afternoon and returning Thursday evening. Pavlov asked if Southerland or I was interested.

I said, "We gotta phone the *Clay*'s office Thursday morning. How can we justify reporting we're alive and well *and* in the area?"

He replied matter-of-factly, "Hey, it may be a stretch, but we're still going to be in the state. As far as being alive and well, that'll certainly be true."

It sounded intriguing and fit into my promise to make the most of my time in Hawaii. I told them that I wanted to go. Southerland also jumped at the opportunity.

McCann had all of the information. He would make reservations the next day.

On the appointed day, the four of us boarded an Aloha Airlines island hopper and departed on our adventure. After a brief stop on the island of Maui, the plane continued to the airport in Hilo. I was in a window seat. As the plane turned to make its landing, I saw a huge whitish cloud rising from the ground to the southwest and near the ocean.

Pavlov saw me staring and asked, "What's ya looking at?"

I leaned back so he could see out the window and said, "Look at that plume rising into the air. I bet it's from a volcano."

"I think you're right. A fire has black smoke and it's too big to be anything else."

Our statements perked the interest of our companions. They joined in gawking at the sight.

McCann thought it was coming from Kilauea Iki, which was not far from where were staying.

Southerland, on the opposite side of the aircraft said, "Hey. Look at this. I think those two mountains have snow on them."

The far one was Mauna Kei. The other was Mauna Loa. People can ski Mauna Kei year round.

The 45-minute drive to the camp took us through a huge macadamia nut plantation. Rows of the trees stretched over the rolling hills for miles upon miles. The wonders of the big island of Hawaii continually revealed themselves.

We checked in. Our accommodation was a wooden cabin. It appeared old but was roomy, clean, and comfortable. Inside, we viewed a strange sight for the Hawaiian Islands: a heater. We cast quizzical glances. The cabin had a musty odor and was quite warm. Southerland opened the windows and we settled in.

It was not dinnertime. Assisted by McCann's brochures, we explored the grounds. Not far away, we came across the cafeteria. A short distance further was the recreation center. It had a three-lane bowling alley and a snack bar. We bowled a few games while eating hamburgers and drinking beer.

By the time we were done, it was dark. It was too early to go to sleep and there wasn't a television in the cabin. We climbed into our rental car and took a jaunt on Crater Rim Drive and the Chain of Craters Road. Navigating the thoroughfares treated us to an eerie landscape. It was a moonless evening. The orange-yellow glow of volcanoes explained how these roads earned their names.

When we exited the vehicle back at the cabin, there was a distinct nip in the air. We found the cabin's inside as cold as the outside. Pavlov closed the windows. McCann started the heater. Clothing-wise, we were ill prepared for this type of weather. Alabama-raised Southerland grabbed a blanket and wrapped it around his shoulders.

Although we knew the rest camp was several thousand feet above sea level, we failed to realize how the altitude could affect the temperature when the sun went down. This was *Hawaii*. At least we understood why the cabin came with a heater.

The next morning, we embarked on the KMC-sponsored bus tour. The stop at Kilauea Iki Overlook was disappointing. A long hike brought us to the active crater. Kilauea Iki Overlook was a misnomer. The caldera was behind a mound of hardened black lava. All we could see was a plume of steam.

I enjoyed the Fern Forest. It demonstrated the Big Island's diverse climate. On one side of the road was the Fern Forest, a lush and humid tropical jungle. Opposite it was an arid desert, barely sustaining a few cacti.

After a bag lunch, we went to Devastation Trail. A boardwalk traversed the hardened lava and cinders, which had spewed in 1959. It was an impressive example of the destruction wrought by volcanic action. Bleached skeletons of trees protruded from the eruption's remnants. They provided evidence that the area was once a lush forest. In one spot, a road complete with a dashed white line down its middle ended under the volcano's deposits. I could extrapolate the road's path by the speed limit sign further down the landscape.

As we stood gazing at the desolate panorama surrounding us, Southerland stated, "It looks like an atomic bomb went off here."

It was notable no one mentioned that the *Clay* could be the merchant of such destruction. The thought haunted me, even though I reminded myself this trip was an escape from that responsibility.

One of the highlights of the afternoon was a trek on a rope-and-wood plank bridge across a semiactive volcano crater. Most of the caldera was a flat sea of coagulated magma. It looked benign. A hole in the surface revealed what was beneath the solidified rock. Red-orange liquid lava bubbled in the opening. Although already walking carefully, I intensified my caution.

The last stop was Lava Tree State Park. Hot, fast-moving lava invaded the area in 1790. A six-foot molten wave passed through, destroying everything in its path. Even though the intense heat of the volcanic emission consumed the trees, it left behind grotesque hollow statues, because the moisture in the o'hia trees coagulated some of the lava. Other than that, the park was beautiful. Lush grass and new trees abounded. I left the park with hope in my heart. The place was a testament to the resiliency and regenerative ability of our planet. If it rebounded from a volcano's destruction, the same could happen at ground zero of a nuclear missile from the *Clay*.

Thursday, our last day of exploration had to wait until after 0800. We had to participate in the *Clay*'s Gold Crew phone muster.

A few strokes after the appointed hour, Pavlov deposited the necessary change into a pay phone. He called the *Clay*'s office. A couple of moments later he said, "Hi, Fred. This is Pavlov. I'm reporting as required. Hang on. There are some other guys with me."

I was next and said, "Dubay reporting."

After Fred acknowledged my statement, I quickly passed the phone to McCann. He followed suit. Southerland did likewise and placed the phone back into its cradle.

I stated, "Well, that's over. We were lucky Fred didn't press us for details. We didn't have to lie."

Before long, we were in the rental car. We had a full day planned. First on our agenda was Akaka Falls, a few miles north of Hilo. Viewing it entailed a several-mile hike. Unlike the one to Kilauea Iki Crater, this one was worth it. Winding through a pristine jungle, the trail was devoid of other humans. It was the complete opposite of the *Henry Clay*'s interior. As we walked, strange birdcalls emanated from the surrounding flora. In several places, stands of tall bamboo lined the route. We heard the roar of the waterfall long before it came into view. At the waterfall's observation point, the sight was spectacular. The cascade, still a good distance away, was a thin white undulating ribbon against the dark volcanic rock. I had to tilt my Instamatic camera to get the 422 feet of falls to fit diagonally into its lens.

Not only did the big island of Hawaii abound in natural wonders, it was also rich in history. The famous explorer Captain James Cook met his demise on its west coast. A monument in his honor rests on the edge of Kealakekua Bay. I was more in awe of the spot than my fellow travelers. Even divulging that his Hawaiian killers ate Captain Cook did not impress them. At least they were nice enough to allow me to indulge in the experience without razzing me.

While eating lunch, I contemplated Captain Cook. Although a brave and bold man, did he possess the special attributes needed to be a submarine sailor?

Next on the agenda was a black sand beach. The beach's material came from waves pulverizing ancient lava deposits. Upon close inspection, the color of the sand was more of a dark olive green. It was also very coarse. The four of us wore shoes to protect our tender feet. We all agreed the unique color of the beach's material did not override the discomfort it caused. There was an upside. I found some nice seashells for my sister.

We were on the north end of the island as dusk was falling. McCann began driving back to the camp, so we would return before the cafeteria closed.

As our vehicle rounded a turn in the failing light, we saw something I will never forget. Unfortunately, my camera was out of film and I could not preserve the scene. The rusting hulk of a car was sticking partway out of a wall of lava. Blackened areas mixed with tarnish provided evidence of its incineration. Although workers had reclaimed the thoroughfare and several feet of the shoulder, the vehicle's remnants were a monument to the cataclysm. Why did it remain in this state?

To me, it symbolized man's insignificance. No matter what we did to the planet, nature was really in control. Billions of years ago, Earth was a lifeless mass of minerals. Eventually life sprouted and matured. If human-kind wiped itself out via nuclear war, the world would duplicate its pre-vious feat and rejuvenate. On the other hand, knowing the USS *Henry Clay* was capable of accomplishing such a tragedy made me shudder.

The next morning we boarded another island hopper back to Oahu. Our mini-vacation was over. It had its desired effect. For the most part, I forgot about my association with the sinister nature of serving on an FBM submarine armed to the teeth with indescribable destructive power.

The residual effects of patrol were finally beginning to wear off. The two remaining weeks of R & R went a long way towards finishing the job.

The next weekend was overcast and rainy. It was typical Hawaiian winter weather. My roommates and I didn't care about the weather. Not being trapped in a sealed container far below the ocean's surface was enough.

It was different for those here for a vacation. Despondent tourists holed up in their rooms littered the Ala Moana Hotel's windows. They gazed forlornly at the dreary weather. Dreams of sun-drenched days on the beach were washing away. Every so often, I spotted a lovely young lady who was looking in my direction and I waved. None returned my gesture. With my short hair, did I look like someone in the military? Hope-fully, they simply did not notice me.

Monday morning broke clear and warm. It was a beautiful Hawaiian morning. Except for the typical clouds over the inland mountains of Oahu, the sky was crystal clear. The temperature was balmy and hovered in the low 80s, tempered by a cool ocean breeze.

Strains of the Temptations emanating from the bedroom helped me locate Southerland. He had a fondness for Motown music. Another of his favorites was the Chambers Brothers.

"Hey, Red. Wanna go to the beach at Fort DeRussey? I'll treat for lunch."

He did not need his arm twisted and quickly agreed. "Best offer I've had all day."

A short drive in his white VW beetle, Hercules, brought us to the military rest camp. We showed our Navy ID cards to the Marine guard at the gate and he waved us in.

We retrieved towels and reed mats from the bug's back seat. While walking to the beach I detected the aroma of the mat wafting into my nose. It reminded me of idyllic days of my youth playing among freshly cut hay. I had come a long way since then. Being a fully qualified crew member of a sophisticated nuclear-powered submarine and living in a high-rise apartment in Hawaii surpassed playing in a country barn.

Fort DeRussey was next to the famous beaches of Waikiki and their associated hotels. As beautiful as it was before we left, the day grew even more gorgeous. The weather drew scores of tourists to the beach as if by a giant magnet. They blanketed the pure white sand. Many more frolicked in the waves of the balmy tropical water. The breeze off the Pacific Ocean was refreshing. I saw Diamond Head in the distance. No wonder people referred to Hawaii as paradise.

We slathered ourselves in suntan lotion. After more than three months with virtually no sun, we had to be very careful about our exposure to its rays. Southerland had the added curse of being a freckle-skinned redhead. His body's reaction to the sun never ceased to amaze me. Regardless of how much lotion he applied, his skin turned bright red. The next day the redness was gone, replaced by more freckles.

Southerland caught a nap, leaving me alone with my thoughts.

I gazed at the ocean. The smooth line of the horizon was eleven miles away, faintly separating the sea from blue sky. The span of water between me and what seemed to be the edge of the earth was empty, save the rollers washing toward the shore. It was a peaceful scene.

Far to my left, Diamond Head dominated the skyline. Something caught my eye. An FBM submarine emerged from behind the famous landmark, heading towards Pearl Harbor. I tried to ignore it. I came to the beach to relax and escape from our association with the submarine service. I glanced at Southerland and others around me. He was sleeping. A few people noticed the submarine and snapped pictures.

I succumbed to the temptation and watched it. The submarine was about five miles from the shore. Memories of the *Clay* tracing the same track six months ago seeped into my mind. We had been completing the final leg of the long journey from Charleston. I was in her conning tower, camera in hand, taking my own pictures of this very beach. At the time, I wondered what thoughts permeated the minds of those on shore. The reactions of the people around me were probably a good barometer. Some were in awe. Others displayed indifference. A few exhibited contempt of the mighty war machine.

I wondered what was going on below the surface of the sea. Although no other vessels were in view, it did not mean there were not Soviet submarines lurking in the area. The United States considered the three-mile limit as our boundary for territorial jurisdiction. Such a restriction allowed Russian submarines to legally prowl up to that distance. A chance to gather valuable information about the lone American FBM might be too tempting to resist. If a Russian hunter-killer boat were foolish enough to attempt such a maneuver, it would not come easy. American fast-attack submarines would boldly harass the enemy vessel in a dangerous game of blind man's bluff. I was grateful that our counterparts in attack boats accepted the role. The unfairness of the situation struck me. Their main duty was to do the dirty work and the Navy awarded FBM sailors a patrol pin.

Southerland's shadow passing over my open but unseeing eyes interrupted my thoughts, "Hey, Ted, are you in there? Your eyes look glazed over. I'm getting hungry. How 'bout you?"

While walking to the club we debated what to eat. Eventually, we agreed it had to include fresh fruit and salad.

After dining, Southerland and I meandered back to our spot on the beach. We enjoyed a little eyeball liberty on the way. He decided to cool off in the water. I let my lunch of fresh fruit salad and BLT, with extra lettuce and tomato, settle.

On my back with hands clasped behind my head, I stared into the beautiful blue sky.

The remainder of the afternoon was uneventful. I alternated between relaxing on the sandy shore and taking an occasional dip in the ocean. Southerland and I accomplished our mission. It was a pleasingly restful day.

Keeping with the mood of our sojourn to the beach, we slowly made our way to Hercules. With the towel draped over my shoulder, I had the mat tucked under an arm. My salt- and sand-encrusted body craved a nice warm shower.

Southerland unlocked the Volkswagen. He inserted the key in the

Breakfast at Oahu's Keaau Beach, with (left to right) Bob Southerland, Bob Frechette, Mike Pavlov, E.K. Lingle, Rusty Wishon, and the author. From the archives of E.K. Lingle (September 1971).

ignition and turned it. The car responded with a pathetic click. Several more attempts yielded the same result. Southerland surmised Hercules had a dead battery. We would have to push-start the car.

I told him he had to teach me. After explaining the actions, he had me sit in the driver's seat and practice a dry run. The key was coordinating the actions. I got in the driver's seat. He pushed. A few grunts later, the Beetle began moving. He yelled, "Okay!"

The engine burst to life. Before I could congratulate myself, it sputtered and died. Puffing, Bob walked up to the window and said, "For your first time, that wasn't bad. Y'all got it started. Ya just gotta be a little quicker on the clutch. Ready to try again?"

Two more attempts met with similar results. He suggested swapping positions. It was worth a try. Even though I was a lot smaller than Southerland and extremely out of shape from lack of activity on patrol, we triumphed.

The remaining R & R went by too fast. It was shocking how we filled the time so easily. Hawaii was a magical place. No wonder people gave up ordinary lives to become beachcombers.

Chapter 16

The Escape Tower

One Sunday in March of 1971, I woke up and realized our month-long vacation was almost over. The next day started our off-crew requalification process.

I dumped the contents of my sea bag onto the bedroom's rug. My eyes watered from the smell emanating off the rumpled uniforms. It triggered a flashback. On patrol, we did not notice the odor. Now, the indescribable stench dominated my senses. Before the room was permanently contaminated, I gathered an armload and stuffed it into the washing machine across the hall. With the wash cycle set for maximum, the cleansing began. I deposited the remaining clothes onto the lanai. Hopefully, some of the smell would evaporate into the earth's atmosphere.

Except for Connell, who washed his things shortly after moving in, my roommates were in the same predicament.

Regretfully, we put fun on the back burner and spent the remainder of the day getting ready to go back to work.

The next morning, we donned freshly laundered dungarees and white hats. Connell departed in his blue Ford Mustang convertible. McCann hopped onto his motorcycle. Not having a vehicle of my own, I rode with Southerland. He needed a partner anyway. The VW still needed a battery and it took two people to start the car.

Upon arrival at the *Clay*'s office, the nuclear-trained individuals were herded into a classroom. An unfamiliar young officer was standing at the front of the room. He nervously introduced himself as Mr. Losen. He had just joined the crew. He was our proctor for a basic engineering qualification (BEQ) exam. It was a comprehensive examination of our knowledge on nuclear theory, radiological controls, chemistry, and thermodynamics. We had four hours to take the exam.

The announcement generated a plethora of groans and comments of "stupid study."

He looked confused. We explained that stupid study was mandatory afternoon training sessions. The classes are mainly for guys who weren't qualified in submarines or all of their watch stations. That applied to him. If any of the fully qualified men failed the BEQ exam, they would have to attend. For them, it was stupid study.

The young officer handed out the exams.

Miraculously, all of us passed the multifaceted test.

Two weeks transpired without hearing anything about my transfer from the *Clay*. I found the yeoman and asked for the status. He told me to come back the next day.

As instructed, I saw him first thing in the morning. True to his word, he handed me a set of orders. I anxiously opened them. Although I was not surprised, my blood boiled when I saw they were to another FBM home-ported in Hawaii. My prognostication of this very outcome had come true. The unfairness of how I'd been treated made my insides churn.

With orders in hand, I left the *Clay*'s office and stomped down the hallway. The USS *Woodrow Wilson*'s office was two doors down and on the left. I found their yeoman and handed him my papers.

He gave me a quizzical look and said, "Something isn't right. We're not expecting anybody new. Take your documents to the squadron office. Maybe they can clear it up."

I explained the situation to a submarine squadron 15 yeoman.

He took one look at the orders and said, "I keep track of all personnel moves. Your name isn't on my list. Besides, these orders don't have a SUB-PAC number. Go back to your boat."

I was madder than a wet hen. Storming back to the *Clay*'s office, I went directly to our yeoman and demanded a meeting with the executive officer (XO), Lieutenant Commander James Cossey. The yeoman picked up his phone and made the arrangements. The XO would see me in an hour.

At the appointed time, I joined Mr. Cossey in his office. He let me vent my frustration without interrupting.

When I was spent, he shuffled through some papers on his desk. Cossey selected one and said, "Maybe I have good news. There's an instructor opening at the S1C prototype in Windsor, Connecticut. You've done a good job on the *Clay*. I have no reservations about recommending you for the two-year position."

There was an equal amount of time left in my enlistment. Two years of shore duty sounded good. I asked him to tell me more.

During his spiel, he revealed that accepting the job required me to re-enlist for two more years.

I stopped him and said, "In other words, you want me to expose myself to potentially the same kind of treatment I'm all upset about right now."

"That's one way to look at it."

Seeing my reluctance for prototype instructor duty, he made another offer. There was an open billet for a nuclear-trained electrician in Antarctica. It didn't require re-enlisting and had a six months on and six months off schedule. If I did not want it, he would keep me with the *Clay*.

I weighed Antarctica duty against my three months on the submarine and three months off in Hawaii. Although I would probably never have another chance of going to Antarctica, bikinis and beaches beat out parkas and snow-covered landscapes. There was no contest. I would stay on the *Clay*. Doing so meant I had fully met the requirements and the government had to ship my car to Hawaii at their expense.

He did not bat an eye and said, "I'll take care of it. If the yeoman doesn't have the necessary paperwork ready before the end of the week, come see me."

Staying assigned to the *Clay* was not bad. If transferred, I had to leave many friends behind. Who knew if I would bond as well with another group of sailors?

There were other benefits of staying with the *Clay*. Some people only dream about *vacationing* in Hawaii. I lived in the tropical paradise six months out of every year.

The icing on the cake was that I could continue to reside in a luxury downtown Honolulu apartment and use the living expenses as a deduction on my income taxes.

On the surface, that seems odd. It came about due to the government's shortsightedness. Submarine officers had to pay for their own meals when on their submarine. An FBM officer tried to use the cost of his meals as a deduction on his income taxes. The government ruled that he could not, because the submarine was his home. The officer used the government's ruling against them by pointing out that he was then eligible to deduct his living expenses when on off-crew. If the submarine was his home and the Navy ordered him to live somewhere else, then his three months away from the submarine were legal deductions. The government's attempt to save a few dollars from a small population backfired. The ruling meant enlisted FBM sailors were also eligible to deduct off-crew living expenses.

The news of my staying with the *Henry Clay* quickly circulated throughout her crew. Not long after I left the XO's office, Southerland sought me out. He was happy I was staying with the *Clay*, but really wanted to know if Cossey said anything about our getting a new XO. Rumors of Cossey's transfer were spreading like wildfire. I hoped it wasn't true, but it was. He had always been a straight shooter. A good example was how he had just treated me.

Two days later, the yeoman informed me the arrangements for getting my car shipped to Hawaii were complete. Then he divulged some bad news. My mentor and friend, Bob Davis, jumped at the chance to take the prototype instructor job that I refused. I would sorely miss the man.

I phoned my parents that evening. Although the government was paying for shipping, I needed someone to transport the car to Bayonne, New Jersey. When I presented the dilemma to Mom and Dad, they were more than happy to help.

My mother was particularly excited.

Her reaction took me by surprise. I did not doubt they would help. Mom's eagerness shocked me.

I quickly found out she had never flown before. They would drive my car there and fly home.

They soundly rejected my offers to pay for the airline tickets. The trip would be an adventure and a mini-vacation.

Knowing my car would eventually arrive in Hawaii was a moral victory. Mom's being able to experience her first plane ride was icing on the cake.

Several weeks later, the entire crew assembled in Ford Island's auditorium for the XO's weekly presentation. Initially, the effects of stimulation of the local economy the previous evening made it hard for me to stay focused. The cobwebs clouding my mind suddenly cleared when he made an announcement. The crew would receive submarine-escape training the next week. Most of our crew, including myself, had not gone through it. The experience was another difficult rite of passage to becoming a true submariner. Butterflies fluttered in my stomach. I took a deep breath and slowly let it out. Knowing many others survived the training and took pride in the accomplishment helped calm me. I resolved to do likewise.

When we were dismissed, groups formed in the hall. As I walked by several, one subject dominated the discussions: the impending submarine-escape tower training.

I spotted Souder, Southerland, Lewis, Pottenger, and Schweikert.

Lewis thought it was about time. The ordeal was one of the premier initiation rites of submarine service and he could hardly wait.

Schweikert was disappointed when we were at submarine school and the escape tower was out of commission. When we got our orders to Charleston, he had given up on experiencing the escape training. Then he found out the *Clay* was going to Hawaii after the overhaul. The first thing that came to his mind was that Pearl had an escape tower.

I never felt comfortable going to sea on the *Clay* without practicing an escape.

Souder had a different opinion. He felt all of our submarine school training and having demonstrated an intimate knowledge on the escape trunk in order to get our Dolphins was adequate preparation.

Southerland provided another insight. Even though we didn't do an actual practice escape, all of us had undergone the fifty-pound pressure test at submarine school. It gave us practice with equalizing our ears.

Pottenger was silent while we debated our opinions. He appeared deep in thought.

"Pottenger, you're awfully quiet. A penny for your thoughts."

He paused for a moment, crossed his arms, and reflectively said, "Well, I don't disagree with anything you guys said. I don't think there's a need for escape training. Ninety-nine percent of the time, we're cruising in water that's too deep for an escape. If the *Clay* sinks, we'll die when the boat goes below crush depth."

His pragmatic assessment was the harsh truth. The statement struck each of us like a body shot from a heavyweight boxer. I felt my body slump as its significance sank in. The others in the group had similar reactions. Southerland and Souder had somber demeanors.

Schweikert composed himself. He was not going to dwell on it. We all knew serving on submarines was dangerous. It didn't stop any of us from volunteering. Going through the escape trainer would be one more thing to add to his résumé. He was still excited.

The next Monday, Southerland and I reported to escape training.

In the classroom, we found tables with two chairs each. On one side of the room, I spied a mock-up of an escape hatch. Above the outside of the opening, someone had painted "Ho-Ho-Ho." On a table in the back

Submarine escape training tower, Pearl Harbor submarine base. From the archives of Ted E. Dubay (August 1972).

of the room were several Steinke hoods. Southerland and I selected the same table at the front of the room.

At 0800, an instructor entered the classroom. After introducing himself as a Navy master diver, he presented the day's schedule. We would spend the morning in the classroom. During that phase, he would cover safety measures, a review of the escape trunk, and escape equipment. After lunch, we would go through the escape tower.

He didn't sugarcoat the experience. There were dangers associated with going through the tower. Men could rupture an eardrum, get the bends, or even die.

After getting our attention, he assured us that none of those would happen if we did everything correctly. His job was twofold. After the training, we would have the tools necessary to escape from a downed submarine. He was also tasked with making sure everybody in the room left in the same condition as they arrived. There have been few injuries and deaths. As long as we applied the proper techniques, trainees would be all right. If not, there were dire consequences.

Before starting the training, he had everyone come to the front of the class and state his name and whether he was qualified in submarines.

We formed a single line as requested. Southerland and I were first. I made my statements and the instructor told me to return to my seat. The same went for Southerland. While observing the procession, I noticed every so often he kept someone at the front of the room. At the end, there were three men standing at the front of the room.

The instructor said, "Those three will not go through escape training today. One has a cold. He won't be able to equalize his ears as pressure increases. The other two have alcohol on their breaths and their judgment is suspect."

He directed the men to go back to the *Clay*'s office and reschedule the training. It was up to them to report the reason.

Then the instructor repeated there was no room for error during this training and wanted to know if anybody had a question.

Southerland wanted to know the deepest someone could safely blow-and-go.

The answer surprised me. It was about 600 feet, although it would rupture eardrums.

I grimaced in reaction to the statement and my hand instinctively stroked my ear. Then I considered the alternative. What was worse? Being deaf or being dead?

I glanced around the room. The expressions on my fellow crew members' faces told me they were thinking the same thing.

The instructor provided more encouragement. Everybody in the room was fully capable of successfully completing the training. All of us passed rigorous physicals, including the fifty-pound pressure test at submarine school. Everyone had completed extensive psychological screening.

He familiarized us with the escape tower. It was over a hundred feet high and filled with water. Everyone was required to perform the act at the fifty-foot level. If there was enough time, men could volunteer to make an escape from 100 feet.

The training had several safety measures in case someone had a problem. An instructor would be in the fifty-foot chamber with the trainees. His job was making sure trainees used the proper procedure. He would also monitor everybody. If someone could not equalize his ears, the instructor would stop and let the man out. It wasn't any different from the pressure test at submarine school. This time, the pressure would only be a little over twenty-one pounds. That was the pressure at fifty feet.

There would also be divers stationed at different levels in the tower. Their job was continuously monitoring trainees during the ascent. If someone wasn't exhaling, a diver would assist. He'd jump on the man's back, pound the trainee's chest, and make him exhale. There was a safety chamber part way up. If someone was in real trouble, divers pulled the man in and administered medical assistance. There was also a decompression chamber in case somebody got the bends.

The instructor had us examine an escape hatch mock-up in the classroom.

In unison, we turned our heads as directed. Above the hatch was "Ho-Ho-Ho" in bold print.

He explained that saying those words continuously was the key to not being injured. As we left the escape trunk to go up, the air in our lungs would expand. If it wasn't exhaled, our lungs would explode.

The statement made my heart skip a beat. Recalling that many others had completed the training without incident helped relieve my tension.

The remainder of the morning flew by. We familiarized ourselves with the use of the Steinke hood. The hood went over our heads and had a clear plastic viewing window.

Next, we repeated dry runs through the escape trunk mock-up, until the instructor believed we had the process engrained.

After eating, we changed into bathing suits. An instructor led us up the spiral staircase on the outside of the tower. Our single-file procession continued until we entered a room at the crown of the structure. Once inside, we saw why the top of the tower was slightly larger than the lower portion. A platform surrounded the water column. Not only did it provide a location for additional safety personnel, but trainees had somewhere to stand when they exited the water.

I looked into the lighted crystal-clear liquid. Although it was distorted, I saw the bottom of the tank.

Our convoy reversed direction and we descended to the escape trunk at the fifty-foot level.

I donned the Steinke hood and crowded into the trunk with several others. The hatch to the stairs clanged shut and was dogged. Someone unlocked the door to the escape tower. Water pressure on the tower side kept the hatch from leaking.

The instructor admitted water into the chamber and the level rose. The minimum level had to be above the top of the exit hatch. I was the determining factor for the upper limit. By the time the water stopped rising, I was standing on my tippy-toes and had my head tilted backwards to keep my nose in the air space.

The instructor opened an air valve and increased the chamber's pressure. To keep the force inside our ears equal to that of the chamber, we held our noses and mouths closed, while blowing mightily. The pressure had to increase quickly. If it took too long, there was more chance of developing decompression sickness (the bends). When the pressure in the escape trunk equalized with the tower, the hatch to the water column easily swung open.

I volunteered to be the first out. It was a relief to stop worrying about drowning while still in the chamber. I ducked my head beneath the surface and made my way to the opening. I faced the trunk and placed my feet on the bottom of the hatch. With back arched, hands hooked in the top of the opening, and head tilted up, I let out a resounding, "Ho-Ho-Ho."

A diver slapped me on the back and I released my grip. The walls of the tower rushed by as I swiftly rose, continuously exhaling. A cloud of bubbles from the air expelled from my lungs kept my face dry. I shot past several rescue men and the safety chamber. When at the surface, I felt like a missile blasting out of the *Clay*. I made my way to the edge and climbed out. A check by a safety officer completed the ordeal. A deep sense of satisfaction washed over me.

Football season began during off-crew. The *Clay*'s flag football team continued its winning ways. We won every game and outscored our opponents 254 to 30.

McCann was the quarterback and the undisputed star of the team. After graduating from high school in Valdosta, Georgia, he received a full football scholarship to the University of Wyoming. While he was there, Jim Kiick, who went on to star with the Miami Dolphins, was a teammate. McCann could throw with touch or heave a football 75 yards with pinpoint accuracy.

Southerland's height, strength, and athleticism made him a natural as a defensive end.

Connell was a running back. He could stop on a dime, reverse direction, and be back at full speed in a few steps.

Rich Lewis played on the offensive line. During one game, he lined up as an eligible receiver. McCann faked a throw to the right, while Lewis drifted into the left flat. All the defenders bit, save one. A speedy defensive back shadowed Lewis. The defender made the mistake of letting Lewis get past him, figuring he could easily run down a rotund offensive lineman. McCann wheeled and lofted a perfect pass to Lewis. The defensive back got the surprise of his life. When Lewis scored, the back was unable to close the distance between them.

The only close game was against the team from the FBM USS *Nathan Hale*. The star of their team was a nuclear-trained electrician and full-blooded Apache, Charlie Vannoy. The University of Southern California recruited him as a running back, but he broke his ankle. If he had made the team, he would have joined O.J. Simpson. With less than two minutes left in the game between the *Clay* and *Hale*, we scored a touchdown and led by a single point. The fleet-footed Noyvan took the kickoff and darted down the left sideline. Bob Davis caught the speeding man seven yards short of scoring a touchdown. The game ended when I dove in front of a receiver and slapped the fourth-down pass to the ground.

We rebounded from the one-point victory by trouncing the team from the USS *John Adams* sixty to nothing.

In celebration of our undefeated season, our coach, Lt. Bill Gruver, hosted a team party at his home. The officer gladly accepted getting in trouble for fraternizing with enlisted men. The act instilled in me a deeper respect for the man.

Before I was ready, it was almost time to relieve the *Clay*'s Blue Crew. The day before our departure to Guam, Southerland and I moved out of the apartment and placed our extra belongings in storage. Souther-land delivered Hercules to a warehouse on Ford Island. I went with him because the car still had a dead battery. After dropping off the vehicle, Southerland and I walked to Barracks 55, where we spent the night.

The next morning the *Henry Clay* Gold Crew boarded buses and made the journey to Honolulu International Airport. A chartered TWA 747 awaited us. When we entered the terminal, officials hustled us onto the aircraft. The plane taxied onto the tarmac and stopped.

After the aircraft had sat there for over half an hour, upsetting news spread through the plane. We could not take off until the Blue Angel acro-bat team completed an air show. Those on the right side of the airliner were able to catch a glimpse of the action. Most sat silently in their seats, stewing over our predicament.

There were similarities between being on the *Clay* when she was sev-eral hundred feet below the surface and confined in the plane. Our present circumstance was worse. At least when on patrol, there were not tantaliz-ing views of real trees, sky, distance and the like. Additionally, roles and responsibilities occupied us while at sea.

After what seemed to be an eternity, the airliner began moving. The 3,700-mile flight to Guam had begun.

Off-crew was enjoyable. Now it was time to get down to business. An inner pride built within me. Soon, we would begin thirty days of ensur-ing the USS *Henry Clay* was ready to sustain a long deterrent patrol, as a guardian of peace.

Chapter 17

Change of Command— The Good, the Bad and the Ugly

I had mixed experiences with the Change of Command ceremony.

On the good side, it marked the end of and provided closure to our part of the patrol cycle. When the Blue Crew captain said "I relieve you" to our captain, it was the official passing of responsibilities to the Blue Crew. I particularly liked knowing my being cooped up in an HY-80 prison was over for the next three months. There could not be anything better than spending off-crew in Hawaii. Southerland, McCann, Connell, Marchbanks, and I would move into the Honolulu apartment.

There were also aspects of Change of Command I did not enjoy.

Nobody got much sleep. Reveille and up all bunks happened at 0230. Breakfast was 0300 to 0330. Clean up ship lasted from 0400 until 0515. The forty-five minutes allotted to change into dress whites and get all our baggage off the boat was barely enough. Then everybody fell in at quarters on the missile deck at 0600. The *Clay* was usually on the east side of the tender and the sun was up already. It's hot enough on Guam without the sun beating down on us.

I could do without the ceremony's pomp and circumstance, especially the speeches. To me, all the stuff they spouted was hollow, insincere rhetorical BS, although some liked it. I eventually avoided the ceremony. Volunteering for standing a watch in parallel with the Blue Crew gave me a valid reason for not participating in them.

There were also several ugly incidents.

Most involved hung-over sailors getting sick during Change of Command. On one occasion, a nuc was puking his guts out over the side while the chaplain was giving the benediction. The sailor almost drowned out the poor soft-spoken chaplain. I think he threw up longer than the prayer lasted. I'll give the chaplain credit. He didn't miss a beat.

Although such incidents were bad, they did not hold a candle to the worst.

The ugliest happened when some of our officers' wives attended. Since Guam is not too far from Japan, the officers flew their wives to Guam. After the Change of Command ceremony, they would spend a nice vacation in Japan.

In order to put on a show for the women, Squadron 15 pulled out all the stops on pomp and circumstance. The squadron commander was the premier speaker. He had a ton of medals, gold aiguillettes, and his sword. Two squared-away aides accompanied him. All of our officers' uniforms were starched and pressed. As usual, chief petty officers made up the front rows of each crew. I think it was to hide the unkempt enlisted men.

The squadron bigwig was piling it on pretty thick. He was going on and on about the importance of FBMs and how wonderful both crews were. He was quite eloquent. During his speech, we started detecting a foul odor. Of course, everyone started looking around thinking someone had farted. It didn't take long to figure out that wasn't the case, but we couldn't determine the source. As the officer droned on, the smell kept getting stronger and stronger. Pretty soon, hardly anyone was paying attention to the speaker. Finally, someone saw a large dead fish floating in the harbor. It was drifting right towards us. As the carcass got closer, the smell intensified. Eventually, the thing banged against the side of the boat. At that point, the situation got really ugly. The bumping action released even more and stronger vile odors. It wasn't long before people started puking.

The squadron commander interrupted his speech and suspended the Change of Command ceremony. The wives, squadron personnel and our officers went to the tender. The crews went below. After one of the submarine tender's small boats hauled the fish out to sea, we reconvened for an abbreviated ceremony.

A few weeks into the ensuing R & R period, Southerland and I got into a discussion about food.

We grew up under different circumstances. He was from the city and never even knew a hunter. I grew up in the country where just about everybody went hunting and fishing. That was how many of my neighbors put food on the table. Although my family bought meat from the store, it wasn't unusual for friends to eat venison, wild fowl, squirrel, or rabbit. My neighborhood friend Jack loved rabbit. One patrol the *Clay*'s cooks served rabbit. Up to then, I'd never knowingly eaten any. Based on Jack's opinion, I had to see what I'd been missing. It wasn't anything special. Southerland refused to eat it. Feeling so bad about the poor bunnies, he avoided the mess deck during that meal and went hungry. He never forgave me for eating the rabbit.

In general, the food on the submarine was good. That changed towards the end of patrols. There was less selection as food ran out. Quality also decreased. At the end of one patrol, the cooks prepared chicken à la king and noodles. They saw the noodles had worms and served it anyway. I ate the stuff just like almost everybody else. At least it was fresh meat. One of the A-Gangers had seconds.

The term for a hot chocolate on the *Clay* was "lovely." It was used in the same context as: I'll have a "black and bitter" or "blonde and sweet." The hot chocolate came in individualized instant packets that also developed worms. I would dump a packet into hot water and every so often, worms would float to the surface. Initially, I would pour out my cup and try another. Eventually, every packet had them. I would take a spoon, remove the worms, and drink the hot chocolate.

Until joining the Navy, the fanciest seafood I'd ever eaten was my mom's fish filets. Other than that, it was whatever I caught fishing and cooked over an open campfire.

That all changed when I was on the USS *Fulton*. After I'd had lobster and shrimp, every kind of seafood appealed to my taste buds. When Southerland, McCann and I were at a Honolulu restaurant, I ordered baked trout. I had no idea its head would still be there. It had an effect on Southerland. He thought the fish was looking at him and begging for help, but it was way too late. After seeing how it affected him, I felt bad. Southerland was grateful when I covered its head with a napkin.

Talking about food made both of us hungry. We decided to walk to the Ala Moana Shopping Center. There was a contemporary restaurant under the stairs. It had good food and a limited seafood selection. The steaks were excellent. What we got on the *Clay* was OK but nothing special. Both of us were in the mood for a grade-A steak. It was probably due an incident the previous week. A couple of our apartment roommates fell asleep while broiling steaks and cooking corn on the cob. It was the middle of the night. The smoke woke me up. I managed to turn off the stove just in time. The steak and corn were charcoal but there weren't any flames. I was amazed how such a little bit of food could generate so much smoke.

At the end of Atkinson Drive, we stopped and waited for a break in the traffic. A group of newly arrived tourists was beside us. They smelled of suntan lotion and were as pale as Southerland and me. It was raining on the other side of the street. We were in bright sunshine. It was typical Hawaiian weather.

One of the tourists shouted, "Look, a rainbow!"

We turned our heads. Nestled against the inland hills was a beautiful rainbow. We crossed the street. Before reaching the opposite sidewalk, the shower was over. The rainbow was fading. Its brief appearance was a symbol of hope. Southerland and I had several patrols left. So far, the *Clay* had escaped some close calls. I prayed our luck continued.

In Ala Moana Shopping Center's courtyard, the exotic sounds of piped-in Hawaiian music caressed our ears. The open space separating the rows of stores had palm trees and a stream, creating a peaceful ambiance. Many people meandered about. Most had the demeanor of tourists. I thought it was strange that so many people flocked to this artificially created commercialized place. The natural beauty of Hawaii abounded nearly everywhere on the island. When several lovely young ladies in miniskirts walked by, I banished the condemnation from my mind and offered a thank-you to God for the women's presence. During the past three months, I did not realize how much I missed seeing females up close and personal. We enjoyed the scenery as we made our way to the restaurant.

The restaurant's dim lights and soft Hawaiian music greeted us. There were tropical plants strategically situated throughout the room. Ironed tablecloths, candles, and fresh flowers adorned tables. A young vahine dressed in a tight-fitting flowered muumuu welcomed us. She led us to a table. The soft, thick carpet muffled her footsteps. The woman's hips swayed rhythmically to the beat of the music.

Her perfume wafted into my nose and I savored the smell.

The restaurant's ambiance sure contrasted the *Henry Clay*'s mess deck.

I got a cozy feeling from the soft lighting. The *Clay*'s fluorescent lights created a harsh, sterile setting. Having our tables bolted to the linoleum deck didn't help. The thin cushions covered in red Naugahyde vinyl on the bench seats were no match for stylish plush chairs. If submarine sailors weren't such slobs, they would have fine linen tablecloths instead of cheap plastic ones. In our defense, it was hard not to spill food when the submarine was at periscope depth, in rough weather. Because we were crammed so tightly together, stuff ended up on the table when we bumped into each other. Having Formica on the walls made them easy to clean. The plethora of equipment and instruments gracing the mess deck's bulkheads certainly didn't contribute to a homey touch. At least we had a velvet painting of a girl.

I listen to the restaurant's music. It blended in and was hardly noticeable. That wasn't the case in the *Clay*'s mess deck. Somebody was always bitching about the music—it's too loud; it should be louder; I don't like that kind. It didn't help that the only music we had were two homemade reel-to-reel tapes. One was rock-'n'-roll and the other country and western. Whoever was in the missile control center picked the style.

Although there was constant bickering between lovers of shit-kickin' and pop music, it never escalated beyond that. I thought the complaints were a safe outlet for guys to vent frustrations.

Another waitress sauntered by and interrupted our thoughts. The *Clay*'s smelly male mess cooks were no match for these perfumed visions of beauty.

We picked up the menus. To our relief, they were devoid of seafood.

The memory of the recent Guam stinky fish episode was still fresh in my mind, if I even caught a whiff of fish, my stomach would rebel.

We put the menus down. Both of us would order steaks.

The menus hardly hit the table before our waitress materialized from the shadows. She was part Oriental and Hawaiian. Her long, straight black hair draped over one shoulder. A plumeria flower adorned her left ear. I could not remember if it signified that she was spoken for or available. The woman sweetly took our order while we soaked up her beauty.

I could not help thinking it was a good thing submarines didn't have mess cooks like that. Some of our shipmates would act like idiots trying to impress her.

Southerland excused himself to hit the head.

While he was gone, I soaked in the peaceful ambiance. Even though the restaurant was nearly full, it was quiet. Unlike submarine sailors, nobody was exhibiting rude, crude, and socially unacceptable behavior. On the boat, the crew's mess was raucous. Someone was always joking around or pinging on somebody. It was pretty entertaining.

Southerland returned before the waitress pleasantly deposited our salads on the table.

After eating frozen vegetables for the past several months, I thought the plates piled high with fresh romaine lettuce, spinach, cucumber, sliced carrots, broccoli, and tomato wedges were more beautiful than our lovely waitress. Spending so long underwater sure had a strange effect on a fellow.

I was crunching a carrot when the peaceful nature of the room drew my attention. The boisterous, fun-spirited behavior demonstrated by my shipmates was infectious. The peaceful atmosphere in this establishment was sterile compared to the *Clay*'s mess deck.

I smiled, remembering the foul, sophomoric behavior of sailors while eating at sea. After my time on the *Clay* was over, I knew I would dearly miss the camaraderie.

Chapter 18

Surprise Package from the Blue Crew

I was riding in Hercules with Southerland. We were on our way to Ford Island. Since our last off-crew, the Navy had instituted a change to the bi-weekly muster. We had to physically report for roll call instead of just phoning in our status.

While we were traveling along the Kamehameha Highway, I found our surroundings engrossing. It was a beautiful Hawaiian morning. The early morning sun was barely cresting the Koolua Mountains. A faint full moon hung like an aberration in the daylit sky. Palm trees along the thoroughfare cast long shadows across the road. Dewdrops adorned the grass and glistened in the solar rays. Pearl Harbor's wavelets sparkled and shimmered.

The sun was the common thread of all the factors fixating me. I sighed when comparing my current situation with living in a submerged submarine. The prestige of belonging to the elite world of submariners did not negate how much I missed direct contact with the natural elements. After my discharge from the Navy, the sun would become a daily companion. I looked forward to the occasion.

The Volkswagen slowed and turned onto the road to Ford Island Ferry's Halawa Terminal. It was 7:30 a.m. The ferry was approaching on its return trip from the island.

We left early for no reason. Expecting the traffic to be its normal crawl, we were trying to catch the 8:35 ferry. As it was, we would be on the 7:40. It was okay with me. I had some logroom yeoman chores to do. I could get them done before muster and we could leave as soon as we were dismissed.

The incoming ferry bounced off the pilings and rammed the dock.

Bob matter-of-factly remarked, "That was pretty smooth. The ferry boat captain must not be *too* drunk this morning."

It did not take long before the ferry was devoid of the cars from Ford Island. Southerland drove the VW aboard. We ended up in the outboard row on the starboard side. I got out and leaned against the rail. Southerland stayed in the still-running car so there was no need to push-start it when the ferry unloaded.

The vessel slowly pulled away from the dock. Gazing at the murky water, I wondered if it had been clear when only Hawaiians lived here. Looking northeast, I saw low-hanging clouds hung over the Koolua Mountain Range. Sheets of rain were drenching the lush jungle's steep slopes. Slightly above, the sun poured out its life-giving energy. I glanced around, looking for a rainbow.

Before I found one, the USS *Arizona* Memorial came into view. Even though I passed this scene every time I rode the ferry, the rusting hulk of the USS *Arizona* under the Memorial always elicited an emotional response. Knowing that the battleship's decaying carcass was the tomb of thousands of sailors made me glad the *Clay* had survived her narrow escapes. If we sank, our bodies would be unrecoverable. There would not be a difference between our coffin and that of the battleship. The ferry neared the relic. I saw a slick on the water's surface as oil slowly emanated from the *Arizona*.

It was almost as if those inside were saying, "We are still here. Do not forget us."

I wondered how many people passed by without paying the proper respect. If they did, it was sacrilege.

The stirring of other passengers alerted me that the ferry was approaching the Ford Island slip. I walked to the Beetle and saw a familiar sight. In spite of having to squeeze his 6'3" frame into the little car, Southerland was asleep. He awoke when I opened the door.

As he emerged from his slumber, I warned him, "You better brace yourself. We're about to dock."

We assumed our prepare-for-collision poses and hung on tightly. The ferry bounced twice and settled into its berth.

He and I looked at each other and said almost at the same time, "Well, we survived another masterful bit of piloting."

He parked Hercules and we made our way to the *Clay*'s office. While walking to the engineering portion of the space, I saw Stan Wryn, the *Clay*'s yeoman. He handled all of the submarine's general paperwork. His job equated to that of an executive secretary. Wryn was lanky with sandy-colored curly hair and extremely personable. His path to duty on the *Clay* was an unusual route. He was one of the few reserves serving full-time in the submarine service.

Word was circulating that Wryn had opened a package and found a very dilapidated *Engineer's Night Order Book*. Along with it was a letter from the Blue Crew saying something about the book having been found folded into quarters in the upper level machinery 2 vise.

A group of sailors engaged in a discussion about the damaged *Engineer's Night Order Book*. It is hard-covered, bound, and legal-sized. It's an official record. The engineer uses it to convey special information. Whenever a new entry is made, watch standers have to read it and acknowledge understanding by initialing the respective block for their station. During a normal patrol, we would need one or two. I, being the logroom yeoman, stocked several spares in the Logroom.

Sometime during the last patrol, nucs started desecrating the night order book. We couldn't recall a specific reason. The nucs didn't dislike or disrespect the engineer. There wasn't an organized plan.

It started towards the beginning of the patrol. Most likely, the initial act was someone with dirty hands inadvertently smudging the book. Maybe coffee spilled on it. For whatever reason, the desecration escalated. The nucs are a close-knit and astute bunch. My guess was we all realized how much it irritated the engineer for his precious book to be treated like that: what sacrilege!

It didn't take long before more and more icky things were adorning the pages. At some point, guys were intentionally getting their hands dirty before handling it. Every substance you can imagine appeared on the pages. Eventually, someone bent it down the middle, then into quarters. If you picked it up by a corner, it just sagged. Before long, the book was ready to fall apart.

The engineer didn't appreciate the treatment of his precious possession. After replacing the dilapidated book with a new one, he designated a guardian—the auxiliary electrician aft. It was a logical selection. Someone was accountable, and the roving electrician toured all the engineering spaces. He could stop at each station and have the watch stander initial the book.

It didn't take long for one of the AEAs to relax his guard, and the destruction began again. The engineer realized seasoned nucs could too easily trick an inexperienced roving electrician.

He refused to be defeated. I provided a new book and it became the responsibility of a senior watch position. It didn't matter. The new one didn't last a week. Another round went to the crew.

With only one spare remaining and the patrol barely half over, the engineer faced a real dilemma. Again, he dug into his persistence and ingenuity. He was determined to prevail. The engineer turned a three-ring binder with loose-leaf pages into the night order log. It was a stroke of genius. After the patrol was over, the engineer would recopy everything into the last ledger and everyone would re-initial the entries, under the engineer's direct supervision. As an additional precaution, the EOOW became the caretaker.

My section was the first to encounter the new logbook. For some reason, the EOOW wasn't thrilled with the responsibility and slammed the binder down on his desk. Everyone in maneuvering turned and looked in the sound's direction. What happened next was like slow motion. After hitting the desktop, the book flew up and to the right. The binder didn't come back down on the desk. The officer made a vain attempt to catch it, while everyone in maneuvering watched incredulously. The book hit the deck directly on the binder's corner. The middle ring flew out and ricocheted along the deck. The poor officer slumped in his chair as the binder joined the ranks of the other damaged logbooks. To make matters worse, it happened in the first hour of the first shift the new log was in existence. The EOOW couldn't claim innocence, but was lucky in one way. I liked him and had mercy on his poor soul. I managed to find a duplicate binder before our shift was over and made the swap.

The binder went unscathed the remainder of the patrol. During the three days of turnover to the Blue Crew, the engineer copied the entries into the last remaining legal hard-bound logbook, just as he had planned.

Southerland recalled seeing the book undamaged on the AMR2UL workbench. It was towards the end of his 1800–2400 shutdown roving watch. That meant the foul deed happened during the mid-watch or after the Blue Crew assumed possession of the *Clay*. If it was unprotected, any-one could be guilty. The group speculated about potential culprits. Although no agreement was reached, everyone was amused about the book's con-dition.

I looked at my watch, hurriedly excused myself, and went off to com-plete my tasks.

While scurrying away, I glanced backwards. The XO and several jun-ior officers were staring quizzically at the mangled book.

I quickly completed my tasks and joined the crew for muster. We gathered loosely in several rows. The CO and XO stood facing us. After roll call and several announcements, the officers conducted the ceremony of acknowledging the successful completion of our FBM deterrent patrol. Each gave a short speech about the significance of patrols. Then crew members came forward one at a time, each to receive his patrol pin for the initial patrol or a gold star signifying an additional patrol. A silver star equated to five patrols.

I paid particular attention to each crew member's reaction as he went through the process. The ceremony had an emotional affect on some. Others appear unaffected. Most of those who displayed pride were the first-timers. The veterans leaned towards impassive. I acted as if receiving the pin was matter-of-fact. My insides told me differently.

No mention was made of the recently received night order book. Muster took less than an hour and we were dismissed.

Southerland and I walked to his car and he got in. It was my turn to push while he popped the clutch. After three months of not exercising, I had to push it more than 15 feet before getting it going fast enough. Prior to patrol, I could do it in five feet. He stopped Hercules while I caught up. I was panting from the exertion.

As the 12:30 ferry passed the USS *Arizona*, the site of the sunken battleship had a somber affect on me. My heart caught in my throat and I bowed my head in reverence while passing by. Thoughts of the sailors' families and friends haunted me. Even after all these years I was sure they still grieved.

Chapter 19

Typhoon

"Ah-oooo-gah! Ah-oooo-gah! Dive! Dive!" The bell of the engine order telegraph sang its tinny "ding" as the needle sprang to ahead two-thirds. In concert, I instinctively acknowledged the speed change. With my left hand twirling the ahead throttle-wheel to admit more steam to the propulsion turbines, I cried out, "Ahead two-thirds."

The submarine descended into the ocean's depths.

It was early June 1972. I was the maneuvering watch throttleman. My final war patrol had begun.

The submarine's sporadic motion slowly subsided as she descended into the ocean's depths. At several hundred feet, Vince Dainotto, the reactor operator, let out a sigh of relief. He was susceptible to motion sickness. Unlike several instances with similar conditions, he was not puking his guts out.

Although I felt badly for him, razzing Dainotto about his affliction helped distract me from my own sensitivity to the submarine's irregular motion. I was fortunate my symptoms didn't equal his. Headaches were my worst malady.

As we snuck away from Guam while rigged for ultra-quiet, it was impossible for any lurking enemy attack boats to pick up our trail.

The auxiliary electrician aft, Second-Class Electrician Ballard, appeared at maneuvering's doorway. He softly requested permission to enter the small space and record his required readings.

Mr. Humphreys, the engineering officer of the watch, responded, "Permission granted. Enter maneuvering."

Unhooking the chain across the opening, Ballard exerted overt care to ensure the metal restraining device and its sign did not bump against the stainless steel doorframe. He expended the same diligence while reconnecting. A few minutes later, Ballard completed recording the temperature and salinity readings.

Before leaving the tiny crowded space, Ballard told us in a subdued voice that he had made a fresh pot of coffee and asked if anybody wanted some.

Dainotto, feeling better, wanted a blonde-and-sweet. Humphreys requested a black-and-bitter.

Ballard performed his exit with the same meticulousness as entering. He returned shortly and passed the cups in.

Dainotto grabbed his, took a sip, and smacked his lips in satisfaction.

Ballard gave me the other cup and I handed it to Mr. Humphreys.

Humphreys suddenly exploded in a mighty sneeze. The cup slipped out of his hand and seemed to hover in mid-air. Lewis made a futile attempt to grab it. As if in slow motion, the full cup fell to the deck. Everyone in the space helplessly watched it hit with a resounding crash. In spite of our supreme efforts to maintain ultra-quiet, we made a transient noise. We held our breaths and hoped the sound did not compromise the *Clay's* position.

Within moments, the intercom from the conn crackled and the captain said in a terse tone, "Maneuvering. Conn. Sonar detected a transient. What was it?"

Before making his report, Humphreys emitted a string of blasphemies and told me not to feel bad. It was his fault. I had already let go. It slipped out of his hand.

His words of assurance did not make me feel any better. I felt partly to blame. It was my fourth patrol with the man. I should have detected something was awry with Humphrey's demeanor. If I had, the incident would never have happened.

His admission of liability provided me another degree of respect for the lieutenant. It would have been easy for him, an officer, to blame a lowly enlisted man. Fortunately, like most of our officers, he conformed to the submarine code of conduct. Whoever was responsible stepped up and accepted his culpability.

As Mr. Humphreys sheepishly reported to the CO what happened, Lewis started wiping up the coffee.

The tirade from the captain did not last long. When it was over, Humphreys placed the 11MC microphone back into its holder and hopped off his chair. With a sullen expression, he grabbed a rag and finished cleaning the coffee and shards of broken glass. It reinforced my perception of submarine camaraderie. Lewis, even though an enlisted man, did not hesitate to help the officer. Likewise, Lt. Humphreys had no problem with cleaning his own mess.

Dainotto tried to cheer him up. "Hey, Humph. It was only a cup of coffee. That's not much of a transient."

Dainotto's comment had the desired effect and Humphreys composed himself. It was another example of how the proper attitude created compassion between members of a submarine crew, regardless of status.

Not long afterwards, we secured from ultra-quiet.

Everybody in maneuvering assured Humphrey that the *Clay* escaped undetected. If there were any question about it, the captain would not have secured ultra-quiet.

Lewis thought the Russians probably heard the noise, but we were quiet enough that they couldn't find us after that. On the positive side, it was a boring exit and that provided some excitement.

Dainotto had his own view. He could not understand why countries could not get along. If they did, there wouldn't be a Cold War or FBMs, and all of us would be breathing fresh air.

I agreed with Dainotto, but there was an irony to my situation. If countries coexisted peacefully, I would probably be stuck working in a grimy steel mill. As it was, I received a first-rate education and had the chance of a good career.

I told them my time in the Navy hadn't always been a barrel of monkeys, but the experience was worth it.

Lewis dryly remarked, "If it was a barrel of monkeys, there'd be a *football* involved."

After being relieved from my maneuvering watch duties, I withdrew a standard U.S. government black ballpoint pen from the breast pocket of my poopie suit. I was always losing my pen and they knew it. Using them as witnesses, I guaranteed I'd still have it when the run was over.

They wanted to know how I could prove it was the same one.

I removed a TL-29 electrician knife from my pocket. I scribed a notch into the pen and displayed the mark to everyone in maneuvering. Without letting it show, I realized my faux pas. Guaranteeing that I would have the pen at the end of the patrol was the same as issuing a challenge to these men. I would have to maintain my guard the remainder of the run. Repeating past episodes of carelessness could no longer occur. I had to keep an eye on my shipmates. They would do their best to sabotage my effort to keep my vow.

When I reached berthing, I suddenly felt very fatigued. I didn't get much sleep the previous night, because I helped prepare the FBM for sea. Hitting the rack right away allowed me to catch a couple hours of sleep before having to go back on watch. Another long patrol had begun. I was grateful it was my last.

While standing beside my rack, I stripped off my poopie suit and hung it on a hook in the darkened area. I climbed into the cave-like space and switched on the small fluorescent bunk light. I closed the rack's curtain and covered myself with the sheet. The tan bedspread and gray wool blanket remained at the foot of the mattress. I would not need them until the boat's air conditioning system was operating more effectively. That wouldn't happen until the *Henry Clay* entered cooler ocean water north of Guam. Reaching under the sheet, I removed my sweat-soaked smelly socks. In the cramped space, I had to contort my body in order to stuff the socks into the laundry bag hanging from the back of the enclosure. Rolling over in the other direction, I scrunched my shoulders to prevent them from being wedged between the top and bottom of my private sanctuary. The maneuver allowed me to retrieve a book stowed under the corner of the mattress by my head. After reading a couple of pages, I returned it to its spot. A few moments later, I was oblivious to the world.

Several weeks later, I was in the logroom replacing the ink cartridge of my pen. So far, shipmates had inflicted several indignities upon the pen. On one occasion, a person removed the spring. Another time, someone inverted the insides. In the current instance, the tip of the cartridge was missing after the pen had an encounter with a pair of wire cutters. I was not upset because it was still in my possession. Even though shipmates managed to get their hands on the pen, I had recovered it. I chuckled at my shipmates' cleverness. In retrospect, my promise had developed into a game, which helped everyone while away the time.

After restoring the ballpoint pen to an operating condition, I worked on several items for the crew's newspaper, the *Henry Clay Clarion*. While hunched over the desk, I heard a commotion in the passageway outside of the tiny office. Someone loudly whispered, "Hey. Keep it quiet."

The sounds intrigued me. By the time I managed to free myself from the confines of the cramped space, nobody was in sight. The only evidence of anybody's presence was the muffled shuffling of feet at the aft end of the missile compartment. Although it was a curious situation, I shrugged my shoulders and returned to my previous task.

An hour later, another disturbance occurred outside the logroom.

This time, I saw the perpetrators. A group of junior officers armed with flashlights was slowly moving through the compartment. They seemed to be searching for something. One of them saw me. We made eye contact but didn't speak. Without appearing obvious, I blocked the doorway into the room. Officers shouldn't see an item for the paper until publication. It was for an advice column. Someone wrote, "I heard the pistachios have worms. What should I do?" The soon-to-be printed response was, "Give them to the officers. They eat them in the dark while watching movies."

One of the officers mysteriously stated, "The logroom's too small."

After returning to my task, the officers' fading voices told me they were moving aft.

Later, the sound of the oncoming engineering watch section heading aft alerted me that it was time for the evening meal. I had been engrossed in formatting an entertaining article written by one of the officers, Mr. Losen. It was his latest story in the continuing saga of Super-Nuc, Ronnie Scrambreaker. Mr. Losen had come a long way since our first encounter. It seemed like eons ago that he proctored our first basic engineering exam in Hawaii. Now he was one of the crew's favorites.

I walked towards the crew's mess, and saw Southerland coming from the other direction. He had an impish countenance.

I asked, "What's up?"

"Haven't you heard? The door to the executive officer's stateroom is missing. All of the junior officers are out searching for it. So far they've come up empty-handed."

I did not mention the odd commotion I detected when working in the logroom, and told him I saw the officers in the missile compartment. It seemed as if they were looking for something. It was strange at the time, but after hearing Southerland's comment, it made sense. I figured the XO forbade them to get help from the crew, because the officers saw me in the logroom and didn't ask anything about it. I wondered how long the executive office would tolerate the shenanigans.

The next day, the XO's loss of patience began to emerge. He stretched a blanket across his doorway. At least it shut out the passageway's light. The XO intensified the search. All available officers joined the hunt. Like before, no one could find the elusive quarry.

I overheard one of the searchers complimenting whoever hid the door: "I've looked in every nook and cranny I can imagine a door can fit into. Whoever stashed it, really knows this submarine. It'll be a feather in the cap of the man who finds it."

After the third day of fruitless searching, the exasperated executive officer took drastic action. An announcement in the Plan of the Day (POD) essentially said: If the door isn't returned, people will start losing sleep.

The notice had the desired effect. His door magically reappeared. Much to the dismay of the officer, the perpetrators of the hijacking sent their own message. The absent object was resting peacefully in the XO's rack, but his mattress was missing.

The executive officer's shoulders sagged in dismay. He went to the wardroom for a cup of coffee. Caffeine would help sharpen his mind in this match of wits. The substance had the desired effect. He formulated another announcement for inclusion into the next POD. As the XO passed his stateroom while on his way to drop off the message in the ship's office, a pleasant surprise greeted him.

The mattress was back in its rightful location and his door was back on its hinges.

Once again, the unknown sly devils performed their feats of prestidigitation without anyone catching them.

I never discovered who stole the XO's door. On the other hand, anybody knowing the identity of the thieves protected the information as if it were top-secret military data. They may need the same consideration later.

After the door episode, the days droned on. Our humdrum sequestered life in a metal container wandering through the ocean depths, at a measly three knots, was like the doldrums. Day after day of repetitive activities followed the same. It was one reason submarine sailors resort to hijinks, such as swiping doors. The antics helped divert our minds from the monotony of the extended foray under the sea. More important, the same went for the constant stress of our dangerous life. The relief was only temporary. Manning battle station missile at random times, and the groaning of the submarine's hull while it changed depth, brought the realization of our hazardous predicament into the forefront.

One day an unusual motion of the submarine awakened me. A check of my watch verified it was not time for the *Clay* to be at periscope depth. In spite of my confusion, getting rest was more important than figuring out the curious situation.

The submarine's motion rolled me forcibly into the backside of my sleeping quarters and interrupted my sleep again. Before I had a chance to understand what happened, the submarine flung me in the opposite direction. I rolled out of my rack and stood. The deck was pitching and rolling under my feet. The previous confusion returned. The *Clay* should not be at periscope depth and *should* be oblivious to the ocean's surface conditions.

Southerland emerged from the shadows and we came face to face. While maintaining my balance, I asked, "What the heck is going on? Are we on the surface?"

"I wish it was that. We're in a typhoon. The boat's at patrol depth."

Usually, when the *Clay* was this deep she was stable as a rock while gliding silently through the mighty Pacific, for mile upon mile upon mile. With closed eyes, it normally was impossible to tell whether I was in a submarine or at home on dry land. The typically benign conditions spoiled submarine sailors. Dainotto and I thought it made submarine duty more appealing.

Whenever the *Clay* rose to periscope depth, it provided a brief taste of more animated elements of nature. Time near the surface rarely lasted long. Nor were they very dramatic. As a result, we never developed sea legs.

Even if we had that nautical trait, it would not help us now. We were rolling severely. The *Henry Clay*, like all submarines, did not have a keel for stabilization. We rolled emphatically when buffeted by brutal weather.

While dressing and reacting to the shifting deck under my feet, I gained a degree of stability. In spite of the newfound steadiness, my gait to the crew's mess was more like that of a staggering drunk.

I sat with Southerland and Schweikert. They were swaying in rhythm with the motion of the *Clay*. To keep things from falling to the deck, each man had a death grip on the table's items.

I had my typical headache. So far, my stomach felt okay. I wondered how Dainotto was doing.

Southerland wondered aloud, "Anybody got an idea how long we'll be in the typhoon?"

We shortly found out bad news. The storm was huge and our track would keep us in it.

As the day progressed, the typhoon's effect intensified. Rolls got worse. More and more men showed the effects. Loss of patience was common. People curtly snapped at each other over almost nothing. Others were lethargic. Seasickness was on the increase. Every job was demanding. Even sitting in the electric plant control panel's chair was a chore. I had to hang onto the panel's railing to stay in the seat.

The captain counterattacked. He canceled drills, which even in calm conditions placed the boat in a precarious position. Unnecessary jobs ceased.

Trying to minimize the effects of the typhoon on us, the CO drove the *Clay* deeper. The tactic only helped a little. There was a restriction on how far down the *Clay* could go. She had a special antenna which maintained contact with the authorities. It was the limiting factor. Escape was not possible. The submarine could not descend deep enough to escape the storm's wrath and was at the mercy of the elements.

Inevitably, a dreaded occasion occurred. We had to rise to periscope depth, where the fierce tempest battered us unmercifully. Thirty-degree rolls scattered men and unsecured equipment. Many crewmen became violently ill. It was a relief when the submarine slowly descended deeper into its natural element. At the new depth, the vicious pitching and yawing subsided to a mere ten to fifteen degrees. Sleeping was possible but was like someone rocking you to sleep five times too fast and too far to each side. Fortunately, our fatigue allowed us to get much-needed rest.

The storm continued unabated for the next twenty-four hours. Once again, we ascended to periscope depth. With every foot of rise, the submarine's reaction to the tempest increased.

The captain planned a quick foray near the surface in the uneven seas. Forty-degree rolls caused by the 20- to 30-foot waves battered us. The typhoon bared its teeth and attacked with increased fury.

Conditions were so terrible, cold-cut sandwiches were the only foods the cooks could serve. I was eating when we increased our expected time at periscope depth twofold. Though not feeling hungry, I nibbled on a sandwich. Schweikert staggered into the mess deck and slumped onto the seat beside me. He looked crestfallen.

While caressing my throbbing head, I asked, "Why haven't we gone back down yet?"

"We cut the floating wire antenna. Can't go deeper till it's fixed."

Schweikert and I commiserated together while hanging on for dear life as the state of the ocean's surface thrashed the *Clay*.

I observed the other men populating the area. Some were obviously unaffected by the conditions. Other than swaying in sync with submarine's motion, they stuffed food into their mouths as if nothing were amiss. A few were miserable. Most were somewhere in the middle, like me.

While walking aft to my watch station, I felt like a pinball as I bounced off the bulkheads.

An hour later, we got word that the repair of the wire was complete. Relief swept through us in maneuvering. I intensely watched the depth gauge. Much to my chagrin, the needle remained static. Not long afterwards, the exhausted voice of the officer of the deck reported the floating wire antenna had sustained more damage.

Mr. Humphreys said, "We're lucky. We don't have much to do back here. The guys in control are working their butts off trying to maintain depth."

I gave up on watching the gauge. We sat at our stations in silence. Each locked himself into his private world of coping with the situation. I continuously monitored the indications on the electrical plant control panel. Sometimes I scanned right to left. Then it was diagonal or up and down. I employed every pattern imaginable to keep my mind off our circumstance.

I noticed a change in the *Clay*'s motion. A quick look at the depth gauge told me we were getting deeper. I joyously blurted, "Hey! Look at the depth gauge! We're going down."

Before long, the submarine settled at a more comfortable depth. Compared to what we endured while near the surface, the *Clay*'s motions felt almost nonexistent. A glance at a half-filled coffee cup showed we were still in much worse than stable conditions. If the mug had any more liquid, its contents would have sloshed onto the deck.

Throughout the next day, the submarine and typhoon mercifully and gradually parted ways. The pitching and yawing slowly diminished. Eventually, the CO returned the *Henry Clay* to her normal patrol depth. As we continued our underwater journey, life aboard the submarine went back to normal. After the three-day onslaught of horrible weather, suspended activities resumed.

There was a downside. Dreaded drills for nuclear-trained crewmen returned almost immediately. In order to maintain our finely honed skills, officers threw particularly demanding scenarios at us. For the most part, we performed well.

During one drill, an officer was monitoring Pottenger in the lower level engine room. The officer thought Pottenger was too slow in shutting the half doors at either end of the condenser bay. The normally easy action was complicated by a loss of lighting and having to wear an emergency air breathing mask. Pottenger disagreed with the evaluation but had no official recourse.

A subsequent trip to periscope depth proved we were not free of the typhoon's grip. Remnants of the tempest still stirred the sea and caused a significant helter-skelter motion of the boat. Most men had acclimated to the erratic motion.

One had not. Dainotto was the lone sufferer.

I tried to help him feel better by telling him he was lucky to have the qualifications for the submarine service. He would really be miserable on a surface ship.

He agreed.

Lewis had some skimmer friends who would rather serve on a surface ship, because they thought submarines are too dangerous.

Dainotto had some buddies serving in Vietnam. They would rather do another tour over there than trade places with him on the *Clay*. He felt the same about going to Nam and would rather be stationed on a submarine.

The discussion ended when we realized it was time to take log readings. I reached for my pen and could not find it. A sound emanated from the deck. Looking down, I saw the pen sliding in beat to the rocking and rolling of the boat. I retrieved the pen. While I was writing the first value, the result was surprising. To my dismay, the pen dispensed red instead of black ink. I scanned the faces of my compatriots for a guilty expression. Each had the look of an innocent angel. There wasn't any use trying to determine the perpetuator. It would only egg them on to more hijinks. All were most likely involved. I was still paying the price for my hare-brained statement at the beginning of the patrol.

Schweikert relieved me; he had good news. In celebration of escaping the effects of the storm, the chief of the boat was organizing an emergency air breathing (EAB) race.

The contest required participants to travel along a pre-planned course, while wearing EAB masks.

We used EABs when the atmosphere in the submarine was potentially dangerous to breathe. The *Clay* had special storage tanks for dispensing clean air, via manifolds located throughout the boat. If the atmosphere became dangerous, we put on a mask, plugged into a manifold, and had safe air to breathe. If someone changed locations, he took a deep breath, because it was impossible to inhale when the EAB was disconnected, moved, plugged in, and resumed breathing.

Southerland and I read the blurb about the race in the POD. Drawing numbers from a hat would determine the starting order. Monitors would disqualify any contestant who removed his mask, cracked its seal, or diverted from the course. Whoever completed the course in the fastest time was the winner. The route started in the attack center, went forward to the torpedo room, headed back aft to shaft-alley, dropped into the lower level engine room, up the ladder by maneuvering, and back to the attack center.

I tried to talk Southerland into entering. He was one of the crew's better athletes. The trait would help him do well.

He turned the tables and encouraged me to enter.

I admitted I'd been thinking about it. He provided some tips: go the farthest on each breath, use the minimum number of stations, pick target manifolds, select some alternative stops, etc.

I decided to enter and thanked him for his support.

At the appointed time, the competitors assembled in the crew's mess. Among the twelve entrants were three officers. The officer who had criticized Pottenger was one of them.

The COB conducted the drawing for the starting order. When it was my turn, I shut my eyes and selected one of the folded slips. I gained a measure of hope when seeing the number 5 on my selection. For no particular reason, I was always partial to the number. I hoped it was a good omen.

The competitors staged according to starting order aft of the periscope, making the space extremely crowded. Not only were the racers present, but also five sailors with stopwatches, the COB, and the normal watch standers.

The participants departed at several-minute intervals. When the man before me left, I pulled the mask onto my head and tightened the straps. I attempted to inhale with the hose disconnected. The mask squeezed my face, proving I had a proper seal. I inserted the hose into the EAB manifold. A few deep breaths saturated my lungs. The mask severely limited my field of vision, so I turned my head in the direction of the COB. With eyes locked onto him, I waited for his signal.

When his hand came down, I took a final breath and unplugged the hose. I ran forward until encountering the route's first obstacle: the descent to the next level. It went as planned. The need for air began to grow while I was sprinting to the hatch into the torpedo room. I passed through the opening without incident. My eyes spied the target manifold. I connected the hose and breathed several times. My strategy of only taking one breath was down the drain. Disappointed but refreshed, I continued. I did not make it to the next scheduled stop and resorted to the alternative.

Before arriving in machinery 1 upper level, I had to abandon even the substitute stops. Fortunately, I could find the location of every EAB manifold with my eyes closed. Every stop found me breathing heavily. My poopie suit was damp with sweat and I hadn't even reached the hottest areas of the *Clay*.

As I scrambled through the hatch into the engine room, the hot, humid atmosphere made me seek the closest manifold. This was the toughest part of the course. In addition to the heat, I had to navigate several obstacles. While replenishing my lungs, I wondered how far behind me the next person was. The added incentive let me make it to the manifold outboard the port main engine. Fatigue and lack of oxygen were taking their toll. Each stop required more and more breaths. When reaching the ladder at the back of the submarine in shaft alley, I mustered the fortitude to make it into the lower level engine room and pass through the condenser bay before needing to stop. I ascended the ladder in the forward part of LLER and emerged from the hatch outside maneuvering.

The remaining portion of the course was a blur. Exhausted, I stumbled across finish line and removed the mask. As usual, some of my hair was stuck in the mask's straps. Despite the pain of having portions of my mane ripped from my head, it felt good to be free from the vise-like grip of the device. Being able to breathe freely was liberating. With chest heaving, I bent over and placed my hands on my knees. I was satisfied. I did my best.

Competitors assembled in the crew's mess. Before long, all had returned, except one—Pottenger's critic.

Someone thought he went directly to his stateroom.

The COB gave our placement in reverse order. Dave Csencsics was the winner. He smashed the existing record of four minutes and five seconds by posting a phenomenal time of three minutes and thirty-four seconds. It was a remarkable achievement and he deserved our enthusiastic congratulations. I placed a respectable seventh.

It didn't take long before a rumor emerged. Pottenger's critic had trouble navigating the condenser bay. He found the area dark and the half doors closed. Somehow wearing a respirator severely affected his ability to pass through the obstructions in a timely manner. Although it was never substantiated, I did not doubt the rumor's validity. If so, Pottenger must have felt deep satisfaction, knowing justice had prevailed.

After the race, I felt the effects of the exertion. Reading in my rack was a good way to recover. It would also temporarily distract me from patrol's strain. We were finally in cool enough water for the submarine's air conditioning system to work perfectly. The cold air emanating from my rack's ventilation duct was the elixir I needed.

With only my shoes removed, I entered the small enclosure. I basked in the peaceful environment. A few contortions later, I retrieved my book.

After reading a few pages, a disheartening sound blasted from the FBM's PA system, "Whoop. Whoop. Whoop. Whoop. Man battle station missile. Set condition 1SQ. Spin up all missiles. Whoop. Whoop. Whoop. Whoop. Man battle station missile. Set condition 1SQ. Spin up all missiles."

I joined the rest of the crew as they ran to their battle stations. The event negated any escape from the unnerving stressful conditions of this war patrol.

Thankfully, the *Henry Clay's* missiles remained resting benignly in their tubes. Once again, Armageddon did not happen.

There was only half an hour before the next meal. I was afraid to lie down and read. If I did, the exhaustion from the EAB race and battle stations would most likely cause me to fall asleep and miss eating.

I went to the logroom to take care of paperwork. While seated in the space, I realized I was completely at ease. During my first patrol, the presence of the lethal contents in the missile tubes just outside the logroom sent a chill up and down my spine. In retaliation, I would close the logroom's door and create insulation from the source of my discomfort. Now, the nuclear-tipped missiles didn't bother me. I wondered which state of mind was psychologically healthier. Was it being comfortable or bothered by my situation? I took solace knowing the patrol and my time in this circumstance were nearing their end.

The next week, I decided to stand the roving electrician watch. More and more shipmates were feeling the effects of our extended period sequestered in a metal monster. Their testy behavior was typical for this portion of the patrol. I was probably acting the same way. Minimizing the amount of time spent with anyone in particular became my defense mechanism. Hence, the roving position provided the necessary attribute.

When it was time to record parameters in maneuvering, I reached for my trusty pen. The object was not in my pocket. I sighed. Either I had misplaced it or someone was having fun with the pen.

I was reluctant to query any of my foul-mood fellow crew members. My own disposition may not allow me to ask them without sounding mean.

The author and his much-abused pen in machinery 1 upper level. From the archives of E.K. Lingle (July 1972).

Maybe I had dropped it somewhere. I retraced my path. While passing the after-work bench in machinery 2, I saw something in the vise. A closer look revealed a U.S. Government retractable ballpoint pen crushed in its jaws. A sinking feeling developed in the pit of my stomach. A ray of hope replaced it. The chances were not good, but there was a possibility the entrapped pen was not mine.

I unclamped the vice and inspected the pen for my special mark. The search was difficult due to the pen's severe damage. Then I saw the notch. Although masked by the imprint of the vise's jaws, it was definitely there.

I was crestfallen. The pen had suffered fatal damage. Not only had the vise squashed the pen, it had administered an ugly end to my vow.

On the way to the trash can, I noticed the ink cartridge was sticking out, exposing the business end of the implement. I tried to make a mark on a piece of paper.

I could not believe my eyes. The pen wrote perfectly. It had survived.

After my initial rush of euphoria, I surveyed its wounds. They were substantial. Its ink cartridge no longer retracted. The pen had a slight bend where the top and bottom screwed together.

Its triumph over the assault helped my mood. My tension, which had been slowly building over the past several weeks, was dissipating.

There were parallels between the pen and me. So far, the pen had survived many trials and tribulations. I had done the same throughout my time in the submarine service. A difference also existed. The pen's wounds were clearly visible. I wondered what unrealized damage I had sustained during my naval service. I cast the thought aside. Innumerable wonderful experiences more than compensated for whatever negative effects I suffered. The prospect of a career in the civilian nuclear industry was highly likely. All in all, I had no complaints.

When I placed the pen into my breast pocket, its metal clip fell off. The additional indignity did nothing to deter my upbeat disposition.

I hurried to maneuvering to record the necessary parameters. Very interestingly, nobody in the crowed space made a comment about the condition of the dilapidated pen. There was no way they did not notice. Their lack of saying something told me each was involved or at least knew details of the pen's encounter with the vise.

There was nothing to gain by holding it against them. I had committed the faux pas and had to live with the entertaining consequences. I refused to admit it, but I'd have been disappointed if my fellow crew members hadn't risen to the challenge. Although it was on its last legs, the pen was still in my possession and in working condition. By that account, I was winning the battle.

The sixtieth day of patrol came and went. There was no end in sight. I refused to succumb to the temptation of checking our location on the navigator's chart. I'd rather not know where we were. If we were far from Guam, it'd be depressing. Being too close initiated a case of channel fever. There was a more important reason to remain ignorant of the *Clay's* track. Not knowing our location prevented me from mistakenly divulging classified information to the wrong person.

At the end of every patrol, the crew underwent a debriefing. The most stressed aspect was forbidding us from revealing the *Clay's* route. Disclosing secret information could have severe consequences. In our case, it could lead to neutralizing FBM deterrence. The Soviets were always trying to gain an edge in this arena and supposedly had spies everywhere. Whether Russian secret agents were as omnipresent as feared was irrelevant. The consequences were too great to take the chance of telling anyone classified data. Unlike me, my family and friends didn't have to swear an oath about not divulging secret information. Therefore, even when pressed

I was careful with what I told them. Multiple facts deemed small or trivial could be pieced together to become something important. I took pride in my integrity and even when pressured was careful with what I told them.

As the patrol continued, my damaged pen continued to provide inspiration. It was in deplorable condition, but still going strong. There was not a chance it would run out of ink. I replaced the refill shortly before its run-in with the vise. Even when I left the pen unattended, nobody messed with it. I wondered why. Were my shipmates too tired? Were they having mercy on the object? Maybe it provided them with the same psychological support. For whatever reason, it gave new meaning to the saying, "The pen is mightier than the sword."

One day, I was the throttleman. Everyone in maneuvering was quiet. The benign atmosphere in the small space was in sharp contrast to how lively it was at the beginning of the patrol. If my compatriots were like me, they were lost in their own coping mechanisms after such a long time under the sea.

Suddenly, the engine order telegraph sprang to life. I smartly answered the bell. A flurry of activities ensued. Watch standers performed necessary actions. When the organized chaos ended, we were making going-home turns.

The end of my last patrol was at hand. I felt the built-up tension within me slowly evaporating. Inhaling deeply left my lungs asking for more. I yearned for a breath of real outside air. Swallowing hard, I summoned an untapped reserve of patience. I needed it to endure the remaining time in this hermetically sealed container.

Satisfied the panel's indications were normal, I observed the other men in maneuvering. After the explosion of activity, each was sitting stoically at his station. It was as if nothing special had just happened. I was sure they were as internally happy as I was about the significant improvement of our situation.

The behavior was typical. Although the event was something long-awaited and yearned for, we had to guard our emotions.

The precarious circumstance of being in our submerged warship was not over until the *Clay* was safely tied to the submarine tender, USS *Proteus*, in Apra Harbor. Too many things could delay, or even worse, prevent that ending. The submarine was as tired as the crew. It had been plagued with far too many equipment failures in the past few weeks. With the sea floor 20,000 feet below, a casualty could mean certain destruction. Escalation of the Cold War always had the possibility of extending our secret mission.

It was time to record the hourly readings. I retrieved my abused pen. The object continued to provide encouragement. It was limping home like the *Clay*.

The messenger of the watch awakened me. He was excitedly telling me something. Fatigue prevented me from comprehending his words.

I shook my head, cleared cobwebs, and said, "What did you say? Tell me again a little slower."

He composed himself, "Dubay. We're almost to Guam. They're going to set the maneuvering watch after breakfast."

I tried getting excited about the impending end to my life under the sea. Strangely, it did not work. It was too much of a demand on my tired mind and I abandoned the attempt. I did not sense channel fever, either. The extra patrol time had worn me out. I lethargically plucked my poopie suit from its hook and got dressed.

After breakfast, my section was due to be on watch. I was supposed to assume the electrical operator. Since setting the maneuvering watch would happen within the hour, I decided to relieve the throttleman and avoid an extra swap of positions.

As scripted, we set the maneuvering watch at 0700.

Fifteen minutes later, a welcome sound issued from the 1MC, "Ah-oooo-gah! Ah-oooo-gah! Ah-oooo-gah! Surface! Surface! Surface!"

As the submarine rose, the effects of surface conditions exerted their effects on the *Clay*. I glanced at Dainotto. He didn't look very good. The closer we got to the surface, the more his complexion turned a pallid white. After the sub was on the surface, the rough seas had him fiercely fighting his affliction.

Feeling bad for the man, the EOOW, Mr. Losen, told him the weather forecast was favorable. It wouldn't be too rough while picking up the Blue Crew officers and leading petty officers. Then we'd dive and show them the condition of the *Clay*'s equipment. By the time we surfaced, the weather would be nice and the ocean as smooth as glass.

Dainotto appreciated the moral support.

To his credit, he managed to maintain his stomach's contents in their proper location. The rest of us in maneuvering appreciated his effort. If he started puking, we could follow suit.

Soon, we heard, "Ah-oooo-gah! Ah-oooo-gah! Dive! Dive!"

The Blue Crew representatives were aboard.

It signaled another small step towards returning to Hawaii and my discharge from the United States Navy. Dainotto was also happy. His motion sickness faded away as the boat escaped the surface effects of the mighty Pacific Ocean.

We put the FBM through her paces. Speed changes, equipment swaps, and angles-and-dangles were part of the exhibition.

Having to demonstrate the state of the boat's equipment to the Blue Crew had its pros and cons. My favorite part was that they were aboard and would relieve us in a few days. On the other hand, the trip prolonged our time at sea. It also gave the Bluies, once they understood the *Clay*'s deplorable condition, the opportunity to rag on us for allowing her to deteriorate so badly. It did not matter that we could not prevent the problems.

The Blue Crew buffered the joy of having them aboard when they delivered sad news. One of their crewmen had committed suicide. A leap off Diamond Head proved to be as effective as planned. The man was despondent. His wife had had an affair with someone from our crew. The somber incident revealed an insight. Patrols strained loved ones as much as submarine sailors. Both cases required an extreme amount of mental toughness. The weak could not survive and must explore easier roads. It was one reason I was grateful for not having a steady girl of my own.

Several hours later, the Blue Crew understood the *Clay*'s tired condition. The Gold Crew was as worn out as the submarine. At least we would get a break in three days.

I was unable to embrace the full effect of the end of my FBM submarine ordeal. The news about the man who took his life put a damper on our happiness. I had known him since our time in Charleston. During the shipyard, we were quite close. When assigned to different crews, we drifted apart. I never met his wife. Maybe if I had known her, the infidelity would never have happened.

I forced myself not to dwell on the tragic news. The situation was similar to when the USS *Scorpion* was lost while I was at prototype. Serving in the submarine service for the past four years had trained me to block out distractions and only concentrate on the present. Getting the submarine back into port safely was the priority. Nothing else mattered.

The realization we were finally heading back to port, thus ending our patrol, caused subtle changes to those of us in maneuvering. Although no one talked, I sensed an improvement in my crewmates' mood. Their tension-wracked bodies appeared more relaxed. My breathing was peaceful. I hoped none of my crewmates would let their guard down. I was confident they wouldn't. We could endure almost any casualty if everyone maintained his professional attitude.

My dilapidated pen continued to provide inspiration. I buried the pen in my pocket.

Loudspeakers blared, "Ah-oooo-gah! Ah-oooo-gah! Ah-oooo-gah! Surface! Surface! Surface!"

The run was over. My vow was safe. The pen, although severely wounded, survived.

As Mr. Losen promised, surface conditions were calm. Dainotto showed no signs of motion sickness.

The submarine finally entered Apra Harbor, Guam. It was the summer of 1972. The *Clay* moored next to the submarine tender, USS *Proteus*. My time at sea on a nuclear submarine was over.

In three days, the Change of Command ceremony was over. The Blue Crew was aboard the USS *Henry Clay* and preparing her for the next patrol. I, along with the rest of the Gold Crew, was heading back to Hawaii. I saluted the *Clay*'s colors and stepped off the FBM for the last time. Before long, I would own a prized possession: an honorable discharge from the United States Navy.

I walked away from the *Clay*, sea bag in hand. I was sticky with sweat. Guam's hot, humid, tropical air was almost smothering.

In spite of the discomfort, I was enraptured with my surroundings. Blue sky, the *surface* of the water, and the seemingly boundless expanse soothed me. The freedom of swinging my arms without worrying about smacking them into something was a joy.

My emancipated soul felt as if it stretched to infinity. Everything around me afforded a sense of freedom, even the aroma of the rotting vegetation of Guam's jungle. Although pungent, at least it was natural air. It was the opposite of the recycled and reconstituted foul stuff inside the submarine.

I tried to resist the urge of saying goodbye to the USS *Henry Clay*. It was impossible.

Chapter 20

Farewell to the *Henry Clay*

I took a final look at the *Clay*. Realizing I'd probably never see her again, sadness overcame me. Together, we had survived life and death situations. Her HY-80 steel hull protected me from the crushing ocean depths. For the past three years, she had been my home.

The boat was motionless, without any signs of activity. She rested quietly in the placid crystal-clear water.

The submarine appeared peaceful and serene. It was only an illusion. In reality, the *Clay* was one of the most powerful weapons on Earth, able to unleash more firepower than that expended by all sides in World War II. On the other hand, her being painted black, without any identifying markings or numbers, were clues to her ominous purpose.

While taking in the scene, the enormous responsibility of maintaining and operating such a potent weapon floated off my shoulders. A sense of relief swept through me.

Then I felt ashamed about nicknaming this fine vessel the *Henry Lemon Clay*. It had happened when the Beatles song *Yellow Submarine* was popular.

During one patrol, someone was singing the tune and I said, "We live in a yellow submarine; too bad it's lemon yellow."

After that, *Henry Lemon Clay* or HLC became standard terminology. At least it was better than calling her the *Henry F...... Clay*. Referring to her as the HFC wasn't right. She never failed us. I was proud to serve on the *Clay*.

The best thing about assignment on the *Clay* was the crew. I talked to guys from other submarines and some of them would give their left arm for *Clay*'s Gold Crew camaraderie. E-Div was an especially close group. The core bunch—Rich Marchbanks, Charlie Ballard, Rich Lewis,

Charlie Schweikert, Greg Metzgus and I—were together for four years. We went through an awful lot. The same went for most of the nucs. I had known Southerland and Souder since 1967.

It didn't matter if the crewman was a forward puke or a friggin' nuc. There was a mutual respect between the two groups. That didn't mean we were shy about trading jabs, barbs, and pings. I don't know about anybody else, but I really valued the closeness. We laughed, played, and fought like brothers. Men have trouble saying the word love. We submariners are prime examples of that fault. Although unstated and rarely acknowledged, the "L" thing existed between *Clay* crew members in a brotherly sort of way.

Hearing a truck behind me, I looked at the *Clay* one final time. The vehicle stopped and blocked my view of the mighty war machine. Poignant emotions flowed through me as I continued to the bus.

Metzgus caught up to me and said, "Isn't it amazing how such a relatively short period of your life can be so significant?"

His comment made me reach over and touch my silver Dolphins. The medal instilled a sense of pride. I had completed a journey few are willing to start. Knowing that many volunteers for submarine duty were unable to complete the ordeal intensified my pride. Some could not measure up to the stringent medical and intellectual requirements. Others were unable to cope with the emotional aspects. It is no small wonder that the submarine service is an elite fraternity. As these thoughts churned through my mind, I wondered how much truth there was in the saying: Once a submariner, always a submariner.

Serving on a submarine is a unique experience. The armed forces have many rigid rules and regulations. The submarine service enforced a relaxed version.

When we were in Charleston, Pottenger went ashore with a uniform deficiency. A surface sailor noticed the imperfection and placed him on report, which could have serious disciplinary consequences.

When Pottenger returned to the *Clay*, our captain summoned him to the wardroom. Feeling apprehensive, Pottenger meekly entered the room.

The captain pointed to a chair and ominously said, "Have a seat. You know why you're here. Right?"

"Yes, sir."

With a stern look on his face the captain asked, "Son, how do you spell submarine?"

Quizzically, Pottenger responded, "S-U-B-M-A-R-I-N-E."

The captain's face transformed into a fatherly countenance, "No, son. You spell submarine: 'F-U N.' Now get out of here and have a nice day."

That was the last Pottenger ever heard of the incident.

Even though episodes like Pottenger's were the norm, every so often someone enforced the rules to a T. One time, when Schweikert was standing watch in maneuvering, there was a need to manipulate a component outside of the tiny room. While leaning out of the room and keeping one foot firmly planted in maneuvering, he performed the action. An officer saw the incident and had Schweikert relieved from watch for abandoning his post. Schweikert was also told he could expect a court-martial if it ever happened again.

The crew of the *Clay* was not the only recipient of similar odd treatment. While the FBM USS *Benjamin Franklin* was on patrol in the Mediterranean, an electrician had to get up from the middle of his sleep period to repair the captain's bunk light. The half-asleep man trudged to the captain's stateroom, fixed the light, and went back to bed. Before long, the captain requested his presence in the wardroom. The electrician thought the captain wanted to thank him for getting up out of a dead sleep and fixing the light so quickly. To his surprise, the captain sternly told him, "You need a haircut. Don't go back to your rack until you get one!"

These were just a few examples of why many good men only completed their minimum military obligation.

I boarded the second bus in line. Southerland had saved me a window seat and I sat beside him. After the typical military hurry-up-and-wait, our buses began trekking to the other end of the island. None of the vehicles had air conditioning. Windows were open in an attempt to provide some relief from the heat and humidity. I was grateful for the lack of air conditioning. Open windows allowed my senses to drink in Guam's unobstructed sights, smells, and sounds.

Knowing it was my last time on the island, I saw Guam with new eyes. Its beauty was striking. The road ran along a pristine shoreline. The absence of civilization's normal din, telephone poles, and signs accentuated the island's primitiveness. I saw the beautiful translucent turquoise ocean. Huge waves roared like continuous distant thunder. The empty non-littered sandy beaches, dotted with coconut trees, were devoid of human presence. An occasional dugout canoe was nestled under the palm trees. Every so often, the jungle's smell mixed with the perfume of tropical flowers.

While staring at the ocean, I recalled an adventure with Metzgus. We were at the beach near Andy's Hut, a small cinder-block establishment that served burgers, hot dogs, soda, and beer. They were within walking distance from the *Clay*. It was a picture-perfect afternoon—brilliant sunshine, cloudless sky, and a cool sea breeze. The lagoon's water was flat as a pancake. He rented a small sailboat and invited me to accompany him. After we set sail, it made me forget I was in the Navy. We were having a great time until I slipped off the back. He heard the splash and came back for me. Metzgus couldn't believe how fast I got back aboard. What I didn't tell him was all I could think about was the movie they showed us when we first got to Guam. Its title was something about the 101 things in Guam's water that can kill you. That inspired me to get back on the slippery deck with ease.

I looked in the opposite direction. Towering lush green volcanic mountains came into view. We used to joke that there were World War II Japanese soldiers still hiding in them. When we returned to Hawaii after one patrol, there was a Honolulu newspaper article about the capture of a Japanese soldier. He claimed to be the last one. The others had either surrendered or died. The man knew the war was over but felt it was disgraceful to surrender. That sense of honor seemed inconsistent with his actions. He was stealing food. What was the honor in that? The natives got tired of his thieving. They set a trap and caught him. He was lucky. When he returned to Japan, his countrymen treated him as a hero for hiding for almost thirty years.

I silently reflected on my own return to the USA. A similar greeting would probably not be waiting for me. The Vietnam War was in progress. The conflict stirred extreme antiwar sentiments in many people. Protests, long hair, and nonconformity were the credo for many young adults. While they participated in their antiwar games, we in FBM submarines were playing our own games, albeit deadly ones of hide and seek. The Russians were constantly trying to neutralize our deterrent advantage. If given the order, any Soviet skipper would not bat an eye about sending us to a horrible death.

What peaceniks failed to realize was they had the same agenda as most of us in the military: peace. Each went about it differently. Antiwar activists attacked their country and fellow citizens. We in the military stood our ground on the frontlines and maintained peace by presenting a strong defense.

Antiwar activists treated those in the military, regardless of role, with disrespect. It did not matter that we defended their right to act any way they pleased. A nervous anticipation stirred in my gut. I wondered about my own greeting and treatment.

As the bus approached the airport, a squadron of B-52 bombers was leaving on a sortie to Vietnam. The scene made me recall peaceniks' accusations that military personnel were baby killers. I shuddered. How many babies would die if the *Clay* ever launched her missiles?

Amid the jets' roar, the *Henry Clay* Gold Crew filed into the airport.

One time, a pleasant surprise greeted us in the terminal. Emanating from the loudspeaker system was a live broadcast of the Super Bowl. After isolation from the outside world for the past three months, even those not interested in sports were enraptured.

I had forgotten all about the game because Guam is on the other side of the International Date Line. For us, it was Monday. This reinforced the significance of the statement emblazoned on Guam's license plates: America's day begins in Guam. When our plane landed in Honolulu that evening, it was Sunday, again. It was strange to arrive somewhere the day before we left. It all evened out. When flying to Guam, a day is lost.

As I sat in the airport for the final time, my mind dwelt on the isolation that submariners endured while at sea. This seclusion was one of the most significant downsides to serving in the submarine service. When a momentous event occurred, such as the assassination of President Kennedy, people associated with the event with where they were and what they were doing.

When the movie *Apollo 13* came out, I could not figure out why I had no link with the noteworthy event. The three Apollo 13 astronauts were on a mission to the moon. Their spacecraft experienced an explosion, crippling it 200,000 miles from Earth. In spite of the damage, NASA engineers safely returned them home. My lack of a connection was unusual. I had had an interest in the space program since its earliest days. On one occasion, a couple of buddies from the *Clay* and I made a trip from Charleston, South Carolina, to Cape Kennedy to watch the launch of Apollo 10.

I compared the date of their heroic rescue to my whereabouts. I was at sea on the *Henry Clay*. Without access to daily news reports, newspapers, or emails (which didn't exist at the time), I did not have a firsthand relationship with Apollo 13. While the rest of the world was on the edge of their seats, the *Clay*'s crew was oblivious. Conversely, in spite of the important role we provided ensuring peace on Earth, the majority of the world was equally unaware of our escapades.

It was time to board our plane. Like cattle, we filed out of the terminal.

The flight to Hawaii would take about nine hours, getting us to Honolulu International Airport late in the evening.

Like many of the crew, I could not sleep during the trip, despite the fatigue of not having had a day off for over three months. It was a combination of several factors. After the *Clay* returned to port three days earlier, we had shifted the clocks from Greenwich Mean Time to Guam time. My discombobulated biological clock, plus channel fever's iron grip, made sleeping on the jetliner impossible.

Chapter 21

Flight Back to Hawaii

Once aboard the plane, I settled into a window seat on the left side just forward of the wing. No matter how tired I made myself, sleep was impossible when flying back to Hawaii. Southerland sat in the aisle seat. He was one of the lucky ones and had already fallen asleep.

The airliner began moving. I watched the terminal disappear from view for the last time

Taking off from Guam was always unnerving. The terminus of the runway was a sheer cliff, which dropped several hundred feet to the rocky shoreline.

An eternity seemed to pass as the jetliner lumbered down the runway picking up speed much too slowly for my comfort. Too soon, the edge of the cliff was in view and I felt internal tension mounting. I muttered to myself, "Get this thing in the air. Now!"

We were at the point of no return. There was no longer any room to recover. If something went awry, we would die.

The aircraft lifted off with plenty of room to spare and I laughed at my nervousness. The margin to catastrophe was not much different between this situation and that of a submerged submarine. The only dissimilarity was that I could see the hazards when in the airliner. I was never skittish in the *Clay*.

The in-flight movie did not start until an hour into the flight. To occupy myself in the meantime, I listened to music. There was a choice of classical, popular, or western songs. I selected popular. It allowed me to catch up with some of the tunes I'd missed during the past three months.

Lunch interrupted the continuous rhapsody. A treat complemented the nondescript prepared meal. I savored my first Coca-Cola in over two months. Southerland awoke, ate silently, and effortlessly fell back to sleep.

I envied his ability to perform the feat. As his chest heaved up and down, a peaceful expression adorned his slightly askew head. I was happy for him. After our three-month ordeal, he deserved the rest.

The in-flight movie—*Paint Your Wagon*, starring Lee Marvin—began. As the plane flew over the seemingly endless and empty ocean, the entertainment helped pass the time.

During the flick, the aircraft banked slightly. I looked out the window. At first, the only thing in view was the Pacific's broad expanse and a cloudless sky. A few low-hanging clouds appeared. I looked below them. After many hours aloft, Wake Island, something to measure our progress, came into view.

The jet's change in attitude and the buzz of shipmates' comments circulating through the airliner awakened Southerland.

In a sleep-tainted voice, he asked if we were landing in Hawaii.

"Not quite. We're not even half way. The pilot is treating us to a view of Wake Island."

He fell back to sleep. This was his first chance to catch up on some rest. His exhaustion was understandable. Between refit, patrol, and the three days of turnover to the Blue Crew, it was impossible to catch up on sleep.

I leaned over to get a better look of the isolated, virtually flat spit of land. The atoll is the remnant of an ancient collapsed volcano. The land barely rose over the sea. It seemed as if a high tide would completely cover the island. Fortunately, for those living there, tides did not rise very high because of the size of the Pacific.

For me, Wake was a welcome landmark on our journey back to civilization. I found the island intriguing. The hope of seeing it one final time was the reason I sat on this side of the plane.

In December 1941, the United States had a small contingent of Marines and some civilian contractors on Wake. The Japanese attacked it four hours after bombing Pearl Harbor. What confuses people is the date of the attack on Wake Island, December 8. Wake is on the other side of the International Date Line.

Wake Island is the Alamo of the Pacific. It has several similarities with the one in San Antonio, Texas. Both were under siege. Each mustered a gallant defense before a superior force overwhelmed them. The defenders of Wake knew they'd be attacked several hours before it happened. They repelled invasions for two weeks. Finally, on December 23, the Japanese mounted an all out-assault and were successful.

This is where similarities end. Santa Anna wiped out everyone at the Alamo. The Japanese captured Wake's defenders. They retained ninety-eight civilians on the island and used them as slave labor. They shipped the rest of the defenders to prisoner of war camps.

The United States forces island-hopped over Wake, leaving the Japanese occupation force stranded. Every so often, the U.S. would harass them with an air raid. The strategy backfired. After a raid in October 1943, the Japanese executed all the prisoners left on Wake. The United States didn't find out until after the war. The men carved "98 U.S. PW 5-10-43" on a rock before being executed. Now the rock is a monument.

I could not stop thinking of the battle. My decision to join the Navy kept me from fighting in Vietnam. Even though the *Henry Clay's* patrols were combat missions, there was a degree of separation from our enemy. I would never be in a face-to-face confrontation, as my father had experienced in World War II. I wondered about my own behavior in battle. I hoped that I would measure up as well as he did. With any luck, the question would remain unanswered. If my performance during crises on the *Clay* can serve as a measuring stick, I would have been okay. I hope that I will never know for sure.

I distracted myself from the thoughts by returning my attention to the movie.

After the film, I passed the time by staring out the window. In some ways, it was worse than standing watch while on patrol while nothing was changing. At least in the submarine, I had responsibilities. It did not take long to appreciate my current circumstance. I could see clouds forming fascinating and ever-changing shapes. The sun's rays made the vast ocean's surface shimmer and sparkle.

One other item added to the positives of my present circumstance. My confinement inside a submerged metal container, isolated from the world for months at a time, was over.

Eventually, the plane banked and started its descent to Honolulu's airport. Bright city lights flooded the area below. Our imminent return to civilization caused a wave of contagious excitement to ripple through the crew.

Some had loved ones waiting in the terminal. Rich Lewis's wife and son would be there. Pat Schweikert, Charlie's better half, would be anxiously waiting his arrival.

Others like me, without anyone to greet them, were just happy to be back.

The plane touched down with a sharp bump. A roar permeated throughout the cabin as the pilot slowed the aircraft. I felt like it took forever to taxi to the terminal. Many had a tough time containing their anticipation of getting off the jetliner. They prematurely unbuckled seat belts, gathered carry-on belongings, and formed a line in the aisle.

Chomping at the bit to exit the plane, everyone waited for our captain to lead the *Clay*'s crew into the terminal. It was his post war-patrol ritual.

The man had the typical submarine captain's cocky maverick attitude. He was clad in a dress white uniform. His hat was perched on his head at a rakish angle. A wig, with hair over his ears and collar, covered his closely cropped hair, giving him a scruffy wild look. Aviator sunglasses were part of the costume, even when arriving at night. He smoked a cigarette in a sterling silver six-inch cigarette holder, which further accentuated the persona.

Chapter 22

Ford Island

As we followed the captain, the crew's appearance added to the mystique of submariners. Our rumpled and yellowed uniforms had spent more than three months crammed in a locker and out of the light of day. Bodies and clothes reeked of that submarine smell.

These disgusting traits did not deter loving embraces from family or friends. To my left, Bill Souder engaged in a tearful loving hug with his wife, Barbara. Schweikert and his wife Pat were locked in each other's arms. An excited squeal to my right caught my attention. I turned in its direction. Rusty Wishon's four-year-old daughter and wife were mobbing the irrepressible nuc machinist's mate.

A sense of relief swept over me. Even though no one was waiting for me, it was enough to be back in Hawaii. One more step of my odyssey was over. I would conduct my own reunion in the morning. It would be in the form of a phone call to my family, back in Hickory Township, Pennsylvania.

The ever-faithful phone tree alerted the crew's family members living in Hawaii. My parents were not part of the network and the call from me would be a surprise.

It did not take long to retrieve our baggage. This was surprising because of items bought in Guam. In addition to being cheaper than the same product in the USA, as long as the total value was less than $200, they were tax- and duty-free. Many took advantage of the situation. The normal fare was stereo and photographic equipment. I procured a Minolta 35 millimeter camera. Lingle had a new tennis racquet. Another benefit was being able to bring back a gallon of duty-free liquor. Southerland always brought back Jack Daniels Black. Since I was not much of a drinker, Lewis and I arranged an exchange for my gallon. His wife would treat me to a home-cooked meal.

Fatigued and loaded down by sea bags plus an assortment of good-ies, we staggered out of the airport. A balmy summer evening greeted me. Compared to the heat and humidity of Guam, it was paradise. A cool breeze blowing off the nearby water kept me comfortable under my heavy load.

Crew members met by wives or girlfriends left with them. I would spend the night in Barrack 55 on Ford Island, Pearl Harbor. Stowing items to their owners' and the bus driver's satisfaction took a lot of time. This more than offset the short wait getting our things from the plane. The delay, channel fever, and fatigue caused some men to fling off-color remarks at no one in particular. My body language gave away how antsy I was to complete the day's journey.

Once underway, the trip to the submarine base did not take long. The bus unloaded near a shuttle boat landing. Water taxis would take us to Ford Island.

Due to their size, the whaleboats required many trips to transport the *Henry Clay* crewmen. We piled as many as possible into each, before the coxswain forbade any more. The heavily loaded boat that I was in sat low in the water. I tried to persuade our coxswain to allow Southerland and Lingle as additional passengers. He agreed to permit one more. South-erland and Lingle had to decide.

After seeing that the next boat would not be as crammed, Lingle sur-rendered the spot to Southerland. He decided there would be less chance of getting his new tennis racquet wet.

Southerland did not argue and hopped aboard.

The coxswain mumbled something unintelligible under his breath, and warned us to sit still or we would capsize the boat.

The launch bounced along as it surged over the choppy water, kick-ing up salt spray. The moisture was refreshing. It was dampening my body but not my spirits. The irony of the situation amused me. While submerged, saltwater spray was my worst nightmare. On the surface, it was benign. I did not need an escape path to limitless air. I was already in it.

The launch arrived at Ford Island, near the tennis courts. The short walk to Barrack 55 took me past the dispensary. It still had visible damage from the December 7, 1941, attack. I silently bowed my head in respect to those who died that day.

Our portion of Barrack 55 was a huge room with a high ceiling, on the first floor. A solid wall formed the perimeter. Separating the center section into cubicles were six-foot high lockers and the outer wall. Each cubicle had four double-decker metal bunk beds.

After doing minimal unpacking, I craved a shower. It would be a treat to use as much water as I wanted. The *Clay's* main distilling unit, even on its best day, which was not often, converted 8,000 gallons of seawater into freshwater per day. We needed most of its output for other purposes, leaving a limited supply for personal use. Sometimes, there was not enough for showers.

Most men did not shower every day for various reasons. I found it unnerving when the only people I could smell were those who had recently taken a shower. What was I used to? Yuck.

When there was enough water for showers, we took submarine showers. They consisted of turning the water on, getting wet, stopping the water, soaping, restarting the flow to rinse, and shutting off the water as soon as possible.

Even drying had its challenges. Limited storage space meant I could only bring a few small towels. To assist the scrap of material, I used a washcloth to remove most of the wetness. When the washcloth was saturated, I wrung it out and repeated the process until I was just damp. Then I finished with the towel.

Guilt tried to creep in when I kept the water flowing after initially getting wet. I managed to fight it off and spent considerable time simply standing under the spray. Afterwards, I was still stuck with drying with the washcloth and small towel. The two items retained a strong submarine smell. As I dried myself, I realized I was rubbing the odor back onto my body.

The same thought emerged while dressing. My clothes had the foul odor. It also wafted out of my cube-mates' lockers. The stench was permeating back into my body, down to the bone, and re-infecting me.

I had a desire to imbibe in some liquid refreshment and headed towards the Arizona Club. It was directly behind our barrack. I changed my mind when hearing the sounds of a lively poker game.

The stakes were high. There were several hundred dollars in the pot. It was a considerable sum, since most players only earned about $400 per month. The game continued for several hours without a clear winner or loser. Each hand was its own entity. Sometimes it was five-card draw, other times stud, with blackjack thrown in. As players tired, others took their place.

During one hand, the stakes became too rich for most. Only Costes and Ty Shinow remained. They continued to raise each other's wager until Costes had bet all of his pay from the last three months. Shinow called. The tension between them was visible as they showed their hands. After revealing their first two cards, Costes had a pair of eights, compared to Shinow's two sixes. At four cards, it wasn't looking good for Shinow. Both had two pair. Shinow had sixes and nines. Costes had eights and Jacks. Shinow sat stone faced as Costes revealed his last card. It was an ace of spades. When Shinow turned over a third nine, the cards fell from Costes' hand. Shinow's full house beat two pair.

Costes was completely broke. All his pay from the time we left Hawaii over three months ago was gone. The festive mood evaporated. Players and spectators drifted away. Shinow silently gathered up the pot, devoid of remorse.

Costes sullenly shuffled back to his cube. He had to survive without a penny until the next payday, which was not for another week. He was fortunate to live on base. The Navy did not require sailors to pay rent when living in the barrack. Plus, there was no charge for eating at the chow hall.

Someone clicked the lights off and I settled into my bunk. It had been a very long day. My channel fever subsided and sleep quickly engulfed me.

I awoke the next morning feeling refreshed. My heart soared like a hawk when I realized what had awakened me. Sunlight, mixed gently with bird songs, and the wind rustling through trees. I inhaled deeply. It was as if these sensations were entering me, flushing out the unpleasantness of the last three months.

Even though extremely enjoyable, I did not savor it long. A touch of channel fever re-infected me. There were so many things to look forward to, I hardly knew where to start.

Another long shower continued the process of eliminating *that* smell from my body.

Next was breakfast. As I stepped into the chow hall, the aroma of fresh-baked pastries wafted over me. The additional stimulus of seeing fruit, eggs, and fresh milk made my mouth water. The last time I had eaten anything this fresh was several months ago.

After loading my tray with a plethora of delectable delights, I savored every bite. Several glasses of fresh-squeezed orange juice and milk helped wash it down. Southerland appeared and joined me. Piled high on his tray was a similar selection.

Both of us had quit eating eggs the third week of patrol. I stopped after watching Al, the cook, dropping three out of five greenish-black eggs onto the griddle. He just scraped the bad ones into the garbage and continued without skipping a beat. It made me wonder if any of them were any good, even the ones that looked normal. I decided right then and there that eggs were not going to be part of my diet until I got back to Hawaii.

If submariners have the best chow, it made me wonder what skimmers ate.

In contrast to rushing through meals on patrol, we leisurely finished our food and lingered.

I wanted to make a quick phone call to my parents and let them know I was back. Southerland patted his stretched belly and we headed to the barrack. I found a pay phone. After I had deposited a dime and dialed O, the operator came on the line.

I told her I wanted to make a long-distance collect phone call and gave her my parents' number. After a bunch of clicking noises and my dime returning, I heard a phone ring.

A woman answered. The operator asked, "Will you accept a collect call from Ted?"

The voice on the other end enthusiastically accepted.

I blurted, "Hey, Mom, I'm finally back from patrol. I'm safe and sound in the barrack on Ford Island."

With a distinct New York City accent, her reply was hesitant and confused. A query determined I was talking to someone in area code 212, New York City, instead of 412, western Pennsylvania.

She interrupted my apology for disturbing her. Being a mother, she was happy to hear of a son returning safe and sound from something dangerous.

I repeated the process with the operator and explained about reaching the wrong number. She assured me she would cancel the charges and tried another call.

It was a treat hearing Mom's sweet melodious voice. She had been expecting the call for the past several days.

I heard Mom say, away from the phone's mouthpiece, "Hey, honey. It's Ted. He's finally back."

Even though Dad was sitting in his easy chair, I could tell he said something about being relieved and glad it was my last secret mission.

As Mom was catching me up with all the news, I heard the voice of my thirteen-year-old sister Leona in the background, "I wanna talk. I wanna talk to him."

"Hold your horses. Everybody will get a chance. Get Curt. He's working on his bike on the back porch."

I smiled, hearing Sweetie's footsteps as she rushed off. A picture of her formed in my mind. I could see her hair bouncing and arms swinging as she scurried through the dining room and into the kitchen. The slam of the screen door announced that my sister had gone outside. Soon it banged again as Curt and my sister clamored into the house.

Mom said, "Sweetie's about to explode. Ready to talk to her?"

She had attended the Cathy Rush Basketball Camp while I was on patrol. Sweetie excitedly told me about it. I wondered how much my own interest in basketball had influenced her in the sport. We concluded our conversation with her challenging me to a game of H-O-R-S-E.

Next, it was Curt's turn. I knew he was dying to ask details about my patrol experiences. He knew it was a forbidden subject. We limited our conversation to a discussion about rebuilding the gears on his ten-speed bike. I promised to help when I arrived back home.

Finally, it was Dad's turn. We mainly talked about fishing. He had stocked our pond with large-mouth bass. My father extolled their virtues as fighters. The call ended with me telling him that I'd see them in about a month. The exact day of my discharge from the Navy was unknown. Treating us like mushrooms, by keeping us in the dark and feeding us poop, was the Navy way.

With much regret, I hung up. We could have talked for hours but a collect phone call from Hawaii was expensive. Although my folks never accepted money from me in compensation, I know it bit into their limited budget.

While walking to Southerland's cube, I realized how much I longed for my family. When on the submarine, I had a defensive mechanism engaged inside me. I knew I missed them but it was an abstract feeling.

Southerland, with eyes closed, was lying in his rack. Seeing his peaceful demeanor almost made me regret disturbing him. I slammed my hand on the side of one of the metal lockers, creating an ear-splitting noise. His eyes popped open.

With sarcastic sweetness dripping from my voice, I asked him if he was ready to pick up our belongings from the warehouse.

His eyes rolled in their sockets and I thought he was going to fling a few well-deserved meaningless intensifiers at me.

As we walked the short distance to the warehouse, I drank in the sensations of my surroundings. The morning sun was warm on my face. Wind rustled through freshly washed hair. The mixed scents of sea and land tickled my nose. I was in bliss.

On the way, we discussed how we didn't see each other very much while on patrol. It was amazing how two guys cooped up in a sardine can for over two months hardly came in contact. He was in the section that was on watch when I was off. When I was sleeping, he was off. Even when manning battle stations, I was in maneuvering and he was stuck in lower level machinery 2. We would catch up while I stayed in the Atkinson Drive apartment. Pavlov was taking my place after my discharge from the Navy.

Since I had shipped my car to the mainland during the last off-crew, I was at the mercy of Southerland's batteryless VW, Hercules. We had to stuff all of our belongings into his Beetle. It was a tight fit, but we were successful. After we'd push-started Hercules, I ended up with a box in my lap. He drove to Ford Island's ferry landing.

The ferry arrived at the landing with its usual amount of crashing and bouncing. I wondered how it remained seaworthy after taking all the abuse. I was not worried about my safety. If the battered ferry sank, we were on the surface and land was less than a quarter mile away.

Residual effects of the last three months tempered the eager anticipation of my discharge from the Navy. A 30-day paid vacation in Oahu was the perfect way to rejuvenate.

Chapter 23

The Circle Begins

The tropical paradise had much to offer and time flew by. Before I knew it, it was my next-to-last day in the Navy. After spending the morning on Ford Island, Southerland and I went to Waikiki Beach. What a way to finish my time in Hawaii! While he dozed, I savored our spectacular surroundings. Beautiful bikini-clad women coated the beach. The water was refreshing. Tourists shrieked during wild dugout canoe rides on the mighty Pacific rollers pounding the seashore.

Then Diamond Head caught my attention. Thoughts of the Blue Crew sailor who committed suicide on its slopes invaded my mind. I wondered if I would ever be able to see the landmark and not associate it with my friend.

His relationship was not the only one which could not survive long patrol separations. Divorce and marital problems ran rampant within the submarine community.

Although single, I was a victim also. Being a submariner partially contributed to my not having a steady girlfriend. When in Guam and on patrol, the crew of the *Henry Clay* was essentially removed from civilization, eliminating any chance of meeting a woman. While in port, most eligible members of the opposite sex ostracized those in the military as warmongers. It was a difficult situation.

On the positive side, I survived. There was much to be thankful for, even though I had some narrow escapes. The snapped line, while tying up the *Nautilus*, missed me by a whisker. A torpedo shot at the USS *Fulton* had a dummy warhead. Evasive actions averted being depth-charged during sound trials. The jam dive brought us to within a hair's breadth of destruction. Encounters with typhoons and Soviet hunter-killer submarines left us unscathed. World leaders kept their sensibilities and the Cold

War never escalated into an all-out conflict. My training and experience were the foundation for a well-paying career. I met many wonderful people. All of these contributed to my growth from a naive country boy into a confident, mature young man.

I went to bed with a smile on my face. There were so many wonderful memories.

The next day, I donned my dress white uniform for the last time. After attaching my Dolphins to the shirt, I picked up the patrol pin. The emblem was missing the star for my final patrol.

A quick search located the tiny star. I stared at it in my open hand. The ⅛th-inch golden icon was pathetically small when compared to what I had endured to earn it. It was a shame that a certificate, stating in words what the award represented, did not accompany the patrol pin or its stars. I attached the new star to the medal. My finger traced the pin's outline and then gently touched each star.

While staring at the miniature FBM submarine with a missile blasting out, I recalled my feelings when the *Clay* fired its test missile. I still recalled the FBM's reverberations. Would the sensation ever fade from my memory? At the time, the launch was an exciting lark. After too many war patrols, the way the submarine shuddered as the projectile blasted towards its target was matched by a reciprocal shiver within me. Mine was due to comprehending the awful conflagration the *Henry Clay*'s lethal weapons would cause if ever dispatched.

Gratefulness quickly replaced the uncomfortable feeling.

I will be thankful forever because we never unleashed the *Henry Clay*'s merchants of unimaginable devastation. Although enemies on political and military levels, the Soviet general population was not any different from that of the United States. If the Cold War had escalated into something more terrible, it would have resulted in the annihilation of millions of innocent victims in both countries. My deterrent patrols had come and gone. During those deployments, I manned battle station missile too many times. Thankfully, none resulted in dispatching the *Clay*'s birds of death. The pin and its adornments were visual reminders of my contribution to maintaining world peace.

My Dolphins were already pinned onto the left breast of my uniform. I affixed the patrol pin to the pocket flap below my Dolphins. Although earned in different manners, both medals made my chest swell with pride.

Southerland entered the room. "Y'all ready?"

I nodded and we walked through the quiet apartment. McCann and

Connell were not home. A final goodbye was not possible. Would I ever see them again?

After depositing my sea-bag inside the VW Beetle, I climbed into the driver's seat. Bob assumed the pushing duties. Our coordinated actions quickly caused Hercules's engine to spring to life. I wondered if my departure would motivate him to replace the battery. I silently shifted to the passenger seat.

Southerland stopped the car in front of the airport terminal. I got out. Neither of us spoke and he drove away.

I did not look back.

Index